COMING CLEAN

Oxford, May 2020

Hello. You saved my life. There's no question about that. Your empathy, your willingness to learn and understand about this disease and have enough faith in me to keep trying through all the pain you endured, saved me, and I'm here doing everything I do now, because of it. I love you. Mike

COMING CLEAN

A true story of love, addiction and recovery

Liz Fraser

GREEN TREE
LONDON · OXFORD · NEW YORK · NEW DELHI · SYDNEY

GREEN TREE
Bloomsbury Publishing Plc
50 Bedford Square, London, WC1B 3DP, UK
29 Earlsfort Terrace, Dublin 2, Ireland

BLOOMSBURY, GREEN TREE and the Green Tree logo are trademarks of
Bloomsbury Publishing Plc

First published in Great Britain 2021

A catalogue record for this book is available from the British Library

Library of Congress Cataloguing-in-Publication data has been applied for

ISBN: HB: 978-1-4729-8637-5; TPB: 978-1-4729-8638-2;
eBook: 978-1-4729-8636-8; ePdf: 978-1-4729-8635-1

2 4 6 8 10 9 7 5 3 1

Typeset in Stempel Garamond LT Std by Deanta Global Publishing Services,
Chennai, India
Printed and bound in Great Britain by CPI Group (UK) Ltd, Croydon CR0 4YY

To find out more about our authors and books visit www.bloomsbury.com
and sign up for our newsletters

Contents

Prologue

I wrote the first draft of this book in my partner's first year of sobriety. When I finished it, I thought I had written an accurate, and indeed fairly tame, version of events compared with what had actually happened and how it had been to live through at the time.

Only three other people read that first draft and their responses suggested it was perhaps not quite as gentle as I'd thought; one said it was so relentlessly shocking she needed a few days off to recover, another called me every day for a week to see if I was OK and the third asked if I knew any psychotherapists I might be able to see as soon as possible.

A few months later, in which time many more bumps in Mike's sobriety journey were navigated and my own recovery from all the trauma had begun – at least a little – I went back to the manuscript and read it again. Now it was my turn to be shocked: burning a hole into my eyes were three hundred and fifty pages of distilled rage, broken only by brief moments of light relief in the form of hate, anger, pain and fear. There was almost no pause for breath in the gunfire of awfulness and it read less like a story of love and recovery than an excuse for murder, or suicide. Or both.

I had pretty much bled my pain onto the keyboard and it did nothing to help the telling of a far more human, layered story – because I'd been nowhere near ready to write it yet.

Emotions need to see out their natural life cycle, be registered for what they are, allowed to express themselves, be processed and understood and, eventually, learned to cope with better. If the scarring is light and we have the required mental tools, the healing happens fairly quickly and successfully; but some experiences are so deeply damaging, the recovery time can be very long indeed.

Recovery from alcoholism – whether as the alcoholic or those affected by their illness – cannot be rushed. It takes its own path and we feel what we feel in each moment. What I had clearly felt, so soon after the events themselves, was a knock-out cocktail of traumas. (Not a beverage I'd recommend, if I'm perfectly honest.)

It took me a lot of time and some slow, difficult self-examination and learning to be able to view our story with any sense of perspective at all and to see it as a three-dimensional, complex, nuanced whole. Its shape still continues to change every day, because this is a real story of real lives that are still being lived, a journey we're still on, both together and independently, and every week brings a new realisation, a new challenge and a new piece in this big, complicated puzzle. And so it will go on, for as long as we do.

So really, there are two versions of this book; the first is a blistering catalogue of everything that happened, for me to keep and, hopefully, never look at again.

The second is this one, for you. A true story of two flawed humans, both battling their own demons, and both now on the long path to recovery. It's a path far better negotiated while holding hands with our fellow travellers, instead of fighting them, or ourselves, all the way.

Introduction

This is a true story about two people driven apart by addiction, and held together by love. It's your classic 'boy meets girl – oh, hang on, boy is an alcoholic' love story.

It's about human fallibility, strength and hope for recovery. But mainly it's about drinking.

I never expected any of it to happen in my life, but it did, just as it does to countless others who didn't expect it either. We're just everyday people with everyday jobs and lives; we pay our bills and take the bins out, we eat vegetables and occasionally think about doing some yoga. We take our kids to the park, call our friends on their birthday, filter our Instagrams and recycle our plastic. We floss. To look at us, you'd never know the secrets we hold or the daily struggles we endure.

I'd never (knowingly) known an Actual Alcoholic before I met Mike, nor had any idea what the word really *means*, far less what it's like to live with one, love one and have one's life smashed apart by one. I *did* know he had 'a bit of an issue' with drink sometimes, but let's face it, so have most of us. Who doesn't get shit-faced at a wedding, drown bad news in vodka or slip into unhealthy drinking habits occasionally? Almost everyone I know has done this at one time or other, or many times, and so have I. But the line between occasional bad habits and addiction is unhelpfully blurred and it's remarkably easy to slide over it – especially if there's an underlying problem being ignored.

When Mike finally fell over that line and descended into an alcoholic vortex of destruction, I found myself alone with our 18-month-old daughter, in a foreign country to which we had just moved to start a new life together, with no childcare or family nearby, working to pay all of our bills on my own, with no idea what was happening or what on earth I should do.

For months, I battled on in silence, too ashamed, scared and gaslit to speak out, until I eventually lost all of my emotional strength, my self-confidence, my health and my mind, all the while trying to keep myself and my child afloat. When I finally broke and started tentatively talking to friends and strangers about the truth I was living, I found a huge network of people who helped and supported me without judgement, and countless others who live, or have lived, with addicts.

We all have different individual circumstances, but it's in the similarities – and there are usually many – where we can find much-needed empathy, spot our own mistakes and learn how we might cope better in the future.

I'm going to tell my story honestly, fairly and, I hope, with kindness and compassion. It's quite shocking in places because the truth of addiction *is* shocking and we can find ourselves in situations so dreadful it's hard to understand how they could be a part of our life, or our children's lives. But these situations happen, and I hope that in sharing all the things I didn't know about, didn't have the words for and didn't dare speak about for far too long – both when Mike was drinking and in the unexpected challenges of recovery – it might help you if ever you need it.

We will travel to some beautiful places where terrible things happened: from the Entry-Level days of alcoholism – occasional disappearances, inconsistencies and changing moods – graduating to manipulation, blame, rage, humiliation and loneliness, and even to the ugly, still largely taboo realms of verbal and physical abuse. These are things nobody ever wants to darken their doors, but they can arrive so fast we don't even hear them approaching.

There are no 'winners' in addiction; everyone, including the addict, is a victim, and everyone involved needs support and love in order to become a survivor. None of us knows when it might be our turn or how we will handle it, and you might never be able to tell anyone about your experiences – and that's OK. You have to do what feels safe and right to *you*.

This isn't a how-to guide or academic examination of addiction – it's a memoir, a diary, an account of one person's experiences of it – but I hope it might change the way we think and talk about addiction, open people's minds to both sides of this all-too-common human experience, encourage dialogue and mutual support, break stigmas and provide support for those who need it. All sides of a story need a voice. This is mine.

Venice, 27 June 2019

On the morning of his 35th birthday, three months since he last drank any alcohol, Mike left our apartment in the quiet south-east corner of Venice to buy a roll of camera film, so he could take a photograph of the three of us on this special day.

'He' never came back.

I found him several hours later, staggering through a silent, sun-blistered backstreet carrying a full bottle of red wine, several empties in a plastic bag and, by the looks of him, a whole lot more consumed previously; a lost, pathetic creature, withering in the sun, steeped in booze. This man, this father, this soul I loved, so drunk he could hardly see or stand.

That day, 'The Venice Incident', as I came to think of it for a long time afterwards, marked the end of many false starts and the start of a final descent into something so dreadful I couldn't understand how it was happening to us – or how we could ever get out of it.

One of the biggest challenges I faced when I started writing this story down was not being able to recall large chunks of it. Bit of a problem, that.

I couldn't remember where I'd been, how I got there, where I went next, why I even went there in the first place, where I stayed and in which month, or even *year*, much of the events occurred. Even when prompted by a photograph, an email from that time or one of Facebook's 'on this day two years ago' posts you'd really rather not be reminded of, thank you, I didn't know how it all fitted *together*. The whole story was like a million index cards of disconnected scenes all hurled into a wind tunnel: I recognised what was on each card, but which *order* they went in or how any of them related to each other was a total whiteout.

Amnesia and confusion are very common when we're exposed to relentless trauma and exhaustion, because our brains, unable to cope with all the shit thrown at them, shut down everything except the essentials for survival. I don't think I was mentally entirely *there* for much of what happened in the worst months of it all: I was sort of everywhere but nowhere, struggling through each newly bizarre, frightening moment, timeless, groundless and directionless, and always either recovering from the shock of the last event or preparing for the next. My fried brain reduced everything to a chaotic photograph album of disjointed, often surreal snapshots: a shout, a phone call, a push, a kiss, a dirty hope, a flood of tears – SO many tears.

I had a baby to look after so I had to keep going, coping and moving forward into the next unforeseen nightmare, never processing or consolidating anything. During the worst months I even shut off many of my senses; I couldn't taste or smell, I was neither cold nor hot, hungry nor full, awake nor asleep. I became almost depersonalised, cut off from myself by constant, high-level anxiety and shock, until I was functioning almost like a robot, marching on and on and on to ... wherever I was going.

Oddly, in all the big-scale memory-wiping, I recalled hundreds of tiny details with almost filmic precision: the exact angle of sunlight on a Venetian roof; shadows moving across my daughter's feet as I pushed her in the buggy under the fig trees; the layout of a hotel room and escape distance to the door; the exact smell of a park in Sweden after it rained; the pattern of a small patch of leaves on a path in Cambridge while Mike was shouting lies at me down the phone; the feeling of a china coffee cup against my lip on a scorching morning after Mike had passed out on the street; the sound of seagulls as I cycled along the seafront in Denmark; the sharp dig of a chair into my thighs as I leaned forward while breastfeeding my daughter so my tears would miss her head and drop onto the table instead; the colour of a jumper; the curl of an angry mouth; the exact force of a push; the sound of a cupboard being smashed by a foot; the sting of a razor blade on my arm.

I was only able to piece the whole thing together thanks to a giant server buzzing away in a warehouse somewhere in Arizona, storing thousands of photos and videos from my phone, letters and words in WhatsApp messages and emails, and kindly providing me with a clear, indisputable and chronological record. Looking through all this material took me months and triggered deep, physically painful symptoms of post-traumatic stress disorder (PTSD) and depression – but it was worth it; it allowed me to navigate it all again, this time with time and distance providing some protection, and so much that I had missed or not understood at the time started to make sense.

We all cut, collate and archive our memories, replaying them so many times they become our Final Cut: our 'truth'. But they're often just our selected version of events, with much missed out or changed. Having all the original material of what *really* happened – the zigzag of his alcoholic peaks and troughs over many years, what seemed to prompt them, how I reacted to them, the signs I missed, my own patterns of self-destruction, and the role that depression and other mental health issues, on both parts, had played in it all – allowed me to me piece together a far truer picture than I ever could have by myself.

One thing I never forgot, nor ever needed reminding of, was my love for Mike: what our love was from day one, and could still be if he could stop destroying himself and come back to us. That's what I held on to, and I'm glad I did.

HOW WE MET

The first time I saw Mike pass out from the effects of alcohol, I still barely knew him – and I certainly didn't even know that's what had just happened.

We'd met a few years before, when he was working in a café in Cambridge and made me my coffee every morning (skinny, extra-hot cappuccino, in case you ever feel like treating me), and for a long time he was just some bearded Scottish barista with an upside-down lamp post tattooed on his right forearm. Just 'Scottish Mike'. He didn't generally say much as he stood there tamping coffee grounds, obscured by a cloud of steam and internal thoughts, but when he did speak it was generally short, bracingly offensive and very funny – a refreshing change from the stifling Cambridge correctness. He had a disarmingly no-bullshit vibe I liked and I enjoyed his sweary, dour company from across the room even before we'd ever properly struck up a conversation.

After a few months of 'Hi. Usual?' we'd bravely branched out into 'Shite day, isn't it?' and gradually, as often happens with people who've become part of the fabric of our every day, we entered the giddy realms of Actual Chat; I got to know where he was from (Fife), that he played golf (very well), had studied architecture (but dropped out) then studied law (but dropped out again) and was actually a photographer when he wasn't caffeinating the city's academics and tourists.

Cambridge is doll's-house small and Mike and I often ended up in the same coffee haunts on his days away from the café, either both working at our laptops or hanging out with a group of mutual desk-hopper friends, him always bantering away and making everyone laugh.

Being in Mike's company when he was in a good mood was like taking a year's supply of ecstasy washed down with dopamine inside a gigantic light box, surrounded by all the people you love most. He talked fast and excitedly about films, books, music, art and people, all with a generous helping of dry Scottish humour – the blacker the better. The first time he told me his parents were both dead it was the funniest account of two people being dead I'd ever heard, and there seemed to be no subject too dark or joke too offensive, because Mike never meant any offence.

A cleansing acid peel for political correctness and pleasantries, his straight-talking was addictive; if someone was an asshole, he'd say so. If *he'd* been an asshole, he'd say so. He was raw and unpretentious – he was once asked by a well-to-do customer if there was a toilet in the café and off the bat he said he fucking hoped so because otherwise everyone had been shitting in a cupboard for the last 10 years – he didn't hold a grudge, seek revenge, feel any sense of entitlement or languish in self-pity, and all in all, Mike was just about the most honest, non-judgemental person I'd ever met.

He was also a total mess.

If people with food issues have 'disordered eating', Mike had disordered *existence*, and while his non-committal, almost detached way of looking at the world was refreshing, it had gained him a dazzlingly catastrophic CV of Life. Less 'lovable rogue', more 'affable mess', it was a picture of almost consistent chaos and very little stability: two abandoned degrees; a 20-page CV of various jobs; a catalogue of places he'd inhabited often for as little as a few weeks; a cast of hundreds of odd bods and vagrants, and the crowning glory of a tattoo scrawled right across his chest in French with a mistake in it, received while drunk. He'd crammed a lot of colourful life into his 30 years, but none of it appeared to have turned out terribly well. He seemed to breed disaster and it sometimes felt to me as if he needed to run out of stories for a while, and just … STOP.

The stand-out feature of almost all of his stories was drink – *lots* of drink. I didn't think much of this at the time, because Mike's from Scotland, and, frankly, if you're not drinking, thinking about drinking or talking about drinking, people will start to ask if you're OK, pal? *Everyone* drinks, the local cemetery is bursting with the graves of those who've been lost to drink, but not once in all his recounting was the word 'alcoholic' ever used – even for those who were permanently hammered for 40 years and died of liver failure. It was just an accepted, almost celebrated part of the culture; so despite all the tales of his pissed escapades, it never once occurred to me that Mike had a *problem* with drink, and certainly not a problem *so* big it was an addiction.

To put it mildly, Mike and I had led somewhat different lives so far. I had a 20-year career in writing and broadcasting behind me and three grown-up children from a now-defunct marriage. The closest I'd ever got to being In Trouble was when I didn't take a Blockbuster video back on time in 1998, and bar a glass of wine with dinner here and there, plus the occasional piss-up at a birthday or wedding, I wasn't really much of a drinker.

Mike, meanwhile, had spent most of his twenties attempting to drink the east of Scotland out of Tennent's, had amassed several student loans during his brief and ill-fated escapades into tertiary education, had no career to speak of yet and had a thrice-broken nose and a huge scar after being knifed in a bar in Glasgow – injuries largely sustained while shit-faced.

None of these differences in our backgrounds or lives so far mattered, because we just *got on* with each other very well, and easily. We agreed on all the important things in life – cricket is shit, Belgian beer tastes better in Belgium but nobody knows why and 'activewear' is mostly worn by people who are never active – and we had shared experiences with depression, anxiety and other mental health issues. We talked about these things quite a lot in those early days and I even interviewed him about his depression for a mental health website I was setting up at the time. For someone so closed off in many ways, Mike was surprisingly open with me about his mental health struggles and he seemed to have a pretty good understanding of his inner demons – though alcoholism was never mentioned, now I come to think of it. I don't know if he was withholding it, in denial about it or if he was maybe not even aware that's what it *was* yet, but either way, the word never cropped up directly with reference to him.

Over all the chats and laughs we slowly became friends – but I didn't really *know* Scottish Mike. And I certainly didn't know about the Drink Problem.

I went round to his house for the first time because he'd been looking more than usually miserable and I'd heard whispers on the coffee-bean-vine that he was in 'a bit of a bad place'. He was down on his life and himself, and knowing how depression can throw you into a dark hole that's very hard to crawl out of, I thought a friendly drink and a laugh might be a good thing, so I dropped him a WhatsApp.

> Hey, dickhead, how goes? Want some company? I can bring my usual fabulous sense of humour to make your day worse.

He was so gloomy of late I wasn't really expecting a reply, but he responded pretty promptly, with a warm, jovial:

> Sure.

Clearly a night of top banter awaited.

I asked if I should bring anything – Crisps? Lobster? – but he said nah, just some wine if I fancied it.

> I've only got beer here.
>
> > Red or white?
>
> Don't mind. No wait, bring both.

By the time I arrived, monosyllabic Mike had morphed into effervescent, comedian Mike: relaxed, easy-going, confident and funny, he was almost a different person from the one I'd messaged only an hour before.

We sat in his front room talking, drinking, eating Kettle Chips, slagging off mutual acquaintances, demonstrating how shit we were at push-ups and laughing a lot, and then he suddenly announced that he needed the loo and off he ran, up the stairs, two at a time.

I didn't make it as far as the kitchen to get some more wine before a thud, loud enough to be a heavy item of furniture toppling over, shook the ceiling.

I called up, but there was no reply. Maybe this heavy item of furniture had fallen … onto Mike?

When I reached the landing, out of breath, I found him lying on the floor, body arranged like the chalk outline of a murder victim in an episode of *Columbo*, but here were no signs of foul play or deadly wardrobes; just a man, now a boy, on the floor. He'd gone from coherent, engaged and very much awake to almost comatose – with absolutely no warning signs.

I stood and stared at this man, dressed like a teenager in a faded T-shirt, well-worn jeans now pulled down to reveal a few inches of pineapple-print boxers with the waistband coming off, and a strong, lean body gone limp. His hip bone stuck out, angular, pale and beautiful. Had he fainted? Had a seizure? Was he *dead*?

I'd never touched Mike before, except the odd brush of a hand as he passed me my coffee, and I suddenly felt nervous and unusually awkward standing in his house, so close to him, while he lay there on the floor for me to look at. I didn't know what to *do*. Nudge him gently? Cough loudly? Swear in my best Fife?

Before I could take the plunge and try to help him up, his muscles suddenly stirred. Confused but alert, almost in panic, he tried to stand up, stumbled and fell hard against the wall, slid to the floor again and went back to sleep.

I called his name, realising I'd never actually addressed him as 'Mike' out loud before, and he came round again. He looked flustered and confused and made some attempts at pulling his jeans up, as if this might erase the whole 'I just passed out on my landing' situation and we could casually go back to crisps and chat.

'Shit, God, I'm sorry,' he blurted. 'I've been working mad hours and I'm so fucking tired. This never happens. I was fine and I just … I guess I fell asleep. Fuck. Sorry.'

Then he passed out again on the floor.

I somehow managed to haul him to his bed, arms hanging like sandbags over my back as we stumbled along the landing, supporting him as best I could – as I was to do in so many ways in the years to come. He fell heavily onto his mattress, dead to the world, exhausted but peaceful in sleep. I tucked him in, like a mother putting a child to bed, and stole a moment to look at his face.

I'd never really *looked* at him before. Not like this. It's strange to look at someone when they're unaware. It's an intrusion into their privacy, almost a violation of their most private state of being, and you have them all to yourself, to *see* them – and it can change everything. Awake, he was rarely at rest – always moving, doing, chatting, working, swearing – and even when quiet he had a constant, palpable sense of discomfort in himself. Now he was at rest he was peaceful, gentler and younger. For years to come, I only ever saw Mike look at peace when he was asleep – or passed out through drink.

Without thinking, almost instinctively in a mothering kind of way, I kissed him goodnight on the forehead.

As I stepped into the cold, sobering night air, I stopped at the front door just before it clicked shut behind me. I remember a very strong sense of not wanting to leave this dark, sad and changeable soul out of sight or touch. I couldn't possibly have imagined, way back then, that one day I would *have* to shut the door on Mike for my own safety and the safety of the child we were to have.

Years later, when he was sober and finally able to tell me the truth about hundreds of events he'd lied about at the time, he said that before I came round that night he'd already drunk eight beers and a bottle of wine, and had been drinking for most of the afternoon. He gave no sign of this whatsoever until he passed out upstairs.

There's no point trying to describe how two people fall in love. They just do. I could write nauseating descriptions of tracing the dip of his jugular notch with my fingertips, memorising the curve of his collarbone, soaking up his smell or how beautiful I found his eyes when he laughed, but it doesn't matter because you aren't me and you might hate jugular notches or collarbones or eyes; if you've ever fallen in love, you know exactly what it's like, and if you've ever been in lust, you know what that's like too. If you have *both*, you've hit the jackpot.

He made me feel at ease in myself and fully able to *be* myself. Some days we'd lie together in silence and those were maybe the best times of all: when he stopped performing and slipped quietly into his own thoughts. It felt comfortable, happy and safe, like sitting down in *myself* for the first time, and in company I'd never known I missed. I remember him saying he'd never felt happiness until now; that this must be what people write songs and talk about, but he never believed it existed and thought it was all a bit wank. He'd dare to let himself feel it for only a few seconds and then his muscles would tense, he'd look suddenly uncomfortable in his skin, his whole sense of ease left the room and he'd sit up, say he had to go. Present Mike was as gloriously present as Absent Mike was painfully absent and the hole he left in me when he wasn't there was bigger than I could fill without him. I had a recurrent, blissful daydream of waking up in bed with him one day in a room with tall windows and thin white curtains blowing in a breeze, and knowing he'd never go again because he'd learned how to stay – but for now he always had to go; to move, move, move away from something. It was just a part of how and who he was: disarmingly open but so closed off he was sometimes unreachable.

It took me years to learn that the pull was towards drink and the thing he was moving away from was himself.

But I fell in love with Good Mike and I've never been able to fall out of love with him. I've hated him, screamed at him, closed my door to him and even performed the Ultimate Fuck You of deleting and blocking him from *all* my social media several times, before immediately regretting it and having to do the 'follow of shame' when things smoothed over again, but I can never fall out of love with the person I met and the man I know Mike can be. I've never felt anything as wholly happy and 'meant to be' as I do when I'm with him and it's why I put up with his problems for so long and kept letting him back in. I'm not saying it's a path for everyone, but it's what I did, and I will always believe it was the right thing to do.

I sometimes think back to how or why our whole story even *happened*. Neither of us was looking for love; it just sort of arrived, moved in, left its dirty coffee cups in the sink and pants on the floor and felt as if it had always been there.

A therapist once told me about 'neurotic love' based on need not want, and I've often thought about that; were we both a bit lost in ourselves when we got together, both in a strange no-man's-land between post-break-up freedom and life uncertainty, grabbing hold of something we needed in a laugh, a story, a flirt, a third glass of wine? Maybe we recognised something of ourselves in the other, or felt safe being with someone we understood, or didn't understand but felt an innate draw towards. Maybe it doesn't matter why, because love is just love and you can't argue with it.

There is, though, an unspoken Code of Comfort between people who understand each other's pains and damaged people often bond over the joys of mutual melancholy and empathy, feeding off a shared sense of 'I totally get you'. Lost souls finding lost souls, and all that.

Mike and I both had a history of mental health ups and downs, depressions and anxieties, and we both used displacement activities to escape an inner disquiet, to numb feelings we feared or couldn't express and thus avoid a reality we found it hard in which to be fully present. For him it was drink – though I didn't know when I met him that it was an addiction as opposed to just periods of heavy drinking – while my go-to reality removers have been anorexia and bulimia on and off since I was a teenager.

At its height, in my early twenties, I'd binge to kill an hour, purge for soporific relief and starve myself to gain some sense of control at times when my life felt uncertain or frightening. I didn't enjoy it, I didn't want to do it, it consumed me, shamed me and tired me, it cost me friends and opportunities, money and happiness, and the more it controlled me the sadder I got, and the more I did it to distract from that sadness.

Mike didn't especially 'like' drinking either, didn't enjoy the act of drinking itself or like being drunk – in fact, he hates being drunk. Initially he drank to quieten his anxieties, then as a buffer from realities and responsibilities, and eventually because he couldn't *not* drink.

Most of us will never know why we end up with the mental health problems we have. It could be genetic predisposition, a major trauma, wonky teeth, being forced to play the trumpet and many other factors – often several in conjunction – and collecting *some* emotional baggage in childhood is almost expected.

Mike, however, carried around an entire left-luggage warehouse after a Bank Holiday weekend. His mother died of breast cancer when he was 13, without any prior warning given to him, and his father, a successful defence lawyer now left with three young sons and a broken heart, died 14 years later.

Previously a conscientious, high-achieving pupil, Mike's grades dropped almost immediately and he couldn't be bothered to do much any more; what was the point of trying, he thought, if the world could just take your mum away? All he wanted was for things to be *normal* – no fuss made, to be treated no differently to anyone else – 'I just wanted everything to be how it was before she died' – and to never talk about it.

To this end, teenage Mike quickly learned how to shut out all emotion and just Keep On Keeping On, hiding his feelings under an armour of humour and, as he entered his twenties, under drink. A *lot* of drink.

He never used his childhood trauma to 'excuse' any of his drinking or associated behaviours, and never played it as a *carte blanche* to do or be whatever he wanted. It just was what it was, it was very sad, he wished it had never happened and he just wanted to move on.

I played it, though, and for a long time I used it to forgive and excuse a lot of what Mike did, because he didn't mean to be like this: *his mother died when he was a kid, Liz. Give the guy a break.*

Looking back now, we were such a cliché of co-dependent character traits it's almost embarrassing. Mike is a classic, emotionally closed, no-strings avoidant; I'm a textbook over-sharing limpet.

Until he went into his recovery and learned new ways to think, Mike was emotionally the polar opposite of me, and also the polar opposite of how he *wanted* to be.

He could walk away from anything or anyone without looking back once, especially things that trapped or challenged him, without a second's thought about the consequences – which were almost always fairly catastrophic. If anything unnervingly good or stable wheedled its sneaky way into his life, he'd set about destroying it – even if it was something he wanted, and *most* especially if it threatened his ability to escape into drink whenever he needed to.

I, by contrast, have held onto things that hurt and damaged me for years, instead of cutting loose and losing them.

Mike's fear of detachment was zero; mine was limitless.

This combination of closed-off avoidant and anxious, over-caring partner is very common where addiction is involved, and it tends to be a perfect storm waiting to happen, because neither is getting what they need. It takes a lot of time, self-examination and sometimes brutal honesty to even begin to unpick these traits and learn new ones – together.

HOW DIDN'T I KNOW?

I'm often asked how on earth I didn't realise Mike was an alcoholic and why, after it had become very clear that he *was*, I didn't run a mile? These are fair questions, and they come with a very simple answer: I knew fuck all about alcoholism or how to spot it.

I'd come out of school knowing Pythagoras' theorem, how Romans made vases and how to ask for directions, in German, to a station I didn't want to go to, but I couldn't spot a single red flag for alcoholism, I didn't know what gaslighting or victim-blaming was, and I had no idea about personal boundaries or how to enforce them. Where's Pythagoras for that, eh? I didn't even know what alcoholism *was*, let alone how to recognise it or what the hell to do if I found myself living with it, and I was definitely off sick the day they taught us about the tell-tale signs of a manipulative narcissist.

I thought alcoholics looked like alcoholics; you know, all bulbous nose and red face, sunken eyes and – always a bit of a giveaway, this bit – *drunk*.

I didn't know about functioning alcoholics, friendly alcoholics, sporty alcoholics, successful alcoholics, recovered alcoholics or vegan alcoholics. I didn't know that Nice people with Nice children and Nice furniture could be alcoholics – even *nice* alcoholics, but still, alcoholics.

As far as I was concerned, Mike *couldn't* be an alcoholic: for a start, he had a good job, he paid rent on a lovely house with varnished floorboards and house plants and he didn't tend to sleeping in a skip with a can of Special Brew or swig gin out of the bottle before breakfast. He *didn't* have a bulbous nose, a red face or sunken eyes, he was fit and strong and he'd even been *vegan* several times, the Gold Star of glowing health. Sometimes Mike drank a bit too much, sure, but so do we all, and anyway, in our drink-soaked culture it's more peculiar if someone *doesn't* drink than occasionally drinks too much. On a drink scale of one to 10, a teetotal zero raises questions, anything above an eight is a bit of a problem, but Mike was a regular three guy with the odd foray into nine, before coming back to three again. He didn't tick a single box on my 'How To Spot An Alchy' form.

To be fair to all of us who don't or didn't know we're sharing our lives with an alcoholic, it's pretty hard to define 'alcoholism'. Some people regularly drink a lot but they're not addicted, they just like a lot of drink, and can happily go without. Some people drink every day but can, and do, stop if they want to and it's not a big problem.

I've sneaked a can of gin and tonic on the train home from work plenty of times and gone through periods of feeling I 'need a drink' to take the edge off as fast as possible after a shitty day, but I'm not an alcoholic. I think.

Further confusion arises about what and when we drink: is two bottles of expensive Sauvignon over an evening less alcoholic than chugging a bottle of Co-op vodka over a weekend? Are six beers of an evening on the same scale of concerning as a gin before lunch?

Is it just that you have to drink LOADS AND LOADS AND LOADS until your life is a massive mess and, despite this, you *still* don't stop? If so, does an alcoholic stop being an alcoholic if they stop drinking loads and loads and loads and their life becomes less of a mess?

Can you be an alcoholic and then *not* be one? (The answer is no, by the way, but I didn't know that for a long time.)

It's all a blurred, drunken stagger through a stained, crumpled dictionary of semi-definitions. Some alcoholics drink when they wake up; many don't. Some get the shakes if they don't drink every day; many don't. Some heavy or binge drinkers consume more in a weekend than most of us do in a year, but they're not alcoholics – they just like *all* the beers on a Friday and Saturday night and it doesn't negatively affect their life.

Most alcoholics I talk to don't know what makes them an alcoholic, they just know they are one. They know that drink has a hugely detrimental effect on their lives and the lives of others, and if they want to remain well, and even alive, then they can never touch the stuff again. *Ever.*

There is no 'qualification' into the Alchies Club, it's impossible to measure or prove whether someone is an alcoholic or not, and it usually takes years of denial before it's recognised, accepted and dealt with properly – both by them and those who can support them.

> I'm NOT an alcoholic. I have addictive tendencies that I can fall into when I'm depressed, but I've analysed my relationship with alcohol many times and I'm not an alcoholic. I know I'm NOT.

Denial is a cunning little mental trick we play on ourselves and others, enabling us to ignore difficult truth and carry on doing what we want. Whether he realised it or not at the time, Mike was in classic denial about his alcoholism for many years, purely because it allowed him to carry on being an alcoholic. For as long as he could dress it up as cultural or circumstantial, temporary or well within his control, he could keep doing it.

I was in denial about his alcoholism too, as is often the case for partners who want to be with someone so much they find ways to ignore all the bad bits screaming at them in the face, because that someone's face is so beautiful and it kisses so well. I wanted the happy, loved-up us and that 'us' didn't include one person having a serious addiction.

I wasn't *oblivious* to his drinking at all: before we got together I'd seen Mike in some terrible drink-holes and I knew from friends that he'd vanish occasionally, staying here and there, having a few lost drunk days; I knew he didn't turn up to work sometimes because he was drunk; I'd cycled past him once when he was slumped under a tree in the park, so pissed he couldn't stand up, but I didn't know him then and I thought he was just unhappy in his life – he was – and fair enough if you want to drink away your woes for a while.

But despite all these warning signs, I didn't think, or *couldn't* think, that there might be A Serious Drink Problem. Anyway, he told me, very convincingly and while naked next to me, that now he was with me he felt truly happy for the first time in his life and his drinking years were over. And I believed it. Nakedness has strong, magical powers.

Even when we were together and Mike had his early drink-wobbles, I always found a ready reason: work was stressful, he injured his shoulder, he had money worries, the weather was bad, his favourite T-shirt had a stain on it, there was no cereal, it was Tuesday, it was SOMETHING. Without these Somethings, Mike was actually *fine*.

Anyway, how could Mike be an alcoholic if he had healthy, dry periods every few months? The fact that I'd never known a single person in my life who has 'dry periods every few months' before returning to very wet periods every time, or that Mike's were less Dry January than Half Dry April and occasional Desert Tuesdays, didn't occur to me even once. It was just the way Mike did things and I guessed it worked for him. Some recovered alcoholic friends have since told me they did exactly the same: dried out every so often as 'proof' to themselves that they weren't an alcoholic, because Look, Mum, no drink.

The fact is that Mike's entire pattern and behaviour around drinking *screamed* of alcoholism, but I didn't hear it.

Shame and embarrassment definitely played their part too: if I was dating an alcoholic, as opposed to a charming Scottish drinker, then I'd scored *nul points* in partner-choosing. I also worried that if Mike were truly a problem drinker – whatever I understood that to mean at the time – friends and family might pull away from us because we were Bad Sorts, or I was a mother beyond forgiveness for staying with a Bad Man.

Lastly, if Mike had a drinking problem even after we had got together, it must mean he was still miserable and thus, I reasoned, he was miserable with *me*. It never occurred to me that he might just be miserable in himself.

Oh, and *lastly* lastly, why didn't I realise Mike was an alcoholic? Because he told me he wasn't and I believed him.

I am very lucky that for 20 years I lived with someone who didn't lie to me. I had no reason not to believe anything he said, and everything he said was generally entirely true. It's a very safe, easy way to live, and you don't realise that until you don't have it any more.

Lies fall out of an addict's mouth, almost sewn into their breath, until it's impossible for them to say anything true, whether they mean to lie or not.

Lying is the only way they can keep getting the thing they crave; it covers up everything they know we don't want to hear and tells us things they know we *do* want to hear. Addicts lie about everything: where they've been, what they've been doing, why they haven't done what they were supposed to be doing, why they are late, who they've been with, what they were doing with them, where all the money has gone, why the job was lost, who they are messaging at the table – what the fuck is actually *happening*.

These lies are also used to placate any interfering health professionals, who might get in the way of the addiction:

I'm feeling much better these days.
I've made good progress.
I haven't had a drink for a week.
It's nothing much, just some depression.
Yes, I'm telling my partner and family everything and they are
  fully behind me.

We, meanwhile, as partners, friends or family, are hurled about in this bullshit tornado and dumped wherever we happen to end up – usually on a friend's floor in tears. Just to make things better, we're often told we are making it all up, and then, for good measure, blamed for it all in the first place.

For the addict, all this heavy-duty deception is a nightmare too, by the way. Constant lying is exhausting and the self-checking and worry about whether you said you were in the gym or the supermarket and whether all evidence of your deceptions has been destroyed will eventually make anyone become anxious, angry and miserable – and turn to their addiction for some blessed relief.

When my anorexia and bulimia were at their peak in my late teens and early twenties, I lied a lot. I'd lie about what I'd eaten, why I wasn't hungry, whether I'd been for a run or not (often I'd been for two); I concealed how much I was spending on food and hid any evidence of my binges quickly so nobody could see them. I got angry if I was caught out, immediately transferring my shame and guilt onto those who'd called me out on it. It was classic, horrible addict thinking and behaviour, so I really do know what it's like to have to lie all the time and why an addict does it. I just hadn't been on the receiving end of it before.

Lies breed lies, and in supporting someone who lies constantly and perhaps also threatens or frightens us into not telling anyone the truth, *we* end up lying as well. I lied about where and how Mike was, how we were and what our plans were to my friends, my family, his family, my employers, my neighbours, our postman, social media – and myself. Then I worried in case anyone who knew the truth would hold it against me that I was covering it up. It made me feel dirty, scared of being found out, isolated and exhausted that I couldn't get the help I needed because nobody knew the truth. It was only when I finally called time on his bullshit and stopped lying to myself that any truth could come out.

WHEN DID IT START?

For years, every time I thought back over what happened or told anyone about it, I always started with The Venice Incident – Mike's scorching birthday afternoon in June 2019 when he fell off the wagon and hit the bottle again – as if this was some kind of definitive moment when Mike The Alcoholic was born.

But as I started to write this book and was forced to recall scores of events as far back as five years *before* The Venice Incident, I looked through all our messages and emails, hundreds of photos and a jumble of memories, and it became clear that the events of that day didn't mark the start of his alcoholism at all. He'd been slipping, sliding, falling and jumping off that wagon for years, but he'd always somehow managed to haul himself back up, just enough to hang on ... until he let go again. As his alcoholism progressed, as it always does, the falls just got harder and closer together, and the only difference between all other episodes and The Venice Incident was its severity, duration and consequences.

Mental health problems don't generally *have* a defined, pinnable beginning or end; they just roll forwards slowly across a life like an evening shadow until you notice you're in the dark, and it's cold, and now you have to try to get back, and stay back, in the light. You don't wake up one morning, skip breakfast and suddenly you're anorexic. You don't get hammered for a week and become a certified alcoholic. There's no fanfare when a binge-drinker finally gets their 'Alcoholic' badge, and a functioning alcoholic can hide successfully behind a job, school sports days and completed tax returns for years, gradually creeping ever closer to being a non-functioning alcoholic.

Mike had been creeping for at least a decade. Peaks and troughs of drinking; decent periods of total sobriety or 'normal' drinking;

wipe-out weeks of booze, then back to sobriety again. You will notice, as you read this story, how many ups and downs there are; how many times things seem to be good but then get terrible again; how 'the worst' times are so often superseded by 'even worse' times, more often than seems possible – and then another good time comes along.

If I drew a graph of Mike's good and bad times from the day we met to today, it wouldn't be a neat line downwards and then another one going up, in a tidy V-shape; it would be two zigzags, jagging sharply across the page, first getting lower and lower, and then, after hitting the bottom, slowly rising again with many crashes along the way. As his alcoholism progressed, this up-and-down war between Jekyll and Hyde got progressively worse and his mood swings, from funny, friendly and motivated to withdrawn, disinterested, frustrated and very unpleasant to be around, became ever more frequent.

It might feel repetitive to read at times: what, *another* crash? Another good time? Now more drinking again? Now you're watching *MasterChef*? What's even *happening* here?

What's happening is mental ill-health and addiction, and for many of us who live with it, this roller coaster we didn't even know we were getting on, or when it left the station, is the reality.

And that's just the alcoholism bit. Many alcoholics, maybe even all, have dual or triple mental health issues and it's hard to dissociate them, decide which causes which and where to start with any kind of recovery. Mike suffered very badly with periods of depression and anxiety, who knows from when, but they were firm bedfellows with his drinking, and all three of them almost always came to the party together. He didn't go off on three-day benders when he was happy; there was always some depression, anxiety, guilt, fear and self-loathing involved too, and the drinking was generally just to get away from all that. And eventually he couldn't live without the drink, because that's how alcoholism goes if left unchecked. So if I had to put a *date* on it and say THIS WAS THE START OF MIKE'S ALCOHOLISM, I couldn't. He was already an alcoholic when I met him. He was an alcoholic long *before* I met him. He was an alcoholic when he was drunk, when he was sober, and when he was neither or both. Perhaps he always had the genetic potential to become an alcoholic, but might never have played his Drinking Card had life not dealt him some spectacularly shitty hands, had he listened to different music or eaten different breakfast cereal or just... *been* different. We'll never know.

And it doesn't matter anyway. What matters is how we handle it from here.

One thing I've finally learned is that *I* can't 'fix him.'

As many of us do, I fell foul of this hollow belief, or perhaps selfish wish, to be Mike's Saviour, the hero who made him better. The one he loved so much he gave up on his greater love, for drink. I worked tirelessly to enable this magic fix. It was always 'if only *this* could happen, or that could *not* happen', if he gets a better job, if we move to a new house, if we have a baby, if we move to a new life in a new country, if The Thing that he needs is in place, and all the things he doesn't need are gone, *then* he will be happier and OK. When each of them failed, as they were always going to, I thought it was either because this particular thing wasn't the right thing after all, or because I'd done it the wrong way.

As I write this now, I can see how ridiculous it is: you can't fill a bucket if it's full of holes and excuses for someone's behaviour, however well meant, only serve to enable and perpetuate a problem. It took me a long time to stop excusing and say 'enough is enough'. I wish I'd stopped trying to find The Fix far earlier, because it wasn't for me to find; it had to come from within him, because the solution to it all *was* him.

LOVE

This book is about 'Love, Addiction and Recovery', and for me the most important one of those is love.

If you love someone, and can see the good side of them even when it's hidden so far under the bad it's invisible to everyone else, and if you believe that the bad is just an intruder and when it's finally banished you will sit together again peacefully in the bubble that you *know* is you, then you stay a lot longer than many others might.

I've talked with lots of partners of addicts who love them and, like me, found it impossible to detach, no matter how much their partner's addiction was hurting them, and even *I* sometimes want to shout, 'Why are you staying with this person? It's *awful* for you. You could be so much happier and more fulfilled on your own. What are you *doing*?'

But then I remember that people said this to me, as you might too when you read my story, and I wanted to shout back, 'but you don't know him and us like *I* do!'

It's easy to offer advice if you have no emotional connection to the people involved, and don't *know* them, as a lover does. It's very easy to say what we might do in someone else's shoes, what the 'best' course of action is, based, often, on either our own direct experiences or those of friends, or something we've read or a statistic or film. But until we are there, in those shoes, in that mind, with that heart, we don't know.

I love Mike. I love him as a human, a partner, a father and a friend.

I loved him all the way through this nightmare, I never lost sight of him and I always tried to bring him back. Sometimes I wished I didn't love him, wished I could cut all ties with him, forget he existed, be free of the pain of him and have no reason for him to be in any part of my life. Maybe, just maybe, if we hadn't had a child together that might have happened, I don't know. Maybe I'd have found it easier to say, 'Sorry, mate, I've tried but this is too shit for me and I'm out.'

I've felt guilty writing parts of this book because I have to tell the story exactly as it was and that means writing awful things about someone who isn't awful but *became* awful, and was awful to me. You might hate him, or hate me for saying it, or for staying with him. I was awful too, and I know it. These are just the terrible things that happen when people become who they are not, until they can come back and become a better version of who they ever were. The decisions I made all the way along, whether right or wrong, were my decisions at the time, made from a place of crisis, despair and exhaustion.

There is no explaining it; it's what happened, and it's a love thing.

Love isn't enough, but it's a good thing to hold on to and build on.

PART ONE

Cambridge

I have to start this story *somewhere*, so I'm going to pick a random day in the late spring of 2016, six months after Mike and I started living under the same roof. We were renting a little house in Cambridge, half a mile from my old family home where my children still lived with my ex-husband. It was very important to me that they retained the stability and familiarity of their own home, during what was unquestionably a tough time for them already. Their dad and I could have spent months arguing over who got to stay and who had to go, or selling the place altogether just because we couldn't agree, and I didn't have the energy or desire for argument or that kind of a split for any of us. Life rarely improves through fighting and sometimes it's better to accept, be grateful for what one has and move on – or, at least, down the road. As splits go it was as cooperative and peaceful as anyone could hope for and I still had my house key, I was welcome to pop by any time, be there when my kids got back from school, hang out with them, have dinner there and so on.

Number Nineteen, where Mike and I lived, was your typical terraced Victorian two-up two-down, complete with pretty window boxes, a red-and-black tiled pathway and some box hedges I never managed to prune properly. Small and simple, it was minimalist and open-plan inside, painted white, and there was a tiny walled garden out the back where we could eat dinner and increase our knowledge of herbaceous border plants from zero to near zero.

Moving in with someone new is always a bit of a learning curve as you discover their ways of doing things, their sounds, habits and domestic irritations, but Mike and I found moving in together refreshingly easy. We'd hang out in the kitchen, Mike cooking and listening to music, talking fast, stopping to show me a YouTube clip I '*have* to see', telling me about some dickhead at work, teaching me many colourful Fife-isms and using a ladle to demonstrate the best way to chip a ball onto a green from a sand bunker.

We met up with friends in the pub, ploughed our way through Netflix, disagreed about how best to do the washing up and shagged against the worktop in the kitchen.

My children, who knew Mike a bit already from his barista days, often came round to eat dinner with us or stay over, and they got to know and like him more with each visit. He was a non-judgemental, calm listener to all their friendship/boyfriend/clothing dramas, provided a very useful channel for any bitching they needed to do about me, and he soon became their close confidant and friend. I was very grateful for how well he managed to absorb three teenagers into his life as seamlessly as he did, and how well they bonded with him and all got on with this new life structure. All in all, the spring and summer of that year were a time of settling in as a couple, and enjoying our new, blended, happy family. Mike was as healthy as I'd ever seen him. After years of bar, café and restaurant work, he had finally quit the hospitality industry, with all its customer frustrations, irregular working hours and seemingly limitless opportunities to drink, and he was working instead in a private health club, complete with a golf course on site.

He had started training to be a golf PT, returned to a strictly vegan diet, got impressively ripped in the gym and stopped drinking completely. None of this struck me as particularly worrisome or unusual at all; we all have a health kick sometimes, especially alongside a new job and 'new start'. There was certainly a suddenness in the change from one extreme to another that was fairly marked, and not like anything I'd seen in anyone else before. Still, I thought, if this is how he does it, and the results were unquestionably positive, then who was I to argue?

But addiction is needy, greedy, selfish and parasitic, and until we've learned to hear its demanding little call and tell it to shut up it will always find any way to creep in. Relapses, whether to alcohol, food, not eating food, sex, gambling or whatever your hit of choice, can happen any time, even when things are going perfectly well, but if the right circumstances or triggers present themselves, they're a dead cert. Triggers are *everywhere*, and are either internal, emotional ones like fear, guilt and anxiety or external: a place, a person, a sound or a smell, family gatherings or major life changes, intimacy, responsibility ... and health problems.

Some time in the early winter months at the end of 2016, two health problems happened to Mike that caused a sudden downturn in his well-being and moods, and a sharp rise in his depression and anxiety.

First, he injured his shoulder at work. This left him in excruciating pain and almost unable to move or sleep, and within 48 hours he had descended into a pit of misery, lying on the sofa all day doing a good impression of a depressed basset hound, his eyes glazed and blank, as if there was nobody home. He stopped chatting with me, wanting any physical closeness with me, and didn't want to *do* anything. The sex stopped, the laughs stopped, the evenings out and cosy nights in stopped. *Mike* stopped, and there seemed to be nothing I could say or do that wasn't either wrong or annoying.

It was a total shutdown from me and everything around him, a side of him I'd heard about but never seen before.

No sooner had the shoulder recovered a little than another problem arrived: a lump. Without going into too much intimate detail, let's just say that Mike was absolutely certain that he had testicular cancer. Oh, and he was definitely dying. Mike's terror of The C-word is completely understandable but the effect on him of even the thought that he *might* have a growth or tumour was like nothing I'd ever seen. Within days of finding the lump he became consumed by worry, could barely eat or sleep and went to the doctor every few days to be told exactly the same thing every time: no, you don't have cancer, it's a benign lump, it's very common and you are fine.

He didn't believe any of it: as far as he was concerned he was dying, they didn't see it, and the longer it went on the more terrified he became. All this health anxiety caused serious knock-on problems with his digestion, so now Dr Mike concluded that he actually had *bowel* cancer instead. He started googling bowel cancer symptoms, went to the bathroom every hour and was barely able to hold a conversation, he was so distracted by all the anxiety reverberating in his head. While he was in such a state of mental distress, I now found myself living with a person I neither felt close to any more or even particularly liked, he was so moody, withdrawn and snappy.

I also noticed he'd started having a beer or two again every evening, and there was almost always an empty green bottle on the floor by the sofa when I came downstairs in the morning. It didn't matter how many times I asked him to take it into the kitchen, there it was. In the space of a few weeks he'd gone from being obsessively careful about his diet and fitness to eating pizza or burgers most nights, not exercising any more, and drinking every day.

He'd just *changed*.

If you've never had anxiety, it's very hard to imagine what it feels like. For me, it's such an extreme level of constant unease and fear it's as if I've had seven thousand coffees, stuck my hand in an electric socket and gone to a rave during an earthquake. Everything just whizzes and hums, flies about and dazzles me, and I can't make my mind be still, or focus on anything except the anxiety. Which makes it worse. My go-to anxiety reducers are running, working or running again. Mike's, back then at least, was drinking.

Around the time of his health anxieties, he started suddenly needing to leave the house for no particular reason but always finding one – to get some milk, to call his gran, to buy chocolate, to get some air – and seemed constantly agitated, unsettled and ill at ease. The only time he could be anything *approaching* calm was after a beer in the evening, and then he was minutes from being asleep. This almost narcoleptic effect of – to my knowledge – *one* evening beer was bizarre, and exactly like that first evening in his house when he collapsed on the landing; he'd go from wide awake to dead to the world within a few minutes, much earlier in the evening than usual and there was always a reason:

> *Work is exhausting.*
> *I've eaten nothing all day.*
> *I haven't had a coffee today.*
> *I had too much coffee today.*
> *I'm not doing enough exercise.*
> *I'm doing too much exercise.*
> *I just can't explain it, OK. I guess I just fell asleep. PEOPLE*
> *FALL ASLEEP, LIZ.*

Maybe he *was* just tired, maybe it *was* just coincidence – or maybe it was just bullshit. I didn't know, and I didn't know *how* to know. I was dealing with something new to me, which didn't seem to respond or react in any ways I recognised, and if I suggested he maybe try to do something to cheer himself up or come out and do something nice with me, it caused quarrels, which only seemed to make him withdraw from me further, so I let it go.

I remember this as the first *Bad Time* – not a bad day or two, but more like a month of Mike being withdrawn and irritable, with a noticeable slide towards him being less friendly or kind towards to me, drinking a little more and us being less happy together. It was a bit 'here's what I ordered but this is what I got', and the huge bunch of roses with complimentary box of chocolates I'd seen on the website he showed me when we met was starting to look like it had been left in the back of a delivery van for a month. It was the first time the thought ever occurred to me that maybe he wasn't the person I'd thought he was, or he'd convinced me he was, and that he had managed to hide something dark from me that he couldn't keep in for much longer.

It was also the first time since we'd been together that I felt lonely and sad.

Loneliness is often a huge part of life with an addict, and whenever Mike was in his alcoholic or depressed phases (which was often and ever-increasing), my loneliness felt like an emptying, limitless abandonment and dragging my soul along the ground until it couldn't get up.

Loneliness isn't being alone; it's being alone when you don't *want* to be, when you're yearning for someone you love, surrounded by people who can't see or hear that you're lonely, and when you've been gaslit and blamed so much you're not only lonely *in* yourself but *from* yourself.

When Mike's drinking increased, I often felt I was living alone in a soundproof box, unable to speak to anyone or make my sadness known, alone not only when he went away and left me, but also when he was with me – because 'he' wasn't there. When he was drunk, angry, aggressive and eventually violent, I could still *see* the man I fell in love with – but he was shut away behind dead or hateful eyes.

Addicts often feel lonely in themselves too, but while he numbed his sadness in drink, I had to keep going, keep coping, keep working, mothering, weeping and hurting, soberly, feeling it all.

People don't tend to flip from '*perfectly* fine and dandy, thank you' to 'so miserable I can't move' without any warning. There are almost always some signposts and markers of a crash on its way, but it can take quite a few of these crashes before we come to recognise them for what they are. Mike's red flags signalling imminent descent into either depression or drink, or both, had been invisible to me against the pink haze of our early love, but as that slowly cleared (as early love has the habit of doing when the toilet roll stops being replaced), I started to see them fluttering, waving at me to prepare me for another bout of bad. Over time I learned how his downward spirals always contained the same few early signs and how relapses were always preceded by lapses: anxiety of some kind, physical and emotional withdrawal from me, depression in himself, frustration, anger, eating badly, not exercising, feeling bad about his appearance and making sudden changes of plan or having to 'pop out' without any clear reason. Once recognised, I became so highly sensitised to these red flags that if I even *thought* I saw a little wave of one I became immediately unnerved and tense. This was the very start of what was to develop into severe and long-term post-traumatic stress disorder a year or two down the line, but for now it was just a low-level anxiety if I sensed the slightest hint of a bad time being on the cards – and one of the strongest of these was when Mike made unexpected changes to any aspect of his life. Especially the big ones.

Right in the middle of his bad-health anxiety patch, when we needed as much normality and stability as possible, he quit his job at the gym. Now, it's perfectly reasonable to hand in your notice from a job you don't like, but the *way* it happened had a familiarly unnerving ring of Chaotic Mike: there was some disagreement about something, someone was being a dick or I don't know what, and he just quit one afternoon in an angry outburst, blaming everyone and everything. It was a spur-of-the-moment leap into the unknown with no planning or thought for the consequences, generated entirely from a place of inner frustration, and with nothing to replace it except a few possible/maybe/vague/unconfirmed photography gigs and 'lots of ideas'.

Mike's unpredictable, puppy-like energy was something I found attractive and exciting about him when we met, but as I got to know it better, I found it often brought with it some very erratic mood swings and events or decisions that didn't quite make *sense* to me, and it was now not so much exciting as downright unsettling and infuriating.

It's sometimes hard to know when to challenge and when to put up and shut up, especially when the other person concerned is clearly struggling within themselves already, and I often found myself performing a precarious dance along the thin line between anger and pity, hate and sympathy, wanting to vent my own frustrations and angers but doing everything I could to lessen his. I flip-flopped over that line many times as my levels of hurt waxed and waned, but my main concern for now was only to avoid this Bad Patch becoming a very long, very bad patch. I didn't know it, but I was fighting a tide it was impossible to stop.

After the sudden job resignation, Mike's moods became even more changeable and he seemed utterly unable to settle, always heading off somewhere, cancelling arrangements to meet up, changing plans or coming home late from some unspecified location. I'd never been with anyone who behaved this way or gave me any reason to worry about what they were doing, so I put it down to my being over-sensitive – but as the weeks went by, my nerves became ever more 'on edge'.

It started with brief flickers of 'Hmm, that was a bit odd', but as these became more frequent they merged to become a constant, low-level nervousness; a background hum of uncertainty, which was incrementally getting louder and more bothersome. If I raised any questions about why he kept having to go to the shop when he'd just been out, or why he was always late when we'd arranged to meet somewhere, I was thrown a quick reason, or told I was either imagining it, or that he'd already told me and it was my fault for not remembering or listening. I tried to shove any unsettling thoughts or upsets to the back of my mind, thinking it might just be me being emotionally over-sensitive after such a tumultuous year in my life, and that they would find a dark little corner and slowly dissolve – but unsettling thoughts and upsets are not very well known for doing that.

I'd never felt like this in a trusting relationship – which should immediately have told me that this wasn't one, but I didn't see it like that. I saw it as temporary and circumstantial. He was just a bit lost in himself and so was I. We were both adjusting to a new life and lots of changes; we just needed something to ground us, and to *settle*.

———

I was in the toilet of a café in London when I found out I was pregnant.

Mike and I had talked about having a baby together from the very start of our relationship; we'd discussed the potential risks involved to both me and the baby, what with me being technically 'geriatric' in pregnancy terms – always a great morale boost, that one – the strains of parenthood, financial burdens, effects on our work, the fact that I already had children, how they might react to me having another one, and so on. But there had never been any doubt from either of us; we wanted to have a child *together*, if we could. And now here they were: 32 cells of embryonic human, the size of poppy seed, embedded in my uterus.

Fifteen years after the last time, I was going to be a new mother again and have a baby with Scottish Mike. Maybe, I thought, just *maybe*, this thing would be The Thing, at last.

Mike was ecstatic about our baby news and immediately put his addictive tendencies to good use, becoming obsessed with every aspect of pregnancy. He went from clueless ('how many months is pregnancy again?') to full-blown fixation, downloading every pregnancy app, checking them every few hours to see if the embryo was now the size of a grain of couscous or a pumpkin seed and watching countless videos of embryonic development and birth. He knew how long our baby's fingernails were, whether it had a bladder yet or not and how often it blinked, and within a few weeks I reckon he could have qualified for a degree in gestation. He bought beautiful baby clothes and a teddy bear, cried when he saw the first packet of newborn nappies and found any excuse to hang out in Baby Gap, cooing over the mini socks. I remember he also made a conscious, thoughtful effort to stay close to my other children so they didn't think we were in any way 'replacing' them with a new baby.

As part of his Project Becoming A Dad, Mike decided to get fit again, in typical Mike style of that time, and leaping straight from 'haven't been for a run for two years' to entering an Ironman competition, buying triathlon books and setting up an Instagram account to document his athletic transformation. I pointed out that I wasn't *quite* sure how Ironman training would fit alongside looking after a newborn, but was told he'd 'make it work'.

This was a way of thinking I heard a lot back then: 'I'll work it out. It'll be fine. We'll sort it'. There was never much actual *plan* or basis for these statements, and they were rarely, if ever, followed through. It was as if he thought saying it was as good as doing it, or at the very least it shoved any uncomfortable, real discussions of *how* out of the way. These good intentions, idealised wishes, dirty hopes, empty promises were all things I got to know very well in the years to come. It's part of the thinking – or *not* thinking – of a person who wants certain things to be true, but doesn't want to put the work in to do it.

I noticed a little addition to our kitchen during this: a yellow Post-it note stuck to one of the kitchen cupboards and in black marker pen: 'Be Better'. Words. Always words, notes to self, and good intentions.

Much like a newborn baby, mental health problems aren't very good at taking a back seat and being quiet; they like to keep waving at us just in case we aren't paying them enough attention. You can think of the happiest, most exciting thing in the world, even having a baby, and mental ill-health will come along and piss all over your beautiful parade.

After all the initial excitement and buzz, about two months into my pregnancy a familiar unsettledness crept into Mike, a jumpy, restless inability to be 'in the room' – as if something else was in and on his mind all the time. If I asked if he was OK and feeling happy about the changes to come, he'd shoot the usual '*Aye, I'm grand!*' – his standard reply to any question about his well-being when he was anything but 'grand'.

The truth, unbeknown to me, was that Mike, like many first-time parents-to-be, was starting to freak out about it all.

Growing a small human inside another human and then carrying the colossal responsibility of looking after said mini-human every day for the next Christ knows how long, with no instructions or annual leave, is pretty terrifying for everyone and parent-panic is as common as morning sickness, but for someone who already suffers from heightened anxieties, and who fears any sense of permanence or responsibility, it's a total head-fuck.

His mind became increasingly frazzled by worry, fears of his own health and mortality, worries about the *baby's* health, whether he would be able to take on such a huge task and so on, and far from my pregnancy being the cue for Mike to call time on using drink as an escape, it was the starting gun for him to want to drink to escape even more. He began to be consumed by thoughts of drink, feeling guilty about thinking about drink and, pretty soon, finding ways to drink. Not a lot, but a bit, and every day, and he noticeably withdrew into himself and away from me over those first two months.

I, meanwhile, was suffering horrendous morning sickness and off-the-charts nausea every day and now I found myself with a partner who, for all the excitement and talk about names, baby clothes, adventures we'd have with our child and so on, was often emotionally absent, preoccupied and 'elsewhere' when I needed him more than usual. I remember feeling a sad, almost cold sense of aloneness in what was already a very hard, tiring process for me, but there seemed to be nothing I could do about it.

Eight weeks into my pregnancy I was putting some laundry away in our room when I found two empty beer cans in Mike's wardrobe, hidden between T-shirts. I've never been someone who goes sneaking around 'looking for evidence' because I've never lived with anyone who had evidence to hide. Even in the months to come, when Mike was drinking very heavily and drunk most days, I was completely unaware of the bottles and cans in coat pockets, bags, under sofas and on top of cupboards, because I never looked for them or even *thought* to look for them.

I sat on our bed that morning, looking at the empty little beer cans for a long time. What were they *doing* there? Were they mementos of some special occasion I didn't know about? Did he put them there by *accident* while he was folding away some clothes and forget to take them to the recycling bin? Whatever pathetically unlikely reasons I came up with, I knew this wasn't just two innocent little cans in a drawer, but I didn't want an argument or to make anything more difficult for Mike when he was already quite down in himself, so I put them back and didn't mention it. I also didn't mention that my worry levels had just gone up a significant notch that day.

The following week, now nine weeks pregnant, I had a bleed. It was so heavy it seeped right through my trousers, leaving a trail of blood on the chair. I'd had bleeds in pregnancy before so I knew it didn't always mean disaster, but this one was different; I felt I was not only losing my baby, but very possibly my last chance of ever having one and my *only* chance of having a child with Mike. I called him to the bathroom straight away as I sat there in tears, blood-stained pants in my hands. He was ashen when he saw them and told me, 'You *must* rest, OK? I'll do whatever it takes to help you.'

Or, he could go to a stag do.

Mike had never been to a stag do before. He hates any big, booze-soaked, laddish events, preferring to drink himself numb on his own – but this was his brother's stag and a clear case for exception. What with the recent bleed, he generously said he wouldn't go, of course, if that was better for me, of course, what with helping me to rest, of course. There was never any chance I'd ask him to miss out on this important brotherly occasion and so, hollow offer made, off he went.

'I'll have my phone on all day and you can call me ANY time, OK? I'll have a drink, aye, but I'll leave really early. There's nothing to worry about, I promise. I'll call you as soon as I arrive, I promise.'

When he left, he had every intention of doing all that. He really did. He only wanted to go, have a nice time, enjoy a drink or two, stay in touch with me and come home the next day. But addiction doesn't care about our intentions or promises, hopes or determinations; it only cares about itself and using us a vehicle for its existence. When my eating disorders come calling, whatever good intentions I have to eat well and healthily vanish immediately as soon as the switch clicks and the anorexia or bulimia voice takes over. I've ruined what should have been very nice occasions countless times because my good intentions and wishes went out of the eating disorder window. It always left me angry with myself, sad, despondent and hopeless – and vowing never to do it again.

Mike left very early to catch the train and by mid-morning, several hours after he should have arrived, I'd still heard nothing and he wasn't answering his phone or picking up any messages. In any other relationship, whether with boyfriends at school, my ex-husband, friends or family members, if someone goes quiet for a while when they're away for the day, especially at something huge like a work jolly or a stag do, this wouldn't be a problem because unexpectedly being out of reach for a few hours isn't ever a Thing.

But with Mike it was a Thing, a *big* Thing. I'd heard all the stories of how he used to get shit-faced when given half a chance, sometimes for days if he was in a depression in himself, and this was his first big chance since we lived together. Given my recent bleed and his very real concern about knowing how I was, he had a very good reason to be in touch and he'd promised I could call him 'ANY time, OK?', so this silence was a deafening Worry Klaxon.

I paced about nervously, trying to keep calm, thinking of the baby and telling myself everything was OK. Maybe there was no signal there, or he couldn't hear his phone for all the background noise of people and chatter. It was odd, though, just vanishing like that at a time like this. An increasingly tense hour or two later, I sent him a few messages. How was it going? Was he OK? Could we maybe call and say a quick hi? Would he like to know how the bump was getting on today? No response.

Everything about this was starting to feel very wrong now, and very Mike on a bender. Several more hours of calling, getting no response and becoming more worried and angry about this total disappearance, I finally caved and called one of his brothers. Apparently, Mike had gone back to the hotel hours ago in a taxi, having 'fallen asleep' by lunchtime.

I remember it was a very short conversation, both of us sounding as if we wished it wasn't happening and neither knowing what to say. I remember I was crying, but most of all I remember it was the first conversation I'd ever had about Mike where I felt utterly ashamed and humiliated.

This humiliation came back to me countless times in Mike's later drinking years; in front of friends, family, shopkeepers, strangers in parks, employers, you name it, and to this day there are people I can hardly look in the face or have even distanced myself from completely, I'm so embarrassed about things I did or said when I was in a panic about Mike. People on the outside can't imagine what it's like to live with an alcoholic partner. They don't know the fears we have, what we've seen and what we know can happen, or understand the devastating impact of worry, abandonment, sadness and nervous exhaustion. They only see the bright, friendly, laugh-a-minute person who got drunk because he was at a stag do – big deal, people go and get hammered all the time! Chill out, love.

But *we* live it every day and we feel it in every nerve in our body; and when you live with someone whose history is to disappear not just for a few hours but potentially days, when you're scared of never seeing the person you love again, you do things that might seem hysterical to anyone else – but we know why we are pushed to do what we do, even when we don't want to.

I did get through to Mike later that day, after eight hours of radio silence. When we spoke he was almost incoherent, his voice a slow, low drawl, nonsensical, garbled words crawling from his mouth onto the carpet where he'd passed out a few hours before. He didn't say sorry once; he just mumbled something about how he didn't understand how this could have happened because he hardly had anything to drink and maybe he just wasn't *used* to drinking any more so it affected him a lot.

Yes, perhaps Mike was just a modern-day Lord Sebastian Flyte, he of *Brideshead* infamy whose drunken mishaps were put down to being 'unused to wine', despite his main source of liquid refreshment being champagne. It took me back to that first time he collapsed in his house and claimed he had no idea why but he **was** so very tired and it was probably that. Or the six bottles of wine I didn't know about.

I know that when he woke up he felt dreadful: angry with himself, regretful, ashamed, hating himself for messing up yet another nice occasion, letting his brother down, letting me down, letting himself down. But for me, that stag do was my first inkling that n*othing*, not even bleeding, pregnant partners, could silence the call of drink and prevent him from getting slaughtered. No matter where we were, how much damage it could cause or what position it left me in, he was powerless to something far greater than us, or himself.

I sat in the bath that night in tears, stroking my tiny bump, talking to it and willing it to stay strong and stay *in*. I knew from that moment that whether he was physically there or not, able or not, sober or not, I could never truly rely on Mike to be there, and this baby and I would have to look after each other and keep each other company at all times. I also knew it needed some rest, and I needed rest.

And that's how we ended up on a plane to Venice.

VENICE, BABY

There is no 'meh' about Venice: everyone who visits her either falls in love for life, returning many times, or leaves as soon as possible and vows never to set foot in that hellhole of canals and rip-off gondolas again.

I first breathed Venetian air in 1984 when I was nine years old and it was love at first gelato. There was just something in the light, energy, colours and sounds that chimed with me, and I was smitten. By coincidence, Mike's parents used to go to Venice every year on a child-free romantic break and they loved it too. He had never been, so it felt like the perfect place for us to go together for some much-needed *tranquila*.

I remember he had a 'nerve-settling/holiday' beer in the departure lounge at 5 a.m., before the sun was even up, and the moment the drinks trolley came shuffling down the aisle two more beers were ordered. He was asleep before we'd flown over the

Channel. (He told me years later that he always bought another beer or two quickly if I went to the toilet on a flight and necked them before I got back.)

As the plane flew on, I drifted into quiet, private thoughts about a lot of things I'd not taken a moment to register before now. So much had happened so fast in the last year and there were things about Mike I clearly either didn't know, didn't understand or didn't want to admit. The good moments, of which there were many, were still very good, the laughs were deep, the sex was good and our love and friendship was unquestionable; I just found it very hard when he pulled away to … something else.

Maybe it had just been a difficult time – he'd had such health worries, been unhappy with his work, and the start of my pregnancy had been rough – but now we had so much to look forward to. As the Alps rose beneath us, I could feel much of the stress from home start to ease and soon I could see the archipelago of Venice, her islands like lily pads floating out into the lagoon. I hadn't been there for over a decade but it really was like returning to a place where I truly felt at home.

Mike was asleep, and missed it all.

I'd booked us a tiny Airbnb in the quiet south-east corner, near the parks and trees of the Biennale – the calmest place on the island, away from the crowds but close enough to walk to San Marco easily for a €25 coffee and some Strauss waltzes outside Florian's. Our street, Calle Paludo Sant'Antonio, was tucked away in the almost ghost-quiet quarter of Castello, completely deserted save for a few cats and elderly couples shuffling along with their shopping trolleys. Despite being one of the less wealthy areas, or *sestiere*, all doorsteps were swept and clean, the window boxes dripped with blooms, and lines of pristine washing hung from one side of the *calle* to the other, like billowing white flags heralding our Insta-worthy welcome. At the last corner before our flat was a bright, mustard-yellow wall, and Mike took a photo of me standing in front of it in a red dress, now 11 weeks pregnant, and looking radiant and happy.

Two years later I found Mike almost *exactly* on this spot, so drunk and broken he could hardly stand up.

Those three days changed our lives – which, for a cheap weekend getaway, is really not bad. My body and mind relaxed and slowed down, the nausea eased off and I managed to eat, and *enjoy* eating, for the first time in weeks. Parma ham, melon, linguine, squid, sun-ripened tomatoes, sardines, pizza … in it all went, and stayed in. I even managed to run again and fill up on a much-missed rush of endorphins, setting out every morning before the heat and crowds arrived to run up and over the bridges along the waterfront into an empty, silent Venice as she stretched and woke up. There was a jasmine running along the railings of the Biennale and every time I passed through its heady morning scent I felt a wellness and happiness I'd craved for years. Mike seemed almost unrecognisably cheerful too: the sea, sunlight and calming pastel palette seemed to centre him; he chatted with people in cafés and stopped to enjoy little details of bridges and angles of steps, his photographer's eye stimulated for the first time in months. We meandered about with no plan, agenda or timetable, getting blissfully lost, enjoying everything and each other.

He ordered a beer in every place we stopped (and we stopped a *lot*), but there was nothing weird or remotely concerning about it: we were on holiday and he was having some holiday beers, as normal people do, and I barely even noticed, to be honest. He seemed very at ease, relaxed, open and at home; we laughed a lot, ate a lot, had sex a lot and generally felt more 'ourselves' than we had since we first moved in together. There was just a vibe and a *pace* to us there that sat right.

On our last morning we had coffee in what had already become 'our' café, in that way any place you've been to more than once does when you're on holiday, under the trees looking out towards the lagoon. I don't know what was in that cappuccino, or if it was pregnancy hormones or a dodgy olive, but I had some kind of Venetian Epiphany. *What if we stayed?* What if we came back and lived here after the baby was born, raised her here in a place with no cars, lots of empty space to kick a ball and chase pigeons, a beach and more ice cream than you can shake a baby wipe at, indulged ourselves in those gorgeous early years before the schooling system sucked us into nativity plays and endless exams. I know I was slightly tipsy on *la dolce vita*, but I was also totally serious. I'd been aching to have a year abroad for 20 years, but jobs and circumstances had never allowed it. We now had a perfect window in our lives to do it, and the perfect moveable jobs to make it feasible. We'd talked about travelling together when we first met; we both sought adventure and change, Cambridge had long since had its day for us and the lifestyle there wasn't proving healthy or happy. There was an opportunity right in our grasp to have an adventure, a total change, a life reset and some FUN, in a place where we felt so at ease and happy together. *What if we just bloody well MOVED TO VENICE, baby?*

I'd half expected Mike to laugh it off and assume I was joking or mad or high on pregnancy, but he did the opposite. He was fully on board with the idea from the second I mentioned it. It would be perfect, he said – the whole place made him want to create, make, do and live. It was a place he felt totally at home in, and yes, he was IN.

And that, basically, was that. The plan was simple and workable: I'd use my share of the value of my old house to buy a tiny flat in this quiet part of town. We'd move out here after the baby was born, and as income we'd work together as a writer/photographer couple, improving the websites of Italian businesses whose English copy is barely readable and whose photography needs hauling out of the eighties – which was nearly all of them. Freelance work had all but dried up at home or paid so little it was impossible to live on after rent and bills, but here in Venice there was a huge, untapped market needing people just like us to come in and sort it out. Two of my older children were already at university so it didn't affect them, and after much discussion their brother decided to stay in the UK to finish his schooling there and be with his friends, but would come out to visit us once a term and we'd go and see him once a term too. Everyone was happy with this and the whole thing was a massive no-brainer.

We had the enviable chance to move to one of the most beautiful cities in the world, whose highlights include 7,000 bridges, kitsch glass models of gondolas, mosquitoes, pigeon shit, rats, floods, unbearable humidity and impenetrable swarms of sweaty, iPad-waving, spatially unaware tourists all crammed in streets no wider than a breadstick. Oh, and which is sinking.

Nothing so wrong had ever felt so right.

No pregnancy is exactly a breeze, but even without any of the drinking factors or stresses involved, it's fair to say this one was a major shocker: my sickness continued right until the birth, I had another bleed at four months, I went into early labour at 27 weeks, resulting in two and a half months of painful contractions before I'd even started squeezing the baby out after an excruciating induction at 38 weeks. To cap it all, I was on my own far more than I would have liked, or expected.

Mike had gone back to work in a café owned by two of our friends, and was now standing all day behind a bar laden with booze.

His working hours increased steadily in the run-up to the birth until he was at work almost more than he was at home, even volunteering to work evening shifts as well. He'd pop home for a couple of hours in the afternoon to shower, have a rest and change into his shirt and smart trousers before leaving again, often until after 10 p.m.

I have vivid, physical memories of being alone at home while he was out at work, chatting with the evening crowd, pouring wine and serving beautiful food, enjoying a hit of normal adult life, while I was stuck in a house on my own, having contractions and being sick.

I didn't know it then, but Mike was drinking when he worked the evening shifts, not a lot but every day, and much of the reason he worked that much at all was to be able to drink.

There *were* good times: we still had evenings out together, and morning coffee on his days off as we'd done when we first got to know each other; we went to the cinema a lot, and out for dinner any time we could, before the baby came. But he was away so much I felt I was creating one life while he was living another, and right from the stag do until these waiting days to the finish line, even though he wanted this so much, came home with baby clothes and planned which of Biggie Smalls' most important works he would be playing his child first, there was already a slight sense of 'just you and me, baby' about it.

I'll always wonder if some of the complications of that pregnancy were caused by the emotional strain I was under throughout it. Either way it was certainly good practice for the blistering first two years of motherhood I was about to live through, as my child's daddy disappeared into drink.

Our daughter was born on a bright, fresh, blue-sky day in November 2017, and for the first two years of her life I spent no more than five days away from her. I woke to the smell of her forehead and fell asleep to the sound of her breathing, read to her, played with her, laughed with her, cried with her and showed and taught her everything I could from the very first days she could see anything at all. She's one of the most extraordinary humans I've ever had the privilege to know, and everyone who's ever met her has felt the radiance and happiness she carries in her.

She gave me strength and motivation every hour of every day to keep going when I thought I couldn't dig for any more, to keep her happy, safe and loved, and give her everything she needed to flourish – and that included having her daddy in her life with us, if I possibly could.

The first year of motherhood is critical to a woman's postnatal recovery. If we're rested, calm and supported we can heal, recover and bounce back pretty quickly, and this is how it had been for me after my other three babies. But this time was to be very different, and my first year with my new baby was the most challenging and exhausting postnatal experience I've ever had.

It started pretty well: for the first week I floated around in a blissful, post-partum haze of oxytocin and sleep-deprived delirium. Mike and I were both so in love with every aspect of this wonderchild we spent hours just staring at her tiny feet, eyelashes and existence, as new parents do. He wanted to show her to everyone he knew, called his grandparents 10 times a day to update them on her latest bowel movements, and I remember watching him rock her in his arms, singing Gregory Porter's 'Hey Laura', her giant blue eyes fixated on his giant nose, and thinking it was one of the most perfect things I'd ever seen, and that everything seemed to have clicked into place after such a strange, tough year. He was happy, he was taking it all in his stride, and he was going to be the best dad there was.

But after that first giddy week of new-parent joy, everything sort of ... changed.

Most people are pretty good at coping with difficult situations if they had some warning, or were expecting them. When we know what's coming and how long it will last, we can prepare, pace ourselves and get through it well. Unfortunately, addiction doesn't 'do' preparation or sticking to plans. It comes along and smashes them up as and when it pleases.

We'd talked a lot in my pregnancy about how things would be after the baby arrived and had reached a very clear agreement, which was that I would not be left sitting at home doing all the parenting. Having taken a step back from my career several times already to raise my older three children – very happily and completely by choice, I might add – I had clawed my way back up the ladder, as all parents, and especially mothers, know it's so hard to do. Mike had been adamant that I wouldn't have to take a big career break again. He said *he* would be the primary child-carer and give me freedom to enjoy the work I'd only just found my stride in again – as a writer and broadcaster on all things family/motherhood/mental health and so on, with occasional pieces of TV and radio work as a commentator for some parenting or 'light-hearted' story of the day. I *love* my work, and it gives me a sense of purpose, strength, focus and great enjoyment. I chose and built this career carefully to fit around my family, so I'd have plenty of time to be a mum, and I looked forward to enjoying that beautiful journey all over again. But not full-time.

This was my time to flourish, he said, and he would support me entirely in this.

Mike went back to work full-time the week after our daughter was born. I realise this isn't exactly unusual in a lot of relationships, but it was at complete odds with what we'd agreed, and, therefore, what I had quite reasonably been expecting, and planning for. It just *happened*: one day he was there, the next he was leaving the house at 6 a.m. to make coffee for people who weren't stuck at home breastfeeding and changing nappies. Again. He'd made it abundantly clear that he would be doing everything he could to help out with the parenting, support me and enable me to have time to work – yet here he was, doing the exact opposite. I was shocked by this unexpected turn of events, delivered to me with no discussion or any wriggle-room at all because it was all arranged with his work. When I asked what on earth was going on and how this was happening, he said, somewhat snappily, that he 'forgot to ask about paternity leave, OK? I guess I had a lot going on, Liz.'

I remember feeling not only ignored and powerless, but hurt and insulted, as if my existence and needs were secondary to his. And, sorry, but *who* doesn't find out about paternity rights – to which they are entitled – when they've had six months to sort it out and have promised to support their post-natal partner? Someone whose mind is consumed with other things, like anxiety and wanting to drink so they can't feel it, that's who.

The extent of the effect on me of this sudden, unexpected effective abandonment from early morning until late afternoon, not only practically but emotionally, didn't come to light properly until a few years later, but it was profound. At the time I just got on with it, as most of us do, but it was without doubt the hardest and most damaging post-natal experience I've ever had – and the least needed. Within a week after a horrific, induced labour, already following those two exhausting months of pre-term labour, I was now on my own with a newborn baby from the second she woke up, having been up with her several times in the night to feed and change her, pitching for freelance writing work in any feeding or burping or changing breaks I could find, still writing my weekly newspaper column to deadline and working on a new book, and all of this with a baby on my breast or asleep next to me in the buggy. Now, when I was called in to London for TV work – which I couldn't exactly turn down in case they stopped booking me, which happens a lot in that industry if you're not available when they need you – I had to take a baby with me. I'd have to be up at 5 a.m. to catch the train, feeding her in the make-up chair, changing her on one toilet floor or another before asking a producer if they could please hold her while I was on air for five minutes, and then travelling back on the train, exhausted. I had no family nearby to help, and a partner who was out of the house more than he was in it. Oh, and it was December, and snowing.

Alcoholics don't 'choose' a lot of the things they do, because they don't have a choice – or can't make a different choice while they are in its grip – and I don't want to be unfair on Mike here. I really don't think he would have chosen this as his ideal way of being a new father, had he had that choice, or been able to make it. But it's what happened, because he wasn't well. That's not an excuse, it's a reason – however baffling, frustrating, exhausting, damaging or hurtful it might be to those on the receiving end of it.

As the weeks went on and the build-up of broken sleep and pressures of new parenthood really kicked in, Mike was at home ever less, and ever less predictably. His working hours started changing as often as our baby's nappy because ... oh, you name it: people called in sick so he had to stay late, the milk had been left outside so he had to go in early to sort it out, his gran called, his brother called, the phone provider called, his bike had a puncture so he had to walk home, and so on and on. His daily cycle home would suddenly take half an hour longer than usual, with no reason given – *it just did, OK?* – and he took on some accounting work for his boss, requiring yet more time out of the house, often at short notice and without any checking with me. If I said I was struggling with him being away so much I was told all of this was benefiting *us*, Liz, because this work was bringing in extra money for the family, and anyway, what exactly did I want him to *do* about it: 'I'm just doing my best here, OK?'

I don't know if it was post-natal fog, which is a real thing for me, or denial or exhaustion or *what*, but I didn't notice at the time that none of this 'extra money' ever came our way, and I never checked or asked about money matters, as it wasn't something I'd ever had to do. In my marriage, all financial things had been open and transparent; we had a joint bank account, divided all bills and outgoings simply and easily, and both contributed fairly in all ways. There was total trust, built on total honesty. So I didn't even question where all this 'extra money' – money I was exhausting myself through hours of extra childcare to enable him to earn – was going. I just assumed it was in his bank account, helping to pay some of our household bills.

It turned out long afterwards that all of this 'extra money' was being siphoned off to settle debts owed to those who'd bailed Mike out at one major drinking time or another. I had no idea about any of this. I also didn't know that while I was doing the shopping or changing a nappy or trying to find a moment to work, he was spending some of it on drink.

Just a few pints at lunchtime, maybe another swifty on the way home – hence the unscheduled and unexplained delays. It was only ever a small amount, but just enough to take the edge off his inner angst and turmoil and take him away from himself. It was also just enough to be part of a far greater problem I still didn't realise was there.

If the loneliness I'd experienced in pregnancy was bad, it had now risen to another level. Of course I had constant, delightful company from my baby, but I wanted *Mike's* company too; I wanted to be near my friend, the person I loved and now missed because he was so often not there, either in person or in spirit

– so to speak. I didn't know where 'Nice Mike' had gone, why I saw so little of him now, and I found his curt rebuttals at any criticism or my expression of sadness or exhaustion very hard. Almost worse, he was always very nice to everyone else, friendly and funny, chatty and kind, the Mike I loved being with – and while he was still like that with me *some* of the time, it was only me who was ever dealt the grumpy, surly, hurtful version of Mike, as if I didn't matter because I would always absorb and keep going, keep taking on the role of coper, carer, shoulderer. He knew I would, because it's who I am and what I do. Until, eventually, I couldn't any more. But that wasn't for some time yet.

Our planned move to Venice was still very much on the cards, and we took two short trips there over the spring and summer of 2018 to look for apartments, make a few work connections and so on. My son and one of my daughters came with us on these recces, so they could see where we were going, feel familiar with the place, and be a part of it. Each time we were there, Nice Mike came back: he was relaxed, funny, caring and easy-going, and we were happy together again. I concluded that it must be the pressures of work back home, of Cambridge frustrations and so on that made him so withdrawn and absent there; *here*, by the lagoon, away from all that, he was himself again, and we were ourselves.

On our second visit, in July, we found the perfect apartment: simple, quiet, light and airy, it even had a small basement where I thought we could make a darkroom for Mike, and maybe even a little home gym, as exercise was so good for his mental well-being. Everything would be OK, I was *sure*, once we were there.

Summer 2018 was a scorcher, in both temperature and bad events, and as I prepared everything for our imminent emigration to the land of gondolas, Mike was preparing himself for his next big drop down into drink.

It's strange to me now that I didn't see his next drinking bouts and mood changes that summer for what they were: not blips or another drinking slip-up or two, but big Steps Down. Alcoholism is a progressive disease and it doesn't 'go away' when things are a bit better for a while. It's always there, and it will make itself known – usually worse each time – until it hits the bottom. The incremental worsening of Mike's mental health and associated drinking, as worries, pressures on him and the pull of his addiction mounted with the mercury was, in the cruel light of retrospect, very obvious – but at the time I neither understood what was happening, nor felt I could *do* anything about it.

There were two big drinking episodes of note and the first was a Nick Cave gig in London. We had bought the tickets while I was pregnant and had intended to go together, but when the time came round I was still exclusively breastfeeding our baby, then six months old, and, a loud, live gig wasn't exactly a good place to take her. We didn't have anyone who could look after her for a whole afternoon and evening, so the choice was made for me: off he went with a friend, while I stayed at home.

Just as with the stag weekend the year before, he said he'd be in touch all evening and I had nothing to worry about because his friend, who was driving and thus not drinking, had young children and needed to be home at a decent time. He said he'd just go, have a few beers and come home to help me with any parenting requirements overnight or in the morning, so I could 'get some rest'.

Problem: there *is* no such thing as 'just go and have a few beers and then come home' if you're an alcoholic. There is only: 'have a few beers and then have *all* the beers'.

I thought that being with someone who wasn't drinking and was a responsible, sensible father meant Mike would be fine. But I didn't know SO much. I didn't know he was drinking most days; I didn't know he had an *uncontrollable* pull towards alcohol, and couldn't fight it when presented with it. I didn't know he was so utterly powerless where it came to drink that after one beer he'd be unable to stop. And I didn't know how skilfully an alcoholic can go to the loo and come back four pints further down, and nobody he's with is any the wiser.

And so it happened. Of course it did. No calls or returned messages all evening, just the lonely, worried, tear-filled silence of a woman left alone at home with a baby again, and who feels like the world's biggest idiot for letting this happen – again.

Mike arrived home very late, too drunk to speak and with beer all over his crotch, and passed out on the bathroom floor upstairs, trousers round his ankles, blocking the doorway – a beer-soaked, limp, pissed father. I tried to wake and move him, so I could get to the toilet, but he was a dead weight and a dead mind. I hated him so much.

The next morning, exhausted from another evening of worry and another night of no sleep, I asked how he thought it was OK to get so drunk he'd passed out. Was this the 'help and rest' he'd promised I'd get when he got back? He was unapologetic, said he only had a few beers over the whole evening, *actually*, and had no idea why he was that drunk because he'd been 'so good about not drinking, you know. I did nothing wrong, Liz. *Nothing.*'

Far from showing any remorse he appeared irritated with *me* for being so tired and upset instead of angry with himself for being so awful. This nastiness towards me was a very significant change in mood and attitude, one he'd never shown towards me, and I didn't understand it. I'd never been treated this way before by anyone who was supposed to love or care for me. I know now that it came from guilt and self-hatred, from being caught out and knowing damn well he'd done wrong, hurt me, let the family down, created yet more problems and reasons for me to hate him, and been so weak as to let this happen – so he lashed out at me.

If I challenged him I got even more nastiness, and that just made me hurt even more, so instead I cried a lot on my own when he was at work or I was out and about in town, and just kept doing what I had to do each day.

That night was still just a baby step compared with what was to come, but it was the worst one yet, and the first time I felt this was more than just being drunk and actually being nasty.

Daily life returned to whatever 'normal' was for us now, as it always did after a Bad Episode back then: we didn't talk further about what had happened and just moved on.

This solved and healed nothing, of course, and all my anger and feelings of powerlessness got stored in another box of unresolved emotions festering away, but arguing was always tiring and unpleasant, and got us nowhere. We did as many Cambridge things as we could before leaving; we met up with friends in the local beer garden, my older children came round for dinner quite a lot, we spent time enjoying the parks and green spaces of Cambridge, doing all the 'last time's and looking forward to our departure.

But in these final few weeks, Mike's bad moods, irritability and flips from kind to cold ramped up noticeably, and my memories of that time are overwhelmingly of crying in parks, sitting on my own in cafés breastfeeding in a strange cloud of numb worry and sadness, and being alone a lot on blistering hot days, trying to keep both my baby and my own head cool.

Mike's last big drinking episode before we left the UK was on his final day at work.

There were to be some low-key 'leaving drinks' in a pub just down the road from us, where we often went for a Wednesday burgers and chips with my children, and we knew all the people who worked there very well. I'd had a grand total of zero evenings out since our daughter was born, now nine months ago, and this was my first opportunity to come out with him, and with his work colleagues, all of whom I knew well from the café and were as much my friends as his. I'd taken it as read that we'd go together, but when no mention of it had come by the time the day itself arrived, I asked and was met with an angry, resounding 'Can't I have this last evening out with people *I* work with? Is it so hard for you to let me have that?'

It was extraordinary. Nobody had ever tried to keep me away from a social event before – let alone someone I was in a relationship with, and with mutual friends. But Mike very clearly didn't want me to be there, and I couldn't get my head around it at all.

I'd held in so much for so long, I finally snapped: we were in a park just near his workplace during his lunch break, and

I started shouting at him, told him how nasty this was, how I felt ignored, trapped and invisible to him, how I was doing so much and getting so little help, and I'd had *enough* now. Enough of his absences, enough of supporting everything he needed while being treated like an expendable commodity.

Far from backing down and saying sorry, his response was bizarre. He showed no sympathy or warmth at all, started swearing at me, told me to fuck off and then sat himself down on a park bench and went into a sort of 'freeze', staring at the ground, not saying anything or responding in any way.

I didn't know whether to stay or go, shout at him more or cry – and he wasn't even *there* anyway, he was sort of ... dead.

Months after he was sober he told me these 'freezes' felt like being trapped inside himself, locked in, paralysed, but aware of everything. He wanted to smash his way out of his brain and body but he couldn't. It was the first time I'd seen Mike like this, while sober – at least as far I knew then, though I *now* know he'd had a fair few drinks by this point – and the first time he'd told me to fuck off, in the middle of the day, when I was asking nothing more than to come out for a drink with him and some of our friends.

The thing was, and I didn't know this then, but Mike *needed* drinking events away from me, because then he could *really* drink. I'd been with him at weddings, out with friends and plenty of other occasions where he'd been drinking, but he never got shit-faced ... except when I wasn't there. His alcoholism desperately needed another massive one now, and that meant me not being there. It wasn't that he didn't *want* me there, it's that his addiction wanted to do what it needed to do, and that meant on his own.

That evening he staggered home, only just made it upstairs and passed out, fully dressed, on the spare bed.

When he finally woke up the next day, several hours after I'd got myself and my child up, dressed, fed and out, he informed me that he'd had 'two small beers' the evening before and had no idea why he'd got so drunk.

He also had no recollection of the argument we'd had the day before in the park, or of any of the evening itself. The whole thing was a total blackout.

Blackouts affect the majority of alcoholics I've talked with since Mike's sobriety journey started, and I'm often told it's the most embarrassing thing they had to face as they sobered up and the most relieving thing not to experience any more: never again to wake up with no idea what they'd done, what they'd spent, whom they'd hurt or slept with or stolen from. Always living in shame, yet not really knowing what they were ashamed *of*, and fearing they would do it again.

Alcoholic blackouts are nothing like going out on a Friday night, getting pissed and not remembering how you got home. That's called being pissed, and feeling like a bit of a dick – and most of us have done that. In alcoholism we're talking daytime, awake periods of complete memory loss. Arriving somewhere, sober, with no idea how you got there, having a conversation with someone, sober, and three minutes later being unable to remember any of it; or threatening to stab someone, say, and not knowing you've said it. They're gaps in memory caused by having so much alcohol in your system for so long, your brain can't transfer memories from short-term to long-term storage, so they're never consolidated properly and just … disappear.

Mike had so many blackouts I'm surprised he can remember anything of the whole of the next year and I bet he's glad he can't, to be honest. As they became more frequent when his drinking was at its worst, he could suddenly snap out of a blackout in the middle of a sentence and have to figure out why he was there and what he was doing. It was horrible for him and deeply unsettling to witness, and it caused a lot of arguments between us because he'd swear blind something had or hadn't happened when I knew the opposite was true because I was sober and functioning. Furthermore, by the time things had reached that stage of frequent blackouts he'd been gas lighting me for so long I'd lost all my confidence and strength of mind and started doubting what I could remember, and the whole thing turned into a big blackout-whitewash-grey zone.

The London gig and the leaving drinks were a huge step down and into a place I'd not been yet; they were the first times I felt like 'one of those women' living with a drunk partner, treated badly and not doing anything to stop it. It put me in a position I'd never been in before, with feelings I didn't have words for, asking myself questions I'd never had to ask myself before.

What was I *doing*? How had I not seen this coming, how did I let it keep happening and why didn't I do anything about it ... or know *what* to do? What was *wrong* with me?

Humans are complex little messes of nature and nurture, made of and controlled by chemicals. We are creatures of the heart, gut and mind, we have a conscience, we wrestle with our morals, duties and responsibilities. Sometimes we think clearly; other times we are at the mercy of hope or blind faith or breakdown.

We make decisions for many reasons: out of necessity, fear, a lack of knowledge or education about things or ways to respond, from love or care for people – or ourselves – or just a gut feeling. Human behaviour often defies cold reason and logic, and 'why' we do things can be hard to dissect or understand. Often we will never understand why – we just did what we did.

And often, we do things that are bad for us – over and over again. From our earliest years we push boundaries until given no choice but to stop. Even in adulthood, we press buttons and test limits for as long as we can get away with it. I played this 'Not Yet' game for years with my eating disorder: I hadn't passed out yet, been hospitalised yet or had a heart attack yet; I wasn't dead ... yet.

And now here I was doing the same with Mike: he hadn't passed out on the street yet; hadn't spat at me yet; hadn't smashed my furniture or run off to another country, yet. I didn't have to throw him out. Yet.

To be slightly fair to me here, I also had little choice at the time; I was legally and financially committed to the flat purchase, had already paid the large and non-refundable deposit and prepared everything for our journey. I had a child with a man who was a good father when he wasn't depressed or drunk, a man with whom I was very happy when he was in a good place in himself, and a man I knew was *there*, under all his problems. The word 'alcoholic' still hadn't been mentioned once, and I still didn't even know what it was or how it worked.

I am sure you're going to scream at me many times from here on for the decisions I made, or didn't make, and I can understand why, from the outside, you'd feel that way. I will *try* to explain my own feelings at the time as some of them might be similar to those of others in a similar position, but that's all I can do. I was there, and I did what I did because of the human and the chemicals I am.

I can argue it all with myself forever and never reach a conclusion. I don't know if I let Womankind down by staying with a man who treated me so unkindly when he was depressed or drinking, by allowing someone who damaged and hurt me to stay in my life, or if I added something positive to *Human*kind by believing in the healing capacity of us all when given help, love, compassion and hope.

I didn't know, and I don't know. I just went on instinct, on what *I* felt was right, on the love we had and the good man I believed was still there under all that damage, self-hate and sadness. I'll probably need decades of hideously expensive psychotherapy to come anywhere near finding answers to 'why', but it's just part of the journey we're all on into self-improvement and understanding. For now, all I know is I did what I did at the time and under the circumstances I was in.

I remember my last few weeks in the UK as a mirage of busy, hot and dizzily tired. In the sweltering heat of July and August, dealing with Mike's drinking and fielding one bout of tears and distress after another, I packed up our life. I sold, donated or threw away anything we couldn't take with us, sorted out mountains of paperwork, admin and banking, van hire, our Shuttle crossing and hotels to stay in along the way, organised a boat to transport all our luggage from the dock to the nearest canal drop-off point to our apartment, sourced a couple of strong local lads with trolleys to push it all from there to our door and negotiated an unregulated, cash-in-hand fee with them in Italian, Romanian, Albanian and Moldovan. By the end of it I'd have paid just to stop Google Translating for six hours a day, and all I wanted to do was crawl into the back of the van and sleep and cry for a year.

But we were ready. This was it: a brand new start and better, happier and healthier times ahead.

PART TWO

Venice

On 2 October 2018 we left the UK: Mike, me and our 10-month-old daughter, in a white Ford Escort van filled to the roof, back and sides with everything we owned.

I have a photograph of us sitting across the front seat and I think it's still the happiest picture of us ever taken.

As we drove through the pre-dawn towards the Shuttle crossing at Folkestone, I remember being acutely aware of the ground moving beneath us, every minute and mile putting more physical and emotional distance between us and so many problems: the bad nights and arguments, conflicts and confusions, stress, loneliness and drink. It was all being left behind us now and we could start afresh – because, as everyone knows, serious mental health problems magically go away if you drive away from them.

Except, of course, they don't. Mike's problems hadn't been recycled with our plastic or donated to a charity shop; they were stowed just inches from me in a crudely sealed box in his mind, waiting for their moment to come out again.

We split the thousand-mile journey in two places to make a real adventure of it, spending one night on the shores of Lake Lucerne, and then, after crossing the Alps into Italy, the next night on Lake Como. We drove through chocolate-box scenery of mountains, lakes and forests, and after a hair-raising last hour dodging lorries on the motorway near Milan, we finally saw the word VENEZIA painted on the tarmac, and then … water.

However you cross the lagoon, whether by road or water, in dazzling sunshine or torrential rain, watching the jumble of ancient bell towers and rooftops slowly rise above the horizon like a gemstone in the water is breathtakingly humbling, and driving over the bridge to the island of Venice was the first time on the whole journey when neither of us could speak. This dizzying labyrinth of waterways, glittering palazzi, tiny side streets, peaceful *campi* and countless bridges linking them all was built in the fourth century on pillars of wood driven into the mud by desperate people fleeing a barbarian invasion from the north, and I still find it impossible to comprehend the work it must have taken to turn a clump of wooden huts on a sandbank into one of the most spectacular cities in the world, controlling a vast empire. And here we were now in our dusty van, a little family of three fleeing the invasions of depression, Life Stress and what I thought was just a bit too much drinking from time to time, seeking to build our own new life in the lagoon.

At the dock, the contents of our van were loaded onto a boat, and the last part of our journey took us over the water to our new home on the other side of the island. When we arrived, I took a small, brass nameplate that I'd had made as a surprise for Mike out of my purse where I'd been keeping it hidden and slotted it into its place beside our door buzzer on the wall outside.

'Fraser-Sim'. We had made it.

The next morning our Polish friend Marta, who knew us both well from Cambridge and loves a bit of adventure and a road trip, flew in from Cambridge, spent 24 hours helping us construct the world's biggest IKEA wardrobe and unpacking countless cardboard boxes with us, before driving our van all the way back to the UK, now empty.

None of us knew it then, but I was to do the exact journey in reverse almost a year to the day later, this time with only me and our daughter.

The House at Number 5, as I came to call it because it's a house and it's at number 5, sits on the ground floor of a tall, elegant building in a wide street, or *calle* in Venetian, in the quietest area of Venice, called Sant'Elena. Few tourists ever go there except by accident and if they do, they always come back.

A lush green space in an otherwise hard, stone city, Sant'Elena has parks, playgrounds, tennis courts and a football pitch, family-run *trattorie* and cafés, a butcher, a bakery and a rip-off greengrocer, two *tabaccherias*, neither of which are ever open when you need them to be, a pharmacy and a post office where you can queue for an hour to get the wrong stamp and then get sighed at. It's a tiny, quiet, respectable and friendly community, its elderly population, many of whom were born here and will almost certainly die here too, slowly being replaced by their children and grandchildren. Only a 15-minute walk from the bustle of San Marco, there are people in Sant'Elena who haven't been 'into town' for 40 years. They remain here because it's paradise, and we now had our own little corner of it, happy and safe.

I'd first set foot in my apartment a few months before, on one of our flying recces, and knew immediately that this was the place. Open-plan, high-ceilinged, tile-floored and painted entirely white, it gave an immediate sense of space, light and rest from the world; a rare find in this city, where life is squeezed into tiny spaces then smothered in ornate floorings and Murano glass just to make it more claustrophobic. This place was pure simplicity and calm.

There was a little balcony overlooking a courtyard at the back and I even had my own washing line; it was stiff, it squeaked and it was a pain in the arse to have to yank it all the way out and in just to get that *one* pair of pants you really wanted, but it made me feel like a proper Venetian.

On the street side there were four tall windows with window boxes I intended to fill with some kind of Venetian flowers, but they ended up being a handy container for our daughter's Duplo, and old wooden shutters to keep out the baking sun.

With two big bedrooms, one bathroom and a handy little basement, it had everything we needed, and, crucially, it needed no work: we could just move in and *stop*.

The day we viewed it, I went through to the main bedroom on my own. I remember looking out of the tall windows onto the street. A huge oleander tree dripped pink blossom onto the ground, gathering in pillowy piles against the wall opposite, and an old lady on the fifth floor, who was shaking out a blanket and hanging it over her balcony rail, smiled and waved, and I waved back. I took in the shape and feel of the room to imagine how it might be to lie in bed there, holding each other naked, hot but cooled by the night air. I had found my white curtains blowing in the breeze, and in my head, at that moment, we moved in.

Less than a year later I was pushed against the wardrobe in that very room by someone so unwell, so broken by drink, he wanted the whole world to stop.

Our first few days in Venice were the happiest we ever had there. Everything was bright, exciting and *happy*: the colours were happy, the sea was happy, the lines of laundry were happy, even the scrawny cats sitting in their window boxes were happy. The late summer sunsets brought Instagram to its knees, and we floated around in a haze of disbelief and Aperol Spritz. *We* were happy.

Venice has no roads – this is probably the most defining feature of the whole place, in fact, and I'll never forget being on a plane just as we were coming in to land at Marco Polo airport, and the lady next to me asked how much I thought it would be to get an Uber to her hotel. I'll never know if she'd been intending to go to Venice, California instead, and was in for a fairly major shock – so to get about you have three options: public water bus, called a 'vaporetto'; water taxi, which is more expensive than hiring a helicopter; or, as is most usual for almost all Venetians, on foot. It's completely normal to traipse 45 minutes for a loaf of the correct bread or an hour to get to work, and you can tell a Venetian from a tourist immediately by their footwear (comfortable and well cushioned to absorb all the stomping on unforgiving stone), walking speed (fast) and the exact line they take. Without warning they'll suddenly duck left down an alleyway so narrow their shoulders scrape the walls, then veer right, take another left, skip up and over a bridge and end up at exactly the right wonky doorway, while nattering on their phone the whole way.

We walked miles in those early days, getting to know every *sotoportego, campo, ruga* and *fondamenta,* as the various types of streets and squares are so beautifully called there, and I carried our daughter in a papoose as we went, her huge, inquisitive eyes taking it all in, fascinated by every cat, window and canal, up and over bridges, up and over bridges, step step step, walk walk walk, up up up, down down down: the constant marching rhythm of this city on foot. Her white-blonde hair stood out a mile, and almost everyone we passed, from tourists to locals, stopped to say hello.

'*Ciaoooo piccolina! Amore!! Ma che beliiiiiiissima!!*' was the soundtrack to our walks. She was the gateway to conversations and friendships, and my overriding memories of her in that year are of watching her explore and play in her new stomping ground, blissfully at ease, at home and happy.

Mike was happy too, or so he seemed in those earliest days; relaxed and calm, he wasn't fazed by things that usually irritated him. He set about learning basic Italian, practising it merrily on any unwilling victim within earshot, and he suddenly wanted to *do* things, see things, enjoy things and explore.

So we did; we took the boat out to the little islands of Murano, Burano and Torcello, we climbed the campanile of the 10th-century Church of Santa Something-or-Other, pretended to care about the Venetian-Byzantine architecture, but really we just watched our daughter happily crawling up and down the hot stone steps in the late afternoon sun; we went to the rooftop of the Fondaco dei Tedeschi and looked down over the Rialto Bridge at sunset, water taxis and gondolas peppering the Grand Canal and the mess of roofs and church towers that provide essential location markers in this almost impenetrable web.

Mike came home excitedly every day with armfuls of fresh *tardivo, funghi* and a random assortment of vegetables we'd never heard of from the 'greengrocer on the boat'. We gorged on porchetta, squid, olives and every shape of pasta you can imagine, which all tasted like ... pasta, and even tried to cook an octopus, whom we named Alan, though sadly he ended up in the bin because we managed to mess it up so badly he was inedible. (Sorry, Alan.) Mike, now fully Scottish-Venetian, would stand in the kitchen, music on, dancing, talking and making me laugh, rustling up some *panzanella*, risotto and huge salads of chicory and orange. It was just like the first time we moved in together, and it was *lovely* to feel that again.

Venetians are people people. They live cheek to cheek, shoulder to shoulder and wine glass to wine glass, talking, gossiping, hand-waving and telling elaborate, wildly embellished stories. In these respects they were not unlike many of the people Mike had grown up around, and he always said he felt socially and culturally far more at home in Venice than in Cambridge. Venetians seemed to love the fact that he was Scottish, not *Inglese*, and he soon became a bit of a local hero, this bearded Scottish photographer who loved to share a colourful anecdote and a beer. And another.

While he cooked, Mike always had a beer or glass of local wine on hand, as people often do when they're cooking at home in the evening. It was to be a long time before I learned how many empty wine bottles were hidden on a wooden beam, just a few feet above my head.

While Mike's eventual descent to the depths of alcoholism was inevitable, I do sometimes wonder if the disasters that followed might not have happened quite so fast, or so severely, had it not been for the Wall Problem.

Long story short, four days after we arrived I was informed that there was a 'problem' in my apartment, in the form of a missing wall.

To my architecturally untrained eye all walls had appeared to be present, but during a conversation with my estate agent in half Italian, half English, half confusion, I learned that in 1984 the previous owners had some internal structural work done, and as part of this reshuffle they were supposed to close off a small alcove between the kitchen and the bathroom, with a 1.5m long wall. But they didn't. *Because Venice.*

Everything had ticked along nicely in the intervening years but now, with a sale imminent (for which I had already paid the deposit and which I was due to complete in the next day or two), some old paperwork had been dug out and the Official Person In The Official Venetian Office of Officialdom had suddenly noticed that the Official Apartment Plans stored in the Official Vault of 10 million pieces of Official Venetian Paperwork didn't match the current *unofficial* layout of the apartment. I could either leave things as they were, but face a possible problem if I ever wanted to sell it in the future, or, to make things 'in order', I would have to put the missing wall back. Due to its position this required smashing out, restructuring and replacing the whole kitchen and bathroom, rewiring and re-plumbing, *and* we would have to move out for several months while the work took place. With a baby. In the winter. Having just moved in.

The wall news was something of a nuclear bomb to my plans for rest and recuperation, if I'm quite honest. I had specifically chosen a place to live that needed *no work doing* so we could stop all the exhausting hecticness of our recent lives, and now we faced having to pack up again, move out and demolish the place. Mike and I talked it all through, talked some more, I cried, then I cried some more, and finally agreed to see it through and make sure everything was as it should be. It wouldn't be *that* bad. It was, after all, just a small wall.

I think it's fair to say that from this point on, things started to go rather ... wrong. Our peaceful start to Venetian life was shattered as my flat and my brain became filled with architects, builders, plumbers, electricians and tile suppliers, all coming and going, poking about, measuring, scribbling and talking fast. My vocabulary grew from *pizza*, *macchiato* and *gelato* to include an impressive lexicon of building terms and materials, and within a week I could talk to an Albanian electrician, a Moldovan plumber and a Venetian architect all at the same time, and work out who was ripping me off the most. My Google Translate read like a cross-border construction manual, and my

WhatsApp beeped every three seconds with another message I couldn't read.

We'd gone from idyllic dreamland to renovation nightmare, our smiles quickly waned and conversation, once excited and happy, became heavy and occasionally argumentative as we struggled to decide where the bath should go, if the tiles should have bevelled or straight edges and if it would annoy us forever to have a corner cupboard that swung the wrong way. (I said it would, because I'm like that with cupboards.)

Mike would sit slowly emptying a bottle of wine as we drew up yet more plans every evening – after we'd already been to our local bar for an *aperitivo* before dinner, after a beer on the way home from another walk.

I don't know if it's because my mind was so preoccupied by the building problems, or looking after my daughter or what, but I really didn't notice the marked increase in volume of Mike's alcohol consumption – and I didn't even *know* of all the rest that was being consumed when he wasn't with me.

Alcoholism doesn't much care about wallpaper, background music or location – it will always find a way to destroy you until you destroy it. But if you had to pick one of the worst places on earth to take someone with major depression and alcoholism, Venice would be a front runner.

If you don't have a drink problem when you arrive, you soon will, and if you're an *alcoholic* when you arrive, you're probably going to die here unless you get out. Truly, if I'd known I was moving into a giant, floating, 24-hour pub with a full-blown alcoholic, I'd never have done it.

I'm not sure what the ratio of bars to residents is, but a rough guess would be at least 4:1. There appear to be no agreed opening hours, no last orders and no official measurements of a unit of alcohol; they just pour and drink. And that's just in the bars; you can also buy a beer in a bakery, a Spritz in an ice cream shop and wine at the bus ticket kiosk. There is almost nowhere you can't buy booze.

With no cars, there is no concern about drink-driving, and the Venetian day starts very early when the fishermen come in off the lagoon and sink their first after-work beer, at 7 a.m. The Rialto market is fizzing by 9 a.m. and so is the Prosecco, booze flowing as constantly as the waters of the Grand Canal: Spritz at 8 a.m., Prosecco with a mid-morning coffee, Cynar on the way to work, a glass of wine at lunch, beer in the afternoon, *aperitivo* at sunset and a last few glasses of wine with dinner. The measures are thankfully small and despite the constant drinking that goes on, in the nine months we lived in Venice I don't think I ever saw more than one local person appear to be drunk.

At least, not *our* kind of drunk. Not Friday night, lairy drunk or shit-faced, offensive, ugly drunk, not Drinker drunk, and never violent drunk.

The only time I ever saw someone being an ugly, offensive Drinker drunk in Venice was five months after we arrived, when a shit-faced Mike was trying to stagger over a bridge in the middle of the day.

The amount we drank in Venice rose very quickly, but so stealthily I didn't even notice it was happening. Within a month or so there were days when we'd quite happily have a drink at 11 a.m., because in Venice ordering a beer in the morning is as normal as a macchiato. If I look back at the photos on my phone of that time, it's a gallery of booze: Lunch Spritz on San Giorgio. Morning Spritz at Santa Margherita. 11 a.m. Grappa. 2 p.m. Spritz on Giudecca. 6 p.m. Beer in Sant'Elena. 1 p.m. Spritz and crisps in Via Garibaldi. 9 a.m. Prosecco and cake on Lido. 11.24 beer and Spritz in Cannaregio.

Et. Fucking. Cetera. I soon graduated from lightweight Aperol Spritz – basically candy in a glass and consumed by tourists in gallons – to the bitter, heavier Campari Spritz drunk by locals, and then discovered the killer *pallina*: literally a 'little ball', it's a tiny wine glass filled to the top with a mix of Campari and either white wine or Prosecco. It costs €2 (and half that in some hidden-away bars) and you can neck one before you've had your first olive.

I almost feel sick at the thought of how much we were casually putting away – but here's the thing about Venice: drinking alcohol is a normal, unquestioned and unconcerning part of everyday life, even if you are working; even if you are a parent with a young child. In the UK, if a mother stopped for a glass of Prosecco on her way to the school run, a lot of eyebrows would be raised at the school gate. If a father had two beers before taking his child to the park of a Saturday morning, and a Spritz before football practice, people might start to talk. But in Venice, ordering a glass of wine on your way to a toddler group at eleven in the morning wasn't even a 'thing' – or, if it was, there was a lot of that 'thing' going on. Everything in life is contextual and there, rightly or wrongly – and I would strongly argue now that it was wrongly – the culture was to drink whenever it took your fancy, and nobody interfered.

Neither Mike nor I were ever even *approaching* drunk, we just drank more than we did at home, drip-feeding the heady Venice vibes slowly every day, as lots of us do when we're on holiday – except we weren't on holiday now, we were living there, so it wasn't just a day or two of drinking more, it was every day, for weeks. Where I could happily go a day or three booze-free, Mike, faced with this endless fountain of his beloved poison, never went a day without, and from day one he drank considerably and consistently more than he ever had at home – or at least more than I'd been aware of. It wasn't just when we were out and about, but at home too.

He found a wine shop close to our flat, where a litre of local Cabernet cost €3 – less than the price of most sandwiches – and he'd bring one home almost every day, drink the whole bottle over the course of the evening, then fall asleep in front of whatever we were watching.

The falling asleep thing seems so innocuous, but I remember it as something that really irritated me, and hurt me; I was always left alone, sitting on our sofa, very tired from parenting and lack of sleep, knowing I'd be up in the night if our daughter woke, as she still often did, yet here he was snoring away right next to me before 9 p.m. I told him I didn't much like this way of being, him being unable to stay awake and have any kind of evening together, let alone any sex together, and he said he didn't much like it either and he wasn't even sure why he did it except out of habit, so he said he would stop. Which he did. For one day.

I *must* have seen the signs. I must *surely* have recognised them from how he'd been before – this creeping, needy way of drinking even when he said he didn't want to, and his inability to stop. I knew in myself that what I was being told either wasn't entirely true, or somehow just didn't feel *right*, but anything I said to this effect was either immediately explained away with a fair degree of irritation, or I was told I was imagining it or making unfair assumptions and he'd done nothing wrong, he was just tired, OK? He also said I should stop mentioning it because it made him worry about something he had no reason to worry about, so it was bad for *him* when I started banging on about drink, when he was perfectly fine.

I didn't know it then, but this re-framing of events to make me look either responsible for making him drink or slightly mad for making things up were the very early days of his victim blaming and gaslighting of me.

I want to say something here about my attitude to Mike's drinking back then, as I now know many partners of alcoholics who did exactly the same in the early days, and also worried, retrospectively, that they had done something wrong, or been in some way responsible for their partner's demise. I never 'encouraged' Mike to drink, but I didn't actively *dis*courage it either. Why would I, if I didn't know he was suffering from a serious illness? Why would I, when he said he was fine? Why would I, when I was told it was only the mention of drinking being a problem that turned it into one?

He had told me numerous times that when girlfriends he'd been with before were obsessively controlling about his drinking, he hated it so much it drove him to drink more. As if he was somehow the victim of their care for him. I don't know if he meant this to be a way of manipulating me, or some kind of emotional blackmail to enable him to drink, but I was very mindful not to be another person who controlled him and made him unhappy. I wanted to be the chilled-out, trusting girlfriend who let *him* decide, gave him control and let him be an adult about his own drinking. Which, of course, he absolutely wasn't.

So yes, I often wondered, in all the problems that followed, whether I might have enabled something I should have stopped. Whether I was the one who allowed alcohol to become normalised, to pull up a seat at the dinner table and crack open a beer, when it should never have been allowed through the door. It's natural for many of us to think this way and to blame ourselves, especially if we have low self-esteem, but I forgive myself now, and know it was quite simply my total lack of understanding of the severity or even *existence* of Mike's alcoholism, far less how to handle something like that, which led me never to bat an eyelid at us drinking together, like a normal couple – because I didn't know he wasn't, and can never be, a 'normal' drinker.

I also didn't know he used to neck another litre-bottle of wine that he'd snuck into the house somehow, every night while I went through into our daughter's bedroom to get her off to sleep.

Or that there was almost always another bottle of wine hidden behind a cushion, just to the side of the sofa, not six inches from where we sat together.

Welcome to the o2 Messaging Service. The person you are trying to call is an alcoholic, and has decided to vanish for a while. There's no point leaving a message – they'll deny everything anyway, and probably do it again tomorrow. Beep.

Nobody can vanish as skilfully as an addict, and there is nowhere easier to disappear than Venice. The city is a giant game of hide-and-seek, and getting lost is an unavoidable part of everyday life – so much so that if you're *not* getting lost, you need to wonder if you're in Venice at all.

The head-spinning twists and turns, dead ends and frequent Wi-Fi blackout zones make it the *perfect* place to go off-grid any time you like, so everyone is effectively wearing an invisibility cloak.

Furthermore, everything there takes *forever*. There's no such thing as 'quickly popping to the pharmacy': it'll take at least an hour. Off to the bank? Set aside a whole morning. At the start, we found it quite endearing and funny, as every day brought some new anecdote or other of waiting for 20 minutes in the post office while your receipt for *one stamp* to the UK is printed out, cut out by hand with a blunt pair of scissors and then handed to you on pain of death if you didn't go home and immediately file it somewhere, but it also provided a fantastic excuse for never sticking to time, and always having unaccountable gaps in a day. You didn't need to explain, it was *just Venice*.

Better still for those hiding secrets, almost everything is paid for in cash, so there's no paper trail of money exchanged. Venetians never sit down in bars because the second your bum touches a chair your drink costs twice as much, so they stand, chug it and leave. You can go into a bar, drink, pay and go in less than a minute, and what with there being so many of these watering holes you could go to a new one every day for a year and still find a place where nobody knows you. For Mike, this entire set-up of endless excuses for vanishing or being delayed, no way of tracing anything he'd bought and no danger of being snitched on was every wet dream come true.

It was also to be a near-death trap for him.

Within a few weeks his disappearances started happening almost every day – sometimes just 10 minutes, sometimes half an hour, always a plausible amount of everyday Venetian delay. If I asked where he'd been or why he was late, again, he not only had a quick and ready explanation, but managed to make these delays out to be annoying for *him*: he was angry at being held up, annoyed at getting lost, frustrated by the crowds, tired, hot, cold, hungry, *something*, and thus I should be offering poor *him* sympathy – when he knew damn well the real reason he was late was the three stop-offs he'd had for a beer on the way home, and he was only angry because he knew he'd done it.

The adjustment to living abroad is very different in reality to what one might imagine in a few weekend visits, and there's no doubt that it was far harder for Mike than for me – and

far harder than he'd thought it would be. I lived abroad twice
as a child when my parents took sabbatical leave to Germany
and France, so I had a rough idea of what total immersion in
a foreign country was like. For Mike, the move was a knock-
out culture shock. He'd never lived in a place where he
couldn't speak the language, either in words or in the day-to-
day mannerisms, gestures or sense of humour. He couldn't
make people laugh as he usually does, or defuse an awkward
situation with a joke. He had no friends to banter with, no
work to occupy him yet, and all in all, he couldn't do any of
the things that made Mike *Mike*. And if you can't *be* yourself,
it's very easy to lose yourself.

Things *were* positive for the first few weeks as I searched for
and found plenty of things to make our life as familiar-ish as
possible: I located two children's libraries, a place to hire bicycles
on the long, beach-lined island of Lido, several public swimming
pools, lots of playgrounds, an indoor play area with toys for
toddlers, a well-stocked gym, a roller-park and even a golf course
for Mike, where I thought he might be able to do some of the
personal training he'd been so keen on, right back in the days
when he worked in the health club.

But even with all this potential and excitement, the relentless
Veniceness of Venice started to wear us down quite quickly;
peculiarities that had once amused us as tourists became a
wearing daily inconvenience: bridges were a nightmare with a
buggy; vaporettos were deafening and cramped; ticket kiosks
closed at random or the barriers didn't work but nobody
explained what you were supposed to *do* so you just got on
and waited to get fined; every alleyway was so rammed with
tourists it was impossible to get past; waiters openly detested
anyone who didn't look 20th-generation Venetian; our local
supermarket was so tiny you couldn't get down the aisle with
a buggy without clearing all the pasta off the bottom shelf and
then you had to wait an hour at the till while old ladies in
puffer jackets discussed the latest cheese; wet laundry never
quite dried in the humidity so everything smelled faintly of

damp and nothing was in any way *easy*. It was like removing the flattering filters on a photograph to reveal a bit of an eyesore underneath.

It's a shame, really, as I love Venice and I always will; but our brief experience of living there had so many problems, it only made the everyday problems even more frustrating and hard to deal with.

———

Mike's first big Venetian relapse didn't happen until early January 2019, but it was already building – or descending – throughout that first autumn.

His initial excitement and enthusiasm for our new life out there had sunk into a sullen disinterest by early November, and he was seemingly lost in almost all aspects of his life: he had no work, no friends, no structure to his day, no common language and no sense of purpose, and while I'd found myself plenty of copywriting work by carpet-bombing every hotel in Venice with emails months ago, he had nothing. I tried hard to open doors for him and introduce him to any useful people I could think of, but grateful as he said he was, it left him feeling a bit pathetic. I was the mother, breadwinner, renovation project manager, cashpoint and driver of the whole Project Venice; he felt like a passenger who was redundant, pointless and bored, and he wanted to get off.

For *anybody*, a total lack of structure, goals, self-worth or ability to control any aspect of their life is hard to manage. For an alcoholic, it's relapse on a plate.

Looking back at my photos from as early as mid-November onwards, only six weeks after we arrived, Mike was already a bit of a mess; he'd let his hair grow long and unkempt and stopped caring about what he wore or looked like – never a good sign with him. His face was noticeably 'puffier' than usual and his eyes were a bit 'lights out'. He started withdrawing from his surroundings and company, retreating instead into his phone, now welded to his palm, being read or typed into almost constantly, so he was effectively 1,000 miles away with his mates, not in the room with me and our daughter, and he stopped wanting to go out and do things together any more.

My messages to him at that time were a stream of requests and positive suggestions – Shall we go for a coffee in San Polo like we used to? Fancy walking to get a hot chocolate in Zattere, on the waterfront? Let's go for a bike ride on Lido, it's a beautiful day! – but it was like trying to drag a sulking teenager out of their room.

I remember I was invited to an event at the Danieli Hotel, and I really wanted Mike to come along so I could introduce him to the general manager and see if he could score some photography work. It took me three days to convince him to come, and on the night itself he was so down and withdrawn he spent the whole evening as far away from the event itself as he could.

I didn't know at the time but smart, civilised social events like that were almost unbearable for him; he didn't want one small glass of wine and a bit of chit-chat, he wanted five bottles on his own.

Mike started going for long walks on his own to 'have some time to clear my head', took ever longer to get back from the supermarket and the gym (which were next door to the wine shop), and went out at night a few times to 'take photos of the lagoon'. I never saw a single one of these photos. He was often in no mood for chats, fun, sex or anything except slumping on the sofa until he fell asleep, usually very quickly.

I was trying everything I could do to settle us here; he was doing everything he could to get away – not just from here, but from everything in his head. I didn't know that he was in a state of constant unrest in himself, unable to settle or stop his mind racing, having to keep moving and moving, keeping busy and busy … but doing and achieving nothing because all he was actually doing was fighting a constant urge to drink – or giving in to it.

In late November, winter decided to set up camp in Venice; by day, the sky and shadows had a beautiful, cutting clarity you never get in the dizzy haze of summer, and in the evenings, a cold fog descended, wrapping the bell towers in a soup of secrecy and silence.

It's all very dreamy and romantic to be alone in Venice but it's a terrible place in which to be *lonely*. It's a city for socialising, holidays, carnival and talk, glitz and Prosecco, and the inescapable beauty of every corner only serves to magnify loneliness as it bounces off the canal water and echoes off bridges. Mike was really in a badly depressed state now, either miserable or asleep, while I was trying to finish the arrangements for the kitchen and bathroom work, still chasing work opportunities any time I could, and trying to make a nice life for us all.

I remember a few misty nights when I couldn't bear to be in the flat on my own with a sleeping, drunk man so I went out for walks in the dark, just to get away and talk to the darkness.

I must have looked strange, this English woman alone and in tears, wandering up and down the paths under the trees, and I got a few odd looks from locals taking their dogs for a late-night walk, or bar owners closing up shop.

Loneliness is hard at any time but when you're far away from home, it's in another league. For all its 'ciao' and exaggerated hand-waving, Venice is a difficult place to make friends, even more so if you're 'an outsider'. My little community of daily 'ciaos' was lovely, but I had no *friends* here yet, nobody to call on, no shoulders to cry on, nobody to help me with my daughter and no comfort of home. My photos from that time, many of which I shared on social media so friends and family could see how we were getting on – or how I portrayed how we were getting on – are of dreamy canals, sunsets along the seafront and play-times with my daughter, but the truth was that I was desperately, painfully lonely and increasingly weary.

––––––

In the winter months Venice floods regularly, thanks to the famous Acqua Alta, rising from beneath, and submerging streets, shops and all hope of getting home with dry feet. Mike's booze Acqua Alta was rising steadily but rapidly, and by December it had reached a point where it almost never dried out. While he was never 'drunk' and always able to do what a day required in practical terms, he was never fully with us either, becoming ever more irritable and unsettled, and any kindness or warmth towards me was now as absent as a smile from a waiter in San Marco. We'd started sleeping in separate rooms because his snoring after a few glasses of wine – plus the litre or two I didn't know about – was so deep and loud it kept me awake all night, and I was already getting up at least once in the night to settle the world's lightest-sleeping infant.

We'd come here to get *away* from all this, he'd said it would be *good* for him, yet here we were even worse than before, and now with no network of friends or other sources of support. I remembering starting to wonder how much longer I would be able to cope with this, and what I should … *do?*

I couldn't just up and leave and go back home because I was in the middle of renovating the apartment I'd just spent almost all my money on, and I *had* no home back in the UK to go to. If I sent *Mike* packing and stayed here on my own, I'd last less than a week in this impossibly impractical city with no family or childcare to help me. Anyway, I didn't *want* us to split up. I loved him, and all I wanted was for him to stop being like this. I was getting very fed up with the way I was being treated, left alone so much and dealing with a surly, grumpy man, and I told him as much, said I didn't know what was going on with him these days or what I could do. I suggested he try to find a counsellor, get some antidepressant medication or talk to a professional about it? *Why*, I asked, was he doing nothing at all to get better?

He snapped back that he didn't need any help and didn't want any medication, he was just sad here, had no friends and was down, that's all, and couldn't I *see* that? And then he blurted out something about money. He said all his bills had come in together and he couldn't pay them because he wasn't earning anything here yet, and his phone was being cut off now and his website was down and he needed £1,000 to cover it all. He was angry, shouting about how pathetic he felt for being in this situation, that all of the shame and money worry was the *only* thing bringing him down. He said *I knew* that, but I wasn't offering to help, when I easily could.

'If you cared about me, you'd just do it, Liz. I shouldn't have to ask.'

I almost couldn't believe he was saying this to me. I had shovelled hundreds of pounds his way for months, covered the entire cost of this move and most of our rent and bills in Cambridge, I still paid for everything out here in Venice and I'd never once quibbled about any of it because I knew that's just how it had to be for a while until he was earning too. I was so hurt by what he'd said I didn't even stop to ask how come he had no money for his phone when he was perfectly happy to drink several beers a day – almost the most expensive drink you can get in Venice – when I was saving every euro I could for our home and our child's nappies and food.

And *I* wasn't helping his depression? I don't know if it was shock, anger, fear of things getting even worse, having no strength left to argue or sympathy for him or *what*, but I transferred £2,000 into his bank account immediately: £1,000 to cover his bills, and another grand just for him, so he didn't need to go through the shame of asking me again for a while.

Two years later, he told me that all the money I gave him that night disappeared immediately into a gambling debt he'd run up in our last weeks in Cambridge. He'd needed money for drink so he had a flutter in his lunch break, and lost it. Then he lost some more, so he took out a thousand-pound overdraft to try and win it all back ... and lost the lot.

Addiction brings a lot of shame and pain, and a big part of recovery is acknowledging our resentments and hates about it all, and letting go. That particular one took me a very long time.

When we say we don't know what goes on behind closed doors, we almost always mean bad things, when public smiles can be switched off. But we can't see or feel the hidden *good*, either. I know it may never make sense to anyone who's not been in this position, but bad can exist next to good, cruelty next to kindness, anger next to love, and there were still many good moments shared, woven between the bad and holding the fraying fabric of us together. They were increasingly spread out as Mike's alcoholism progressed, but for now, they were still there, and the relief brought about by being freed of his money worries seemed to lift him suddenly into a lighter, calmer place for the second half of December. My eldest daughter came to stay and we all went ice-skating in Campo San Polo, drank Glühwein under blankets in Campo Santa Margherita, ate panettone washed down with hot chocolate (laced with schnapps) and had a very happy, family time.

On Christmas Eve we went to the Midnight Mass in St Mark's Basilica, because, frankly, you can't *not* go, and when we came out into a misty piazza San Marco, with the bells chiming midnight and the whole place looking ludicrously like a film set, Mike took a little blue box out of his coat pocket, handed it to me and asked me if I'd like to marry him. Reader, I said *si*.

The ring was so huge it looked like a piece of plumbing on my tiny finger so I wore it on a piece of leather around my neck. The only time I took it off was to hurl it against a wall in our flat many months later, after he'd walked out, yet again too drunk to think.

———

You know what they say: New Year, same old mental health shit. And so it was to be.

One evening in mid-January, while lifting our daughter out of the bath, Mike put his back out again. From one second to the next he became almost immobile, and in constant pain. Going to the gym was out of the question, he couldn't help me carry the buggy over bridges any more so I had to lug it myself or not go far from home, and he was back to being trapped in an uncomfortable, claustrophobic body, this time in an uncomfortable, claustrophobic city. As tensions inevitably rose and moods sank, Mike, who had just come out to play again, retreated almost immediately back into his dark hole.

During our relationship so far, Mike's big drinking blow-outs had been stand-alone events of total inebriation, like the stag do or the Nick Cave gig, separated by months of almost 'normal' drinking, or certainly no drunken binges.

But that January saw the first run of them, where he drank to the point of collapse several days in a row, and barely sobered up in-between.

It was the worst I'd seen him since we'd got together and the next Big Step Down towards the bottom. Bar a few short dry-ish spells, he never properly came back up from this point onwards.

January 20th was the start of it. I was putting away some clothes when I heard the roll of an empty beer bottle in his sock drawer, just as I'd found those empty cans back in Cambridge when I was pregnant. Even since then, I'd never gone looking or poking about for evidence. I know partners of alcoholics who used to go through rubbish bins, search cupboards, look inside the toilet cistern, even dig about in the grit box at the end of the road trying to find hidden booze. I only ever found evidence by accident and it never occurred to me that he'd be so brazen as to hide evidence, empties or full bottles of alcohol in our own home.

God, what an idiot I was.

He told me years later that there were 'always two beers, Liz, the one you saw and the one I knew about.'

Unlike the beer cans in Cambridge, which I'd ignored, I challenged Mike this time, and it didn't go well.

First he denied its existence altogether and then, when that became clearly ridiculous as I had it in my hand, he said oh yes *that*, God, he totally forgot about it and no, it had no significance at all, actually. 'I drank it one night when I went out taking pictures, then I felt guilty so I hid it. I'm conditioned to be ashamed of having a drink even if there is no problem but now, by hiding it, I've turned it into one.'

Clearly his definition of 'no problem' was different to mine.

We had a big argument late that night and a lot of very nasty, hurtful and angry and pent-up words were exchanged. I was so hateful of him and I think he was hateful of himself too, and of *me,* for finally being brave enough to confront him for what he was: a liar and a drinker.

The next day he got up and left the flat early, and sent me a message to say I'd never see him again. He'd never said anything even remotely like that before, and however pissed off with him I still was, it really worried me. He was so deeply depressed, angry, in pain and now either very hungover or drunk, and anyone would worry about a person in that state who said they were never coming back.

I messaged him every hour throughout the day to ask where he was, was he OK, would he like to come back, but received not one message, call or reply. Just radio silence and 16 hours of high anxiety, tears and fears.

He came back home at midnight and fell asleep on the sofa, extremely drunk and fully dressed.

The next day was even worse. This was the Big Kitchen Buying Day and we'd planned to go to IKEA in Padova to design, measure and order everything for the new kitchen. It had been in the diary for weeks, and I'd been really looking forward to doing this big exciting thing together. Mike woke up in surprisingly good spirits and was even fairly friendly and chatty at breakfast, and I thought perhaps he'd had a word with himself and was going to pull his shit together today, say sorry and come and be useful.

At the very last minute before we were due to leave, he suddenly suggested I go on my own. It would be much easier without a toddler crawling around, he said, and anyway she was coming down with a cold so it would be better if she stayed here, warm and looked after.

He certainly had a good point and he made it very convincingly; going on my own *would* be much easier in some ways, and maybe a day apart would be good for us to cool off a little and think calmly.

There was something else significant about this day, which had nothing to do with IKEA kitchen units. It was the 20th anniversary of Mike's mother's death. Mike never dwelled on anniversaries or significant dates of any kind, but I'd been worrying about this day for weeks, just in case it really upset him – as, to be honest, I'd fully expected it might – and it pushed him to get hammered again. But he really did seem to be in a good mood, with nothing weighing on his mind, and he was very happy to stay at home and have a calm day with our daughter. Maybe that was exactly what he needed, I thought.

So off I went on the train to Padova, on my own.

All morning the messages between us were a fairly mundane mix of: how are you? all good, off to the park, what kind of hob do you think we should have? we're having lunch now, do you like mixer taps? and so on.

Mid-morning he said he was heading out now to 'take her over to Giudecca to the playground. Change of scenery.'

This sounded like a good idea to me, so I carried on ordering counter tops and drawer handles, not worrying about what was going on in Venice.

At half past two he messaged to say they were getting very cold and tired so he'd head back to the flat in 10 minutes.

If my phone dies don't worry, my battery is very low. I'll be back in touch ASAP. X

I asked if he'd like to come and meet me at the station around seven-ish, to help carry a few bags and then we could stop off for some dinner together?

At half past six, four hours after he last messaged, there was still no answer.

I called. Nothing.

At half past seven, while I was struggling to carry all the bags from the train to the vaporetto, he sent me a blank message, and nothing more after that.

They didn't come to meet me, of course. It turned out that Mike had been drinking all afternoon, had carried on drinking on his way back to the flat and was so drunk when I got in that he was already asleep on the sofa, having, thank God, got our daughter fed, bathed and into bed safe and sound.

He told me years later, during another 'let's talk about what *really* happened back then, now you are sober' session, of which there were many, that the anniversary of his mother's death, as a date in itself, had no particular significance to him in terms of how he felt, memories and so on; it was quite simply a perfect hook on which to get hammered and have a totally reasonable, understandable excuse for it.

I had to leave our flat the next morning at 8 a.m. to walk across town to an interview at a real estate agency where I'd just started a new job, copy-editing the English on their website and visiting new properties coming on the market to then write the English descriptions for the website. It was a dream job for me and I both wanted and now needed it, what with the huge, unexpected cost of the kitchen and bathroom renovations to cover, plus the countless beers Mike was emptying my bank account with every day.

They don't really do Bring Your Kid To Work days in Venice: almost all children go into full-time nursery from as young as six months, and *mamma* either stays at home or goes to work, very much *not* with her child in a papoose. But I had to, because her daddy was too drunk to get up.

You might ask why we didn't just get some childcare for her, but it wasn't that simple out there. We looked at a few nurseries and even took her to one for a few trial days, but she wasn't happy there and it wasn't the right thing for her at this time. Anyway, we *loved* being with her, and as far as I'm concerned the more time I can spend with my children in those first two years the better. So parent-juggling it was. Except one parent kept not being able to.

I was livid to have been left in such an unprofessional position, bringing a baby to one of the most prestigious real estate agencies in Venice, not to mention how boring it probably was for my daughter, and when Mike finally managed to wake up and ask where I was, I told him I was at work and how angry I was. His reply was that I should fuck off and I knew what he was like when I met him. He then disappeared out of contact again, and we didn't speak for the rest of the day. From the state of him when I saw him that evening, I think it's fair to say he was drinking for most of that time.

The following week was a strange mix of awful and fairly OK. Mike continued to drink in the day, every day, was surly and rude to me at home and we avoided each other as much as possible. He wasn't *drunk*, in fact he was more often than not 'sober', and now his back was considerably better he often took our daughter to the playground of a morning while I went off to do some property viewings, with no problems at all. In fact, when he was with her, he was happiest of all. But there were growing numbers of days when I had to either cancel work arrangements or hand in work late, or even bring her with me to work again because he'd gone out 'for a wee wander' and I couldn't get through to him for hours, and in these times I worried a lot – about where and how he was, about us, about why he so often didn't answer the phone, about what the day was to bring, if he'd come home sober or drunk, if I'd get any help with the cooking or bath time, if he'd be kind or angry, and how this was ever going to get any better. All this time, I had to keep working, sorting out many further last-minute problems with the plans for the renovations, which were due to start very soon and negotiating Mike's ever-changing moods, and I was really struggling to keep it all together.

I notice from my photos of that time that I have a large scratch on my face, a bit like a Harry Potter zigzag, right across my forehead. I can't remember exactly when it happened, which argument or frustration or moment of despair prompted it, but I do know that I did it to myself.

I don't understand self-harm, and it's very hard for me to explain why I used to do it, or why I sometimes still fall back into wanting to do it if I'm feeling stressed or sad. I just know that if you've ever done it you know why, and if you never have you might never understand why anyone could.

Bafflingly, in this day and age, there are still people who think self-harm is done for attention, that it's narcissistic or controlling, and I almost feel sorry for anyone so ignorant and uncompassionate as that. A person has to be in a *lot* of mental distress to slice their own skin and make themselves bleed just to feel better, and it's certainly not for show.

I remember needing a way to scream silently, to focus my swirling feelings of fear, sadness, anger, powerlessness and anxiety, to have a *place* for all that hurt, and scratching at my skin was the instinctive way I did it. It was almost to feel and see the pain I was cutting out.

It started with that scratch on my face, but the little scratches soon became more frequent and deeper. I'd sometimes dig my fingernails into the back of my hand, pressing in the hurt as hard as I could, leaving white crescent moons of distress on my skin; sometimes I'd scratch a line with the end of a corkscrew or a fork, anything sharp enough to feel that sting.

I don't remember the first time I cut myself with a razor blade in Venice; there was no big, showy 'I am going to cut myself now' moment, it just happened, and I think it felt good, though I hate to say that and I hope it doesn't harm anyone else to read it. I carried a little box of razor blades with me in my wallet or coat pocket after that for at least a year, in case I needed some pain relief through pain.

There's something so almost 'un-human' about cutting oneself that people sometimes think a self-harmer must be crazy, dangerous perhaps, and to be avoided. Mike's damage to me was psychological, and thus invisible, but my damage to myself was glaring and disturbing, and it made *me* look like the mad one. That always hurt more than any cut. I didn't do this 'to myself', I always felt it was done *to me*. So to be blamed or mocked or avoided because of it was just another blow.

———

One of the saddest things about many alcoholics' drinking days is how many of them were painfully aware of their situation, and of the pain it was causing others. They weren't there getting hammered every day, making those they love cry and scratch their own faces without giving a damn, or thinking what they were doing was *OK*. Mike was aware almost all the way through – until he lost his mind and stopped feeling or caring about anything at all – just how unwell he was and how much damage he was causing me. That awareness was of course, ironically, one of the driving factors for him to drink more.

Somewhere in the mess of those very bad weeks in February, he wrote me this message, I suspect from a bar somewhere, and it still makes me cry to read it:

> It's all been too much, Liz. I'm lost here. I'm lonely and frustrated and I feel completely worthless. I am beyond ashamed of my behaviour and SO sad. This is just another failure. I'm a total fucking waste of air. You told me I was a great dad the other week, but clearly, I'm not. I *want* to be a better, kinder person but I worry that I'm just too fucked. That I'm actually just a lazy, selfish, angry liar with a propensity to drink too much when life is tough, and I will hurt, damage and destroy everything that I truly want, out of fear. I steal happiness, I lack empathy and warmth, I bring misery, difficulty, anger, resentment and hurt.
>
> I'm not sure I even know when I'm telling the truth or not, and I will lie again. I will be angry. I will be drunk. I will let you down. One thing I do know is that I want you. I want everything we said we would have, I want things to be OK, and all my energy will be concentrated on making this better. I will do whatever I have to do to get my mind into a place I can be better. I'm so sorry. x

I was to hear or read words very similar to this many, many times in the year or two to come. 'I want things to get better.' 'I will try to make things better.' 'I will do my best.' and so on. He meant them all. But he had absolutely no chance of seeing them through, until he got sober.

It's hard to imagine anything we needed less at this point in our Venetian doom-venture, but the builders were finally ready to start work and we had to move out of our home for the big smash-up to commence. Everything was put back in boxes and stacked in a sad, dusty pile under sheets of plastic, the kitchen and bathroom were completely emptied, the whole living room was cordoned off, bedroom doors were taped up, the heating and electricity were switched off, and my beautiful home was cold, dark, echoing and grimy. Everything we might need for the next few months was loaded onto a trolley and pulled up and over bridges through the mist to our new temporary home in a first-floor flat about half a mile away, in Via Garibaldi.

God only knew what fresh liquid horrors awaited us there.

With our home all packed up anyway, we decided this was probably a convenient little window in which to take a desperately needed break from Venice, to re-calibrate, re-group and re-connect with some tarmac and wheels, and some time away from bridges. So off we flew to the UK. I really thought and hoped this trip would be good for Mike: get him back on familiar ground and reconnect with a part of himself he was quite clearly missing and replacing with alcohol. Our first stop was in Cambridge, where we spent a few days catching up with old friends and old lives. I saw my children every day, they played with their little sister a lot, we all hung out like we used to and there was a blissful pause in all the struggle and tears of the last few months.

I haven't said very much about my older children in this book and that's as it should be, but they were clearly involved at times and it's important that their part isn't ignored. Any time Mike was with them he was always lovely to them and they never once saw him drunk or behaving badly towards me. But they were all adults, or very nearly adults, and were well aware by now that he had a pretty bad drinking problem and it was impossible not to notice their mother get ever thinner, more tear-stained, scratched and utterly exhausted. They also watched their friend Mike become someone they didn't understand, and it must have been very hard for them at times to know what to think, say or do. Always, when we were all together, the Bad Things were very much played down and we enjoyed a happy, relaxed and friendly time together, as we'd always had since they knew Mike. I don't know how much they truly knew, or what they talked about between themselves, but whenever I was in the UK they were brilliant to me if I ever needed an hour alone to be with Mike to deal with some very difficult situations, often at short notice and always with me in some distress, but they took it all in their stride and tried never to take sides or judge. I'm immensely proud of them and sorry for any sadness, anger or distress it caused them. They showed themselves to be far stronger and more mature than me in many respects and I learned a lot from them about boundaries, self-care and love. Maybe some of it was useful to them in terms of Life Lessons, and who knows if and when they might ever face something similar. They know I will be there for them, always. And so will Mike.

I did everything I could to make our short trip home special and helpful for Mike's mental state; we went to London so he could see one of his best friends and I even bought us train tickets to Scotland to see his family, and a very special journey back on the sleeper train from Edinburgh.

There *were* good moments, and he was always fine when we were with friends and family; he'd return to being chatty and funny, Good Old Mike, and I loved seeing him like that – the gorgeous, funny guy I loved, and in those circumstances he was nice to *me* too. It was only when we were alone that he turned off the show and dropped almost all efforts to be nice. He turned up late to every arranged meeting we had, even when I was struggling in the rain with the buggy laden with food-shopping bags and packets of nappies, and there was always a reason: he bumped into X, he was chatting with Y, he stopped to look at something or buy some water or scratch his balls, and when he did finally turn up, all pumped with stress and anger at having to be somewhere when it didn't exactly suit him, he was angry with *me* if I was annoyed that he was late, saying *I* had made him this stressed or I was wrong in some way.

Anyone on the outside would have seen us as a happy family of three on a jaunt back home, but I spent the bulk of it in tears any time I was on my own or alone with him. If I so much as *suggested* I wasn't happy about one thing or another he'd either get angry, with me or himself or the world, or go into such a sulky gloom that I was left on my own all evening while he went to bed, so I was constantly trapped in a tiring mixed state of anger, sadness and worry about what on earth was happening and what I was supposed to do. I had no choice but to go back to Venice and see the renovations through, I had a job there that I needed for income, and I just wanted to be able to enjoy our *life* with a healthy, supportive partner.

He knew he wasn't healthy or being supportive at all, and a few nights before we went back to Venice he texted me from somewhere in town, saying he wanted to smash his entire existence to pieces:

> Everything feels too difficult. I'm not cut out for it, Liz. I'm trying to destroy and sabotage any happiness I might want or could have. It's awful for you. I'm sorry. x

Before we left the UK I asked him to please go to the doctor, to see about getting some antidepressants; just to give himself some help to lift out of his depression a little, and maybe that would reduce the drinking too.

He did go, and he was prescribed some Sertraline, a common antidepressant, and even collected it from the pharmacy. I don't know if he had any intention of taking them or if this was just some kind of 'see, I'm doing something about it, OK?' gesture to me. All I know is that he didn't actually *take* any until several weeks and more terrible drunk-days later.

———

Via Garibaldi is one of only two 'Via's in Venice. Straight, wide and lined on each side with restaurants, bars, local shops and tall houses with a hotchpotch of shutters and balconies, it's a busy, colourful strip of local activity, where life is lived, talk is talked, ice cream is eaten, children zip about on scooters, dogs bark, gossip is exchanged and drink is drunk – in gallons.

It's a strange mix of uptown smart and unashamedly skanky: the cool kids sipping Prosecco up at the lagoon end, while grandads, single mums and construction workers neck breakfast Spritz in a haze of acrid smoke down by the ironmonger's and tea-towels shop.

From 7 a.m., when the supermarket deliveries are loaded from boats onto trolleys and pushed all the way down the road, until midnight, when all the restaurant tables and chairs are put away for the night, Via Garibaldi almost never sleeps. This is LIFE and everyone comes here to live it.

If you want to drink all day every day, this is the place to be, and you soon figure out which bar – or bars – are 'yours'. The staff soon know you, your children's names, your mother's shoe size, what you drink, how much you drink and who you drink with, and never a word is ever said to anyone about it. We had just moved from the edge of the pub right into the brewery, and not only that, the brewery was about to go mad.

What you really need when everything in your life is going a bit bonkers is to be in a place where bonkers is the norm: just after we got back to Venice, the annual Venetian Carnevale kicked off. Carnevale is basically a two-week festival of madness where thousands of people from all over the world gather together dressed from head to toe in outlandishly garish costumes and elaborate masks, and prance around filling every tiny street with a heady haze of bizarre, creepy and sexually charged illusion. Some people get off on all that stuff, but for me it was a ghoulish, claustrophobic freak show of make-believe and lies and I wished they'd all sod off, quite frankly, as I already had quite enough of that in my everyday life.

Mike's drinking, already swaying perilously high, ratcheted up another few notches during those few weeks we stayed in Via Garibaldi: the wine shop, once a 15-minute walk away from our apartment, was now just at the end of our road, past at least six bars, and he was always popping back to the shop to get something he suddenly remembered we needed, but definitely didn't, always took a little longer than expected and then often had to go *back* because whaddayaknow he left his bank card there – amazing. He'd fall asleep by 9 p.m. almost every night, while I was settling our child, and on more than one occasion in that first week back he was so drunk he fell asleep fully dressed on the bed, after telling me to do various forms of fucking off when I asked him to move.

During the day he was withdrawn and dark, seemed to exist under his own Carnevale cloak and mask of misery, didn't want to do anything with me at all and seemed to have given up on even trying. I, meanwhile, had to work a few hours a day to keep the new job I was really enjoying and which happened to be paying for all the Co-op trips and drink, and at least once a day I also had to traipse all the way across to Sant'Elena to check on the 'progress' in the apartment – now a freezing, gloomy building site with a tiling job so bad it gave you motion sickness and needed to be completely redone, sockets in the wrong places and paint splatters on half of our belongings.

Conversations with Mike had been reduced to a tiring mix of hot confrontation and irritation at each other, oddly calm discussion about what kind of radiators to have in the bathroom, then more outbursts of anger, apology and general hopelessness, then back to taps and grouting. I've had more fun getting root-canal treatment without anaesthetic. I wanted some *help* – instead I was getting more arguments and worry about where Mike was half the time.

Repetition can lead to carelessness and it's easy to get complacent and drop our usual vigilance and attention to detail; to start pushing things a little further, thinking we can get away with it, or maybe not thinking at all. I remember the first time my husband found some sick in a toilet because I'd got so used to wiping the rim carefully, I just forgot to do it one day.

Mike's 'secret' drinking was already very much not a secret, but his need for another quick beer or another swift Spritz was now so strong he'd started grabbing any nanosecond he could, however risky it was that he'd be seen.

One evening around our daughter's bedtime he went to 'get some milk'. I stood with her, looking out of the window as we often did in the evenings after her bath to watch the bustling street life, wave at couples and families heading out for dinner or taking an evening *passeggiata*, as normal families did when one of them wasn't sneak-drinking at every opportunity. We waited also to wave to Daddy on his way back.

'He's coming soon. Can you see him yet?' Not yet. We waited more.

'Where's Daddy? Can you see him? He's coming...' She was getting restless, but still he didn't come.

Then I saw him, about 50 yards down the road in the semi-darkness at the side of the street, slinking out of one bar and disappearing straight into the one next door, head down, hunched, on a mission. He was almost right in front of our flat, where he knew we were waiting for him. There wasn't even any attempt at subtlety, just blatant bar-hopping in full view of our window. This was one pissed stagger too far.

With child on hip, I ran down the stairs barefoot, across the courtyard, through the heavy iron gate to the passageway outside and right out onto the street, straight into the bar. There he was, Spritz freshly poured, at least two already in him.

I've never thrown anyone out of a bar before, because I've never had to, but I shouted at him to get out and GO HOME NOW.

Everyone was staring at me like one of those deranged wives having a go at their poor, long-suffering husband who was just trying to get a minute's peace from her nagging. The humiliation, in such a small place where everyone knows everyone, was total and I remember from that evening on I never felt quite comfortable or at ease in that street, in case people knew who I was and thought bad things of me, or of us.

We were now about six weeks into this horrible run of drinking, and March only saw things get worse. In the mornings, while I did my work, Mike was usually on fairly 'normal' form, sometimes meeting up with other parents we'd befriended in various playgrounds so our daughter could have some playtime with other toddlers. But in the afternoons, when I was back home, he'd head out on his own, never with any specific, specified or demonstrable destination, just his usual 'wanderings about' look for work or inspiration. While I had secured a steady stream of copywriting and editing jobs, photography work was still proving impossible to get, despite many emails and knocks on doors, meetings and talks, none of which ever resulted in any actual *work*, and it was all just compounding the deep, crushing depression and pointlessness to everything Mike felt about himself.

Separate to the exhaustion of my home life, I was actually enjoying my work, the contacts I'd made in some exciting places, and the chances I had for really building on this and establishing myself out there. I think this probably just made Mike feel even more impotent and useless, and unable to do anything he wanted to do, got satisfaction from or gave him a sense of purpose. But even when he was given a chance, a door to walk through, a window of opportunity or any other gap in brickwork you care to mention, alcohol managed to mess it up.

Venice is a merchant city, and it didn't build its kick-ass empire by everyone sitting at home being shy and retiring. The whole place breathes and grows through socialising, social interactions and social climbing, and if you're not out there meeting someone, or arranging to meet someone you don't even want to meet but might be useful in the future when you want to do some not-entirely-by-the-books accounting, you might as well pack up and go home. To survive, you need to play your socialising cards right: keep your 'frenemies' close, your friends at a little distance and play a strong 'ciao' game, all of which I'm hopeless at. I'm socially pretty shy, I can't be bothered with fake pleasantries, I wear my heart on my sleeve and I have the world's worst poker face.

Abiding by the Accepted Social Rules in Venice is key, and one of the keyest of these key rules is not getting shit-faced at a smart Sunday family picnic, attended by very well-connected, cultured and influential Venetians.

We'd been invited by a friend of a friend of a sort of vague friend – as most connections happen in Venice – whose family has lived there for about four thousand years and owns several palazzi and a small island. I owned a flat full of smashed concrete and dust, and a drunk partner.

It was one of those blissful 'coats off for the first time' spring days where your skin remembers what it feels like not to be rigid from cold, and we all gathered on the grass in the shade of the trees, as everyone pretended not to network, while networking constantly.

Mike had promised to be on his best behaviour because these were 'important people, OK?' and it was a very civilised event (there are few other kinds there, to be honest) where nobody would be attempting to get hammered as fast as possible. Within half an hour of our arrival he'd drunk almost an entire bottle of Prosecco, followed by several glasses of local wine he'd feigned vague interest in beyond getting it down his throat as fast as possible, and before I'd got near the Co-op grissini sticks we'd brought with us he had invited himself to join a vigorous, rough-and-tumble game of football with a group of 12-year-old boys, launching himself about almost manically happy, jumping, kicking, rolling and laughing with them, and working up an impressive sweat. All the alcohol seemed to have numbed his back pain and released a hyperactive jack-in-the-box, and lovely as it was to see him enjoying himself so much, it was quite the change from the sullen, listless Mike of the last few months. I was talking to the director of the Guggenheim, trying to score work, while he was tackling schoolboys and trying to score a goal. I remember watching him and wondering who this even was.

Nothing bad happened at all and we actually had a lovely afternoon there, we had a few hugs and laughs and felt close again, but that was almost the problem in itself; just as in Cambridge a few weeks back, when he was out with other people, when we were in company, Mike was fun and friendly, and you'd never know there was anything wrong or troubling him or us. It was only behind closed doors that he could be so miserable and disinterested in everything, including me, and by the time we got home the rush had worn off and he was back in his box again, and went straight to bed.

As I was going through all my photos and notes from this time and trying to piece together the mess and confusion of that month or two, my overriding sensation was one of real shock at how I just ... carried on. On and on and on. My work, my full life as a mother, the intense flat renovations, trying to keep any handle on what Mike was doing, and just getting by every day.

Mike was carrying on too, drifting through each long, boring, miserable day, drinking as he went.

I couldn't even stop to *think* most of the time, because there was no space or time to do that; every day was filled with things to do, places to be, nappies to change, parks to go to, library books to return, pieces of work to complete, plumbers and electricians to speak with, and Mike to try and find.

If I ask myself, 'What were you *doing*, Liz, letting all his drinking carry on like that?', I don't have an answer except I was just busy living and doing everything I had to do.

It's impossible to say what triggers an alcoholic to stop drinking (again), but it's fairly true to say that if their behaviour is allowed to continue, and nothing of any consequence happens, they'll just carry on. So he did.

But in March, two events happened that did bring consequences, and I wonder sometimes if they were, in a terrible way, a blessing in disguise.

First, there was the Rugby World Cup match. Looking back, it was primed with inevitable disaster from the start. Mike had gone out for a 'research walk' straight after breakfast, and sent a photo not long afterwards of him chatting with some old blokes at a football social club about a 'potential photography project' he wanted to do. It was a tiny room with a makeshift bar, lined end-to-end with wine and beer taps and a row of wizened men doing their best to empty both. Eleven a.m. is not exactly a great time to be in a boozy social club on *any* day, and definitely not if you're on a two-month bender.

An hour later I got another message (Mike always used messages instead of calling when he was somewhere he shouldn't be, or wanted to be able to disconnect when he couldn't keep all the lies in a row any more) to say he wanted to watch the England-Scotland World Cup rugby match that evening. There was nothing especially unusual about that, but he was insistent that he watch this match *out*, and definitely not at home, and had even very helpfully taken the time to find an Irish pub in town showing it. Oh, did I mention that it was St Patrick's Day? What could *be* more calm, sober and family-friendly than an Irish pub on St Paddy's Day on rugby night?

I suggested several times that we watch it at home, as it would hardly be the place for a toddler, and I'd quite like to see it with him so we could have a bit of *fun* together for the first time in ages, but there was no way around it: he was watching it in that pub and that was that.

I really didn't want to be stuck alone at home on yet another occasion when he was out having a good time, socialising and chatting while I was mummying in a flat I didn't even want to be in, so I said OK, I'd like to come along for a while and see how it went.

How it went, was disastrously.

The pub was absolutely heaving when we arrived – how surprising – and so deafening we had to shout straight into each other's ears to be heard. This is the kind of atmosphere Mike detests, but here he was, point-blank refusing to be anywhere else. After half a drink, one try for England and a quarter of a conversation with a lady from Devon, I decided it was just far too loud and chaotic and I had to take my daughter home. I went outside to get her all wrapped up and back into the buggy, and gestured to Mike to maybe come out so we could figure out what to do?

He came out into the narrow alleyway with me for a few minutes, agitated and clearly desperate to get back in, and I asked if we couldn't please go home *together* and keep watching the match there? Did I really have to go home on my own in the pitch-dark?

You'd have thought I was suggesting we put him in solitary confinement for a year with no Wi-Fi. I don't know if it was the fact that we were in such a public space and he felt embarrassed to be having this conversation but he just flipped, became angry and aggressive, telling me he just wanted to do this ONE THING, and couldn't I just let him have that?

'I'll be home in a hour. Is this *so hard for you*?'

It was just like his leaving drinks in Cambridge again, but this time I was being left in the dark with our baby in favour of the 'one thing' he wanted more: drink.

For the first time that I can remember, I *wanted* to get away from him. I walked away from the people and the pub, pushing and carrying the buggy back through Campo Santa Maria Formosa, over six bridges, through the backstreets of Castello, past the sleeping lions at the Arsenale, down another pitch-dark alleyway or 10, past groups of friends out for dinner, laughing and enjoying life. I cried all the way back to Via Garibaldi, carried our daughter up the flight of wonky stairs and took her into bed with me. We lay there together, her soft and warm, me holding her tight and crying as quietly as I could.

Mike's heavy, drunk frame banged the door open several hours later; he stumbled and crashed his way down the corridor and passed out on the sofa, limbs sprawled off the sides, his loud, deep breaths filling the air with booze. Everything was dirty, nasty and wrong about the whole of him and I'd had enough of all of it. Mostly, I'd had enough of being treated like a piece of shit.

One of the saddest things in the 254,684 sad things about alcoholism is how it forces us into positions we don't want to be in, and makes us do things we don't want to do – to ourselves and to others. When you're lied to and lied to and lied to for weeks and months, even years, but you're told that YOU are making things up and YOU are the problem and YOU are crazy, eventually you want to see the truth for yourself – and you *should*. Everyone deserves to be informed about things that have a colossal impact on every aspect of their life and the decisions they might need to take to have a better one.

I knew the code for his phone, and I looked. Of course I felt guilty, ashamed and scared to be caught doing it, but I didn't care. I just wanted TRUTH, and there it was: his bank card app showing lists of payments made in Cambridge a few weeks back, in pub after pub, always at times when he was alone even for five minutes; when I was looking after the baby and he was 'bumping into people' or 'on my way, OK?!', he'd gone straight to the pub. There was also a large payment at the Hard Rock Café in Venice – somewhere that doesn't take cash, so it left a trail – when I was missing my work to look after our daughter so he could 'go and see a place that does good film printing'. He'd been drinking *all* this time, spending money I was busting a gut to earn. Not only this, but the messages he was sending to his friends bore no resemblance to the truth of our life at all. It was all how great his work was out here, he was making some amazing contacts, how he was having to look after his child a lot to support me and it was tough out here but heigh-ho, he was doing great. Excellent idea. Why not keep telling everyone how great life is, while you piss it all away? Why not just STOP BEING A FUCKING HORRENDOUS PARTNER?!

I was shaking so much while I was looking at it all I nearly dropped the phone several times; I was livid not only at the evidence I'd just seen of all the ugly lies and even uglier truth of what he'd been doing and hiding from me, but that I'd been put in a position to do something as shitty as look on someone's phone. I was ashamed that I'd looked, but also scared of what to do, because if I told him I knew all this it could *only* be because I'd spied on his private information and then *I'd* be the one in the dock, *I'd* be the one in the wrong – in his eyes anyway – and everything could get a lot worse. If I said nothing I'd have no way of telling him I knew he was a liar, and if I told him I'd be the guilty party.

I had to go to work early the next morning and as Mike was still comatose from drink, I took our daughter with me again. To be honest, it was comforting and cheering to have her lovely company anyway. She was so gorgeous, so sweet and smiley, you could take the worst day in the world and she'd put some sun and love in it.

At midday Mike surfaced, demanding to know where I was and where his child was, because he had 'a right to know', followed shortly by:

I want a MASSIVE drink. I'm going to a bar. I want to see you. Where are you. Where are you. Fuck you.

While I was at work I got several more drunk, self-pitying, righteous messages, and then an apology saying he wanted to try and make it up to me, he was just very tired and he wanted to meet up and walk home together.

I agreed to meet him on my way back from work, if for nothing else than to guide a pissed man back through a labyrinth of streets, and started walking in his direction, baby in the papoose, the Wheels on the Bus still going round and round. A long way before the place we'd agreed to meet I clocked him, swaying through tourists who were moving aside to give his heavy, lurching form some space, faltering, swerving, dragging his feet, hands in pockets, slaughtered. When he saw us he didn't seem to register or care at all. There was no shame or humility, just a strange amusement at this charade, and a drunken determination to get to the next bar.

I remember he was wearing a grey beanie, a burgundy jumper and the same old grey jeans with holes in the pockets and crotch that he'd been wearing on the evening he collapsed in his house years before. They were hanging low, he was swaying like a

ship at sea, and it seemed everything he could do just to try and
stay upright.

I asked him if he thought this was OK. He mumbled no. I
asked how he thought I was supposed to do my work and go to
the flat to sort out the builders, *and* look after a child when he
was so pissed he could barely stand, let alone look after a child.
He didn't say anything, he just smiled a bit and kept stumbling
along, hands in pockets.

He staggered all the way back home a few yards ahead of
us, fell over twice on the way, and when we got in he tumbled
onto the bed as if he'd been gunned down, and fell asleep.
His daughter, now 14 months old and so gorgeous there are
no words that could ever do her justice, was standing beside
him, trying to shake him awake to play. He half opened an
eye, made a kind of moaning noise and fell asleep again. It was
disgusting, and I couldn't bear it any more. I'd had no decent
sleep for weeks on end, I'd been left outside a pub, left to go to
work with a tiny child, left with a drunk man slumped across
my sofa and here he was, smiling in his pissedness, ignoring
the calls of his beautiful baby girl. This was no longer Mike,
and I was no longer able to deal with him on my own. For the
first time since we'd been together I needed to get away from
him, from all this drink and ugliness, somewhere I could stop,
breathe and *think*.

I still didn't have many 'close friends' in Venice, not the kind
you call on for refuge or confess to that your home life was a
disaster, but one person came to mind who might be able to help
me in this embarrassing, desperate, lonely little moment in my
life. We'd met through mutual friends when we first arrived in
Venice, and though I didn't know her very well at all, she was
a working mother of four, like me, a strong, calm woman; I just
sensed that I could call on her if I needed to. I think women are
good at feeling these things.

I still have the voice message I left her on my WhatsApp, and
it's very hard to listen to now: I'm in tears throughout, my voice
is cracked and rough from crying, shouting and lack of sleep, and

I say 'I'm sorry' and 'I don't know what to do' five times in the two-minute call.

I didn't tell her Mike was drunk, I didn't say anything about what was going on, and she didn't ask. She just said I could come round straight away and stay for as long as I needed to.

I packed a little bag in case I decided to stay overnight and set off across town with my daughter to find some space and calm away from the vile, drunk, snoring liar in my life.

Going to Mia's house was the first time I'd stepped out of the Mike Bubble since we'd left the UK, and actually for a long time more than that, I think. It was a space and time in the world where he held no power over me at all, and it was the first time I could take a few hours to step back and look at my situation now that he wasn't there to upset me, lie to me or confuse me, where I was treated kindly and with care, and I could think about what was happening, and what I wanted.

I still wanted us. I wanted our life, and our family. *I just wanted the drinking to STOP.*

Having that tiny bit of space and protection behind different walls gave me a little bit of confidence to say things I'd felt for a long time but had never dared express. I'd also seen the truth for myself now, seen the extent of the drinking and lies at every opportunity, even when it so clearly damaged me, so I knew what I was saying was right – and I said it:

> Mike, you've lied to me for months, treated me like a piece of pathetic, dispensable, worthless shit. You dodge all accountability for what you do: Venice makes you drink. I make you drink. We make you drink. The world makes you drink. Here, watch this video of you trying to walk home this afternoon – I missed the glorious moment you fell over right in front of 50 people on the Arsenale bridge while I was carrying the buggy on my own. Yet you tell *me* I'm difficult. You have used me beyond all understanding I'm capable of and broken my brain. This is how you treat *me*, not how I treat you. And I won't have it any more.

I read that now and I'm not sure whether to laugh or cry. It's so transparently the faux gung-ho words of a person bolstered by keyboard confidence but who, in reality, is miles from being able to act according to any of the 'fuck you's she's tapping on her phone.

'I won't have it any more.' Oh yes, you will, Liz. You will have a lot, lot more of it yet.

I didn't stay the night at Mia's. I decided it was better for my daughter to be back in her bed with her things around her and anyway, I wanted to see where and how Mike was. If he was ready to say sorry, or talk in any way sensibly with me about what was going on and what he was going to do about it.

He was asleep when I got back, and then out for most of the next day, drinking.

I remember the exact spot on the waterfront where I was standing when the phone call from my employer came in, telling me I'd been fired.

Apparently there had been a complaint from the owner of an apartment I'd been sent to visit, because I'd turned up with my child in tow. There I'd been in a £5 million penthouse apartment, bouncing a baby in a papoose and wiping crumbs off a Dior rug. It was so far off professionally acceptable I'd have fired me as well.

I was mortified. I wanted to weep down the phone and tell her the truth, tell her that my partner is an alcoholic and it's not my fault and I know I've been crap and I'm never usually like this and I will try to make it work better, I *promise*. But I didn't. I just said I was terribly sorry and I understood completely, thank you and goodbye.

Fuck, it was awful, though. I'd lost my job, which was something I loved, but worse than that my reputation was now shattered with someone very well connected in a city where everyone knows and talks to everyone, and if you have even one professional disgrace, especially as an 'outsider', you'll be lucky to ever work again.

I don't know if the combination of me seeking respite and comfort at a friend's house while he was comatose on a bed and then losing my job as well was a wake-up call to Mike of how seriously his drinking was now affecting both his life and mine, but that week he decided to stop drinking. Just like that. It was like I'd seen him do before, back in Cambridge when he had his 'dry periods'. He'd just stop drinking if he decided this was his moment to, and within as little as a day or two he would go back to being the Mike I know and love. It's a transformation it's very hard to believe unless you've seen it in someone you know, but that's how it was: drunk, vile, angry, cruel and aggressive … to sober, calm, thoughtful and kind.

It didn't mean he was 'well', obviously, but when the drink was removed from his system it made a huge positive difference to our life almost immediately.

On 29 March the building work in the flat was complete. I put on a skirt and silver DMs and strode through the hot spring sunshine to the Notary's office in town, where I signed the final contract for the purchase of my apartment at last. One of my favourite photos from our whole Venice adventure was taken by Mike just after that – me and our daughter sitting together on a little jetty sticking out into the Grand Canal, sparkling in the sunlight. We were now official Venetians.

We said goodbye to the dark days of Via Garibaldi and moved into our *home*. The kitchen and bathroom were beautiful, the living area was repainted white, my books and magazines were back on the shelves and our daughter's toys were back in her room. It was clean, light and bright, and though I hardly dared to think it, it did seem as if this might, after *all* the incessant, exhausting, stressful, dusty upheaval, the stress, the drink and the darkness, be the start of better, brighter times. We needed them so much.

What with this fresh start and renewed sense of hope, I decided to do some spring cleaning of myself too; I found myself a psychotherapist and booked in for a first appointment.

I've had a few stints of therapy before, so I know that a little professional help and support with our emotional and mental well-being can be a lifesaver. Much as I liked to think of myself as strong, capable, maybe even unbreakable, there was no denying, even to myself, that my well-being was suffering as a result of the stressful circumstances I'd had to deal with and I was now starting to crack a little under the pressure of it all. I had started sweating a lot at night, my pulse was higher than normal, I had a tremble that was sometimes so strong I couldn't do up a button on my coat or pour milk into a baby bottle without spilling it, I had terrible insomnia despite being very tired, and when I *did* manage to sleep I often woke up with my whole body and bedding drenched in cold sweat. The trembles sometimes even grew into mini convulsions and I often had flu-like pain just from nervous exhaustion. I was still cutting myself occasionally if I got upset and my own drinking had taken on a new, far less healthy light; it was no longer a relaxed, social, enjoyable thing as it had been for me for years, but now almost a medicine to numb some pain and remove me a little from the reality I was in, and which I found so hard to cope with.

I know a lot of partners and children of addicts whose own drinking habits were well and truly messed up by it all, and it's hardly surprising; being soaked in the strains of alcoholism 24 hours a day will push even the cleanest-living person to a point where they need a bloody *drink*.

As partners of addicts, we can become so embroiled in *their* problems, cleaning up *their* wreckage and supporting *their* (many) attempts at recovery that our own ill-health – often caused by theirs – can take such a back seat it falls out of the car. Emotionally too, we can almost cease to exist in all the noise of Them, and become so caught up in caring for everyone else we stop caring for ourselves.

I knew that I, as the mother, the breadwinner, the family organiser and responsible adult in almost all ways, had to make sure *I* was OK, especially as Mike so clearly wasn't, even when he wasn't drinking. I knew it was time to get some help.

I saw Sofia about six times in all and it was worth every euro. Raven-haired, pale-skinned and clad head-to-toe in black, she was a sort of Morticia Addams meets Sophia Loren meets firework, and talked fast in an Italian-German-Romanian-slightly-Insanian accent held together by copious amounts of hand-waving and eyebrow action. She was tough but fair, confident in herself as a woman, mother and therapist, fiercely direct, mildly terrifying, and the exact opposite of everything I now felt myself to be, and I clicked with her immediately.

It took me a few sessions to even *start* talking honestly about my home life, it was so ingrained in me to smile in public and cry in private, and I approached this unchartered Safe Talking Territory cautiously, words sliding out like droplets of blood squeezed from a scab.

It's hard to describe what 'happens' in therapy, exactly, because it's often a long, meandering conversation over many weeks and months, going off on side tangents, pockmarked by tears, laughter and note-scribbling, and in the relatively short amount of time I spent with Sofia I thought and learned so much it's impossible to fit it all in here. But the key things are fairly common to a lot of people in my position, so I'll try to outline a few as best I can.

First and maybe most importantly I was hearing a fresh, neutral voice, not tied up with any of the problems themselves, and well versed in the typical patterns they bring. She opened my mind and eyes to things I wasn't able to see before, under the cloud of lies and manipulations I was being constantly confused and silenced by, and she taught me that I could exist and survive – no, *thrive* – separately to Mike. She gave me an identity and a voice I'd lost in the mud of his drinking, showed me how small I had become in the shadow of his addiction, and how everything I had been so sure about in *myself* had become twisted by his gaslighting to the extent that I didn't know what I even believed any more.

It was like having my lungs filled with air, replacing the lead they'd been suffocating my soul with, and I slowly but surely started to uncurl a little and breathe deeper.

Learning about gaslighting was a game-changer. It's become a bit of a buzzword in recent years, which is both good and bad; greater awareness means more people might be able to recognise if they are victims of it, but there's a danger that by using it when not appropriate, its power might become devalued. Gaslighting is not the same as lying. It's also not being told something we don't like to hear, or think isn't true. That's just called a difference of opinion. It's a powerful form of psychological manipulation designed to make someone question their reality, and it's extremely damaging to those who experience it. It's also ingenious because by its very nature a person being gaslit doesn't know it's happening to them, because they're being gaslit. It's a sort of mental catch-22, where if you could stop it for a moment you'd be able to see it; but until you can see it, you can't stop it. (I told you it was clever.) By sowing seeds of doubt in someone's mind, repeatedly denying things they know to be true, a gaslighter makes their victim start to question their own memory, perception, judgement and sanity until they have so little self-confidence or self-belief they're basically non-existent. It's dehumanising, psychological torture that attacks our emotional and psychological coping skills until we can't cope any more.

Listening to Sofia, I saw for the first time how many of the tell-tale signs of this kind of manipulation were present in every day of my life: straight-out bullshit and denials cleverly mixed with occasional truths just to remind me that he *did* tell the truth sometimes, so when I said he was lying *I* must be mistaken, he lit almost every gaslighting fuse there is. Intentions and promises rarely matched actions, but there was always an excuse at the ready, or a claim that he'd *told* me and I'd forgotten because I clearly can't remember things, and I should get more rest because I'm the one causing problems by being so knackered.

Conversations were twisted to turn a justified criticism of him (he was drunk, he'd wasted money, he'd lied to my face) into an attack on something *I* had done wrong, so now the victim of his hurt was the target of his blame. Over the last year he had increasingly started to say I was mad, a nutter and 'fucking crazy', and there's nothing more crazy-making than being told you're crazy when you're the one keeping things sane. It was absolutely maddening, but if I ever spoke up about all this I was told my feelings were pretty much invalid because look at you, Liz, you cut yourself and don't eat well so you CAN'T be sane.

That is gaslighting too.

And then there were his frequent claims that I was a narcissist, because I only saw things from *my* perspective and I wanted him to stop doing things that *I* didn't like him doing. I wasn't exactly sure what a narcissist *was*, so being repeatedly told that I was one had made me wonder if it was true. Maybe I *was* a narcissist? When I asked Sofia about this, her answer was as sure as it was welcome.

'Liz,' she said warmly, 'I'm a clinical psychiatrist, and I can assure you that you display no characteristics of narcissism at all. For a start, narcissists don't wonder if they are narcissists. You are being *told* you are a narcissist, and *that* in itself is classic psychological manipulation … by a narcissist!'

Boom. At least half the medicine I felt I needed was right there in those words.

I'm not ashamed to admit that half the reason I went to see a therapist was so she could tell me I was amazing, brave and strong and extremely admirable for sticking with Mike despite all the shit-awful things he did when he drank; I wanted hugs and high-fives and maybe a packet of Haribos, and I'd have paid double for a hug. But that's not why you pay a shrink.

Good therapists aren't there to tell us what we want to hear. Sometimes they have to say things that challenge our thinking, maybe even hurt a bit, but we need to hear them in order to make personal progress.

Perhaps sensing that I was ready, Sofia raised the subject of 'co-dependency'. This is a complicated little bastard, and crops up a lot in conversations about addiction, because it's present in many relationships with addicts. The whole subject can be fairly uncomfortable because it asks us to admit that *we* might be dependent on something too, when we thought we were kick-ass and independent, thank you very much. But many people stay with those who treat them badly because, without realising it, they are addicted to that person, or something they feel they get or want from them, just as an addict is addicted to their substance of choice.

The first time it was put to me that I might be 'addicted' to Mike, I felt almost insulted, as if I could be so pathetic as to be 'addicted to my man' and in some way incapable of being happy without him. But maybe she had a point.

I've read a lot about co-dependency since I first discussed it with Sofia, I've talked to people who live with addicts, to psychotherapists and counsellors, I've bought the *Codependents Anonymous* book and worked my way through some of the questions it asks, and I've pushed myself hard about whether I really am, or at least was back then, *co-dependent* on Mike. I'm still not sure exactly where I fall on the scale, but I certainly do fear detachment, I have great separation anxiety and I am happier in a relationship than outside one – sometimes so much so that I stay in it for far longer than I maybe should. These are all things I am now working on as part of my recovery, but I am very sure about one thing: I *chose* to stay with Mike throughout it all. It was a choice, and it was made for a reason: *love*.

I *love* Mike and I always believed in his potential to be the Good Mike I know he can be when he's not ravaged by a disease. If that makes me 'co-dependent' then fine, I'm co-dependent, but I think above all it just means I love someone, and am prepared to go a long way to help him. Co-dependency is not an easy concept, but it's worth at least reading about and digging into honestly, I think, if one lives with a manipulative narcissist, as almost all active addicts are. It might be that we're entirely co-dependent and addicted to them. It might be that we just love them. Or, most likely I'd suggest, it might be a combination of both.

Of all the things I learned on those hot Tuesday mornings in Sofia's gleaming black-granite kitchen in the heart of the old district of Castello, one in particular I was to hear many times from other people too, as I became progressively weaker, sadder and more lost in myself.

'Liz,' she said, putting her hand on mine for the first and only time, 'you are intelligent and strong, a mother and a very loving partner – but look at you. You have become *tiny* in Mike's shadow. You let things happen to you that make you feel small, powerless and sad, when really you are very *powerFUL*. You just don't know it any more. *You* are the core of the family, the mother lion, and everything starts with *you*. Mike can do what he likes. If he wants to drink, he can drink; if he wants to stop, he can stop. But you need to care about YOURSELF, be strong enough to look after your four children. Please start to think about *yourself*, so you can roar like a mother lion again. You are a writer, so go and write your book. You can do this, and it will be good for you. I want you to send me the first chapter before I see you next week, OK?'

That was the only time I cried in all of our sessions. For months, almost all I'd heard from Mike was things that brought me down, made me cry, hurt me, exhausted me, cost me, belittled me or told me I was mad. Here was someone I admired and whose professional expertise in these matters I trusted, telling me things that gave me strength, and a grain of confidence to remember who I really am. It took me well over a year to even start taking care of myself properly, putting myself first for more than a brief period of time, and starting to regain any sense of self that lasted.

But I walked back home that day, over the Arsenale bridge where Mike had fallen, pissed, just a few weeks before, taller and lighter than I had for quite some time. I stopped to take a photograph of my old black Converse on the edge of spring-green canal water, and posted it to Instagram. (It's still there if you fancy a very long scroll back.)

'Today, I am going to be a writer again, and start finishing my 4th book.'

April and May were glorious.

Mike was still sober, healthy and happy again, I was back to writing again, our daughter was now a blissful one-and-a-half-year-old ray of happiness, bursting with the joys and excitements of everything around her, and we were in our new home. The builders had gone, the bluebells in our courtyard were in full bloom and the air was filled with Jo Malone's lesser-known scent of 'Jasmine and Relief'.

Our Venice life had at last become what it always should have been, and we went back to doing all the things we'd abandoned when the Wall Problem happened, depression had descended and everything had gone to *mierda*: we hired bikes on Lido and cycled along the seafront as a family of three; we swam in the sea and collected shells; we took evening walks through Santo Stefano to the wide-paved lagoon-front at Zattere to buy a gelato and watch our daughter enjoy a spot of pigeon-chasing, walking back over the wide, wooden Accademia bridge where Mike's mother had once taken a photo of his father, and which still stands in a frame in his grandparents' living room.

Everything was so *easy* now Mike was sober. It was as if his drinking made everything drunk, and his sobriety made everything clean. If you could just take the poison away, the whole place could breathe again and everything could be that thing he craved ever since his mother had died: NORMAL.

I also stopped drinking, which had a definite positive effect on my own moods and my ability to deal with his, and my therapist had prescribed me a low dose of Valium, which helped calm and ease my jittery, frayed nerves, allowed me to catch up on months of missed sleep and to feel and look a little more rested again.

We had a few friends now and felt part of our community; our neighbour often dropped by for our kids to play together and Mike and I starting talking at long last about travel plans to Croatia and the Dolomites, where we'd book-marked as 'must-see' places if we moved out here. With his back now fully recovered, he started exercising again, drinking plenty of water and cutting out all junk food, and he looked healthier and happier than I'd seen him since we first arrived. He borrowed a skateboard and got back to one of his old favourite pastimes of falling off but having fun, and I took a lovely photo of him on it under some old arches near our house, our little girl standing behind him, beaming. I posted it to my social media, of course; keeping up the 'happy family' face for those back home was still something I did, because it hadn't yet come to the point where I couldn't pretend any more.

'When you think your Daddy is the best thing ever. And you're right.'

I remember a little Post-it note appeared on one of our kitchen cupboards again, with the same message as the last one: 'Be Better'. Still, it was a blue one this time, not yellow. Maybe the new colour would make all the difference.

I really believed it, by the way; I believed that now everything was in place, we were settled in our home, the weather was gorgeous, our daughter was a little older and easier, Mike wasn't drinking, I was happy working on my book and he had a couple of photography jobs on the cards to boost his mood, we could have a normal, happy life again. I even still believed Mike could start having the odd beer here and there if he wanted to, as he had many times with me before, without any disasters occurring.

I genuinely believed that, because I still knew no different. For now, as far as I was concerned, everything was safe, happy and well at long, long last. Again.

I'd love to be able to write, 'And they lived happily ever after. The end.'

But you know that's not how it works.

June brought a heatwave – '*Agosto in Junio*', they said. It took everyone by surprise and brought the whole place to its sweating knees: hospitals were full of wilting elderly residents, babies overheated, and with very little air-conditioning in the city, office workers suffered heat exhaustion.

The paving stones were untouchably hot, and even shade provided no respite; the light breeze was like a bush-fire, and gentle, spring-like Venice was suddenly a stifling, baking furnace surrounded by water you couldn't cool off in because you're not allowed to swim in the canals or the lagoon surrounding the City itself. There was no getting away from the heat: by 5 a.m. it was already unbearable, the playgrounds were impossibly hot by mid-morning, and we found ourselves unexpectedly confined to being indoors more than we had been all winter. Our daughter flopped about like a roasting beetroot all day and spent hours sitting in a big plastic box we filled with water to cool her down. We sweltered all the way to the hardware shop and carried two big fans home, but still we couldn't sleep: if we opened the windows the mosquitoes came in for a feasting and if we left them closed the still heat was suffocating and we lay in pools of our own sweat, unable to touch each other it was so unpleasant.

Weather aside, things on the home front remained fairly calm and stable. There were no major dramas, Mike wasn't drinking – that I knew of – and in mid-June I completed my book's manuscript and we all looked forward to good times ahead.

It's still almost impossible for me to look at photos of Mike that week, cooking at home, reading to our daughter or skateboarding on the basketball court, and to believe he was so close to the biggest, longest and most terrible relapse of his life.

I didn't notice it very much at the time, because everything becomes a little more tense in unbearable heat, but Mike's mood and personality changed a little over those first three baking weeks of June.

He became withdrawn again, frowny, suddenly disinterested in doing the things we'd just started enjoying, he was 'elsewhere' and preoccupied, and didn't seem to care or show much interest in anything around him. He started gradually eating less healthy food, let his hair grow longer again – which he rarely does when he's in a good, strong, focused place within himself – and then shaved it all off. His WhatsApps had started beeping more than a Geiger counter in a nuclear power station, and when I cautiously mentioned this familiar collection of little slides and changes I was immediately met with all the curt retorts and knee-jerk explanations I'd heard before.

But this time it was *different*. Instead of just being down on himself there was a defiance in his voice and body language, almost an *intent* to be aggressive towards me that I'd not seen in him before – certainly not when he was off the booze. Mike was never soberly nasty to anyone; it wasn't in his character. But now he seemed to be almost wantonly unkind, self-righteous and rude to me, as if he were somehow *owed* it, or wanted to cause destruction for destruction's sake.

I searched through the world's entire Catalogue Of Possible Reasons why this might be – the relentless heat; the fact that I'd handed in my book, so the pressure to 'be nice' and support me for this brief time had lifted; a frustration in his own work, or lack of it, by comparison and so on – and tried to find things to do that might cheer him up. Now, with what I've learned, I know my efforts to find reasons and solutions were all futile and there was only one 'reason' for his change of mood: he was an active alcoholic who had just managed two months of sobriety and was now bursting for his next relapse. Or, very possibly, had already relapsed and was drinking on the sly and hating himself for it.

That first time he pushed me I'm not sure I even realised that's what it *was*, and I'm certain he didn't mean it to be what it was. We were having a stupid little disagreement in the flat, I've no idea what it was about but in his current state of almost *looking* for a reason to be annoyed it could have been almost anything.

It was early evening, the air temperature inside was still well over 30 degrees and it was so humid I could have rented the flat out as a Turkish steam room; all the windows were fully open and we were wearing little more than underwear and T-shirts to avoid melting our internal organs. It was 26 June, the night before Mike's birthday, and I remember I was holding his wrapped presents in my hand as we argued.

I don't know if I was narking too much, picking him up on every little thing he was doing wrong – which, at the time, was a *lot* – and if he felt there was no let-up or escape from me, the intensity of the heat, the mosquitoes, the tourists, the million irritations of everyday life there. I don't know if he felt claustrophobic, anxious and suddenly panicky as he often did when his mind wasn't in a good place and there was too much noise and *stuff* going on in his head and he just needed some space to *think*. I don't know why he snapped, but I was in that room, I know him, and I know he didn't mean to be as rough as he was.

To be clear, I know that pushing someone is never OK, and I'm not here to condone it, excuse it or enter into endless debate about it. I *know* it's wrong, and I know it shouldn't have happened. But I also know that we are all capable of doing things we never normally would if our mental health were good, if circumstances were a little different, if we were thinking more calmly and could behave accordingly. Things we regret. It's called being a fallible human, and I can forgive genuine human mistakes.

Our sofa is one of those contemporary, square-edged IKEA ones that look more expensive than they are and have a much harder edge than one might expect. When he pushed me away from him, I fell across it and landed with my thigh against the edge, making it dig hard into my bare skin. I cried out, more in shock than in pain. What the hell did he think he was doing, and did he know he'd just really hurt me?

He blurted back that it was just 'a little nudge, for God's sake. You're doing my head in.'

I could hardly believe I was hearing it.

It was as if a switch had turned in him, and there was no kindness or concern for me at all. Just a weird, almost delighted anger and total lack of compassion. He looked strange and distant, jumpy and almost joyfully combative, and I remember looking up at him and feeling I didn't know this person at all.

As with most pivotal moments in life, I didn't realise how pivotal it was at the time. I went out for a walk on my own, had a cry, and went to bed without any further exchange between the two of us. But something very bad had happened that evening, I felt it. And I didn't feel truly at ease, for months after that.

———

And so here we were: 27 June 2019, Mike's birthday morning, and The Venice Incident. You can now see how it wasn't the 'start' at all.

I went out at 6 a.m. with my daughter, to give her some playtime while it was still only a sweltering 25 degrees. Mike was asleep and I wasn't exactly looking forward to seeing him after the night before. He woke at some point around nine-ish and there were some text exchanges of:

Sorry, I shouldn't have done that, I was just frustrated

and

Let's just forget it. Happy Birthday

and so on. I know I should have made it very clear that it was not OK, being 'frustrated' is no excuse at *all* for pushing someone and he'd stepped *way* over a line, but I wanted things to come back to some kind of calm and normal as soon as possible, especially on this day, so I let it go.

At around 11 a.m., after I'd got back to the flat, we'd had a 'hug-and-make-up' and the day was a little more on track again Mike said he'd like to go into town quickly, to buy a roll of camera film so he could take a family portrait for his birthday.

Sure, I said, of course, that's a nice idea. So off he went.

It all started fine: he got the film, went to H&M to get a birthday T-shirt, and by midday he messaged to say he was finished already, it was a circus out there and he was heading to the vaporetto now, to come home. He added,

I feel really sad today. Yesterday was awful. I would love to have dinner and a nice night with you. x

This sadder, quieter turn after the anger the night before and slightly strained morning had a ring to it that I recognised. A sort of 'slipping away' into a longing for a way of being he wanted, but was being pulled away from.

I heard nothing more for half an hour, which might sound insignificant but it was odd, because it only takes eight minutes on the vaporetto from where he was.

At half past twelve I asked if he was OK, but got no answer.

A one o'clock I messaged again. Still nothing.

At quarter to two, nearly two hours after he was 'getting on a vaporetto', he sent a message:

I lost my phone. I coming home now. [sic] I'm ok

Then nothing again for an hour, until, at three o'clock:

Sa [sic]

And there it was. Relapse. Absolutely shit-faced, lost to me, himself and the world.

If it happened now, I like to think I've learned enough and have healed enough that I would leave him to it, ignore him and he'd come home eventually. But then wasn't now, it was *then*, and all I could feel was the first little glimpse of a happier life being destroyed in one morning, just as it had got going again, and I wanted to stop it as fast as I could.

It was far too hot to take a child out on a drunk-man-hunt, so I called the owner of the local café we went to almost every day and who had become almost an Honorary Auntie to my daughter. They adored each other, and I knew it would be absolutely fine to leave them together for an hour or so.

Gina came to my flat immediately, and gave me a big hug. I didn't even try to hide my distress, or need to explain why Mike had disappeared. It seemed to be almost instinctively understood between women, but that made it no less humiliating and embarrassing for me.

I set out into the crushing heat, fairly sure of the most likely places Mike would be or routes he might take, and after half an hour of frantic walking, pacing, turning, running and searching up and down the back alleys of our neighbourhood, hitting dead ends and sweating in my rising, breathless panic and the extreme heat, I finally saw him, staggering heavily down the exact street we had stayed in when I was pregnant and we'd first come here two years before, and had fallen in love with it. Pale-blue shirt now dark with sweat, eyes unable to focus, legs too weak to hold himself upright, he was lurching between doorways, leaning against terracotta walls as weathered and crumbling as he was, and clutching a plastic bag containing a half-empty bottle of red wine.

Several more bottles – and all the rest – had quite clearly already been consumed; this last one was for the 800 yards between here and home. Folding and withering like the lines of laundry blowing above him, fading with hunger, steeped in booze, he was a wobbling mirage of wretched human hopelessness and despair, and watching him stumble and fall against the mustard wall where he'd taken that lovely photo of me, pregnant with our daughter and glowing with happiness, I felt the whole island sink beneath my feet.

I knew calm words were the only way to get him to come back home, at least at this point in his alcoholism journey, so I took his arm. It was like rescuing a child. He asked me to buy him some more wine to 'get through the rest of the day' and I said sure. I'd have said anything to keep him with me in that moment and not lose him into the heat again.

As we walked slowly back he kept lurching into walls, his weight pulling me sideways with him until I managed to hoist him vertical again, and the two of us swayed down the street like that, his feet dragging like an old woman's slippers. As he slurred his body around the last corner he let go of me, walked a few feet ahead and then turned and laughed at me. He'd never actually laughed *at* me before. Not like that. Not to hurt.

Mike was done giving a shit about giving a shit. And he hadn't even started.

PART THREE

Madness

Mike was drunk. *Everything* was drunk.

I remember the next days as a haze of hot, numb detachment punctuated by moments of gin-clear focus: a thin, green tie-dye dress my daughter wore; the sauna-still air, a yellow football we kicked around the park, a square picture book with a ladybird and a blue dog, my daughter's sweaty skin stuck to mine as I fed her, the crunch of the buggy wheels as they crossed the swaying vaporetto platform, while we waited to go … somewhere.

I remember swimming in the dizziness of impossibility, and all I could do to stay afloat was keep moving and doing what I had to do.

This was to be no short relapse or week of heavy drinking, but a long, devastating descent to the bottom over several terrible months; an unstoppable vortex of destruction that broke everything we had, including each other. Mike's brain, from now on constantly topped up with poison, seemed to go into a sort of shutdown, then meltdown. Even when he was present his mind was now elsewhere, and he became strange, volatile, nasty and unlike any Mike I knew or wanted to be near.

Living with an alcoholic in full drinking mode can make us crazy too. Nothing makes sense, everything is confusing, contradictory, hurtful, exhausting and relentlessly brain-spinning, and my descent into something one might describe as a sort of 'madness' was probably inevitable, given the situation I was in. I'd danced on the edge of the drop for a long time already, picked myself up countless times, coped as well and as far as I could – further than

many might, I think – but as Mike became ever more drunk and
horrible, and ever less recognisable as the man I loved, my mind
cracked so hard I couldn't hear it. One day I was holding up the
world, the next I was in free fall.

I don't know if we can tell if we're mad; if we can be aware of
losing our minds, or feel when we tip over that edge. Either way,
there's no doubt that while I carried on parenting and surviving,
and he carried on drinking and dying, neither of us was of entirely
'sound' mind for quite a long time to come.

The day after Mike's birthday wipe-out I was up and out of
the flat by 5 a.m. It was 32 degrees already, and I'd had no sleep
at all. My daughter's soft legs and bare feet dangled over the lip
of the buggy seat like mosquito-bitten sausages, swaying with the
waves lifting the vaporetto platform as we waited for the next one
to arrive. My mind was at sea with it, rising and falling, rising and
falling. Where even was I?

We went one stop to Lido. It was quiet, still, and heatwave
hot. There was a café open already and we sat at a table on the
pavement, her still in her pyjamas, nestled onto my lap, dropping
croissant crumbs into the sweat pooling between our thighs, and
me drinking coffee as if it was oxygen. I read her a Maisie book
through stinging, tired, tear-stained eyes then paid, strapped her
back into her buggy and pushed it up the main drag, past cupcake-
pink villas, purple bougainvillea, yellow oleanders, white roses,
lush greens and black pools of shade to the playground. So much
colour, all in grey. It was still only seven o'clock in the morning
and the heat was already baking into our bodies, making them
ache for some cool. Everything felt drunk and strange. As my
daughter climbed a ladder to the top of the slide I saw a dry, golden
leaf suspended in mid-air, twirling on a single strand of a spider
web. I watched it for a while, spinning in the roasting silence. It
looked how I felt; blown about this way and that at the mercy
of things I couldn't control, kept in place by the thinnest thread.
What should I do? If I stayed I'd be trapped in this nightmare,
twisting and struggling to get free; but if I let go, I'd fall and I
didn't know what would happen then. I was one decision, one
phone call away from a freedom I didn't want. I wanted him and

me. I wanted our love and our family. I wanted Mike to be able to be all that I knew he could be.

For now, all he could be was asleep. Or out drinking, who knew?

At 9 a.m. Mike sent me a message, asking what had happened the day before. I gave a brief outline of the key events including passing out in the street, talking shit to some tourists and inviting them to our house to stay, and laughing at me. He said he remembered none of it, but it 'sounds pretty terrible'. He offered no apology.

After an hour or so it was already too hot for a baby to be out so I popped her back into the buggy yet again and started heading back. She fell asleep almost immediately so I sat on a bench in the shade, opened my laptop, which I had brought with me just in case I got this chance, and got to work on an overdue copy-editing job I'd managed to get from a local hotel. Family life doesn't stop for drinking, and there were bills to pay, responsibilities to meet and adulting to be done. And I had to do it all.

I was so tired. I was so hateful of him, and of what he had done to our dream.

Mike was out when we got back. I was glad. I couldn't manage any more fighting. I asked him where he was and he said he was in a park 'feeling horrendous'. Poor thing.

At midday he wrote again:

We're over. I'll book flights home today.

I was sick in the kitchen sink.

At 2.30 p.m. I looked out of the window and saw a man lying on the ground in the middle of our street. The oleander tree opposite was in full, joyful bloom and spread-eagled underneath it was a corpse-like heap of Mike, head crooked to the side, legs and arms splayed limply, palms up, his phone lying across one of them. It was the ugliest, most incongruous and shameful sight I'd ever seen in Venice – and a fairly poor impression of someone who's about to get on a plane and go home. Two people walked by, pausing for a moment to stare at this sad little scene, and I prayed they didn't know or recognise him. When they'd passed I went outside and tried to wake him gently by kicking his shoulder as hard as I could. It was pointless; I could have broken a rib and he wouldn't have felt it.

I spent the rest of the day playing with my daughter in the relatively cool 30-degree heat inside the flat, peeking out through the shutters occasionally to see if Mike was still there. He didn't move for two hours. At 5 p.m., when the sun had lost its bite, we ventured out for some fresh air before her dinner. Mike wasn't on the street any more. He sent me some messages from a bar somewhere, staving off his impending horrific hangover and full, painful consciousness of what a disaster he was, and whatever he was imbibing seemed to have had a remarkable effect on his mind and mood.

He casually asked if I'd like to go and get a drink together:

It might be good for us. We can try again. If you want to. I want to. x

Five hours ago he said he was leaving the country, having ended our relationship; now he wants a drink together so we can make it work. Chop, change. Jekyll, Hyde. Up, down. Christ, what next?

I was in the playground now and it was rammed with local children all out after school for some entry-level bullying, as seems to be the way there. I tried typing a reply, but I didn't know what to say or even think, so I just tried to express what I was feeling. I told him I was heartbroken after the last two days, exhausted beyond words, and it was all sinking in now just how bad his drinking problem was.

How many times will this keep happening, Mike? How can I make a life with something that destroys it every few months?

He said he didn't know, but things had been good and they could be good again.

He was beyond sorry, he'd been weak and thought he could have a drink. It was 'just a lapse of concentration and conviction', and he only said those awful things to me when he was angry, down and drunk:

> I HATE that I say them. I don't mean them. I'm scared of what
> I say in those moments. I'm terrified of me.

He often said this, when he was drinking, managing to somehow sound at once helpless, ominous and overly dramatic. Was I supposed to be impressed by how awful he could become? Should I feel sorry for him? *Did* I feel sorry for him? And how many agains were too many agains, I wondered.

My daughter moved from swing to climbing frame, while I tried to work out what to do with my life. I'm surprised now that I even had to question it; I was with a man who frequently relapsed into drunken chaos, seemed incapable of preventing it, became vile when it happened and was now telling me he was terrified of himself. If he was so scared of himself, surely *I* should be too? And if a 'lapse of concentration' was all it took, it hardly painted a reassuring picture of a stable future. My mind felt as if it was going up and down like the kids on the swings. Stay or go? Support or reject? Stay for the man I loved, even though he kept disappearing, or give up and find someone who could love me back better? I really didn't know; I kept flipping from sympathetic and longing to independent and almost ballsy.

One of the longer messages I sent later that day reads like a clear, calm ultimatum, and I really find it strange to read it now; it appears to be written by someone with a strong understanding of her own needs and wants, and an awareness that neither were being met:

> Mike, the fact is that you can't NOT have these relapses. Even when I was pregnant. Even with a baby. Even for our daughter. For *anything*. I wish for you that you didn't have this problem, I truly do. I've tried everything I can think of

to make things good for you, often to my own detriment, but nothing ever helps and the toll on me is becoming too great. It can happen again at any time, and it most likely will, over and over again. I want to be together, Mike, I want our life together, I love you and I love what we are when you're OK, but I don't know how much more I can take. I just don't think I can do this any more.

I don't know what 'version of me' managed to write that, or how much of it I believed at the time. Maybe I thought a WhatsApp algorithm would spit out a conclusion and plan of action for me that I couldn't come to myself. Or didn't *want* to.

In these penumbra days of Mike's active alcoholism, before he really vanished into his darkness, bearable normality could still park itself hard against bat-shit awful. 'Fine' would snuggle up in bed next to 'unbearable'. They could even share the same *day*, with one dreadful hour followed by a hug, dinner and a film.

It was like living with two people who kept popping in and out of the room every few hours; when the nice one came back, it was such a damn relief it was hard not to invite them to stay for a cup of tea. If you've never experienced it you can't believe it's possible, but it is. I know lots of people who go through similar things with their alcoholic partners, and it makes it extremely difficult to reach any kind of decision or come to any conclusion.

Mike describes the battle that was going on in his head between his attempts at a life of sobriety and the incessant pull of addiction as being like turbulence on an aeroplane: he could be gliding through clear, calm skies, happy, not drinking, thinking positively, and then suddenly he'd hit a storm of anxious thoughts and feelings that knocked him this way and that, tumbling into pockets of panic and anger, unable to pull himself horizontal again.

Back in the heady, early days of his drinking, these phases undulated slowly over weeks, sometimes even months, but as it got worse it sped up and he was eventually swinging in and out of calm then mania as fast as every 20 minutes. In the calm moments you'd literally not know he had a problem at all; he was there, he was Mike, we did normal things together. But when the turbulence struck again he was gone, back into awful, and it seemed impossible that the nice days had ever been there.

Mike went back to being sober (or less drunk – I didn't know how much or what he was drinking when he wasn't in my immediate line of sight) for those dying days of June, and we had a normal-ish week doing normal-ish things; there was civil conversation, morning coffees together, we did the laundry and made risotto and nobody passed out on any streets or pushed anyone across a sofa. But it was strained. I was so deprived of rest or calm, I was just robotically 'carrying on as usual', too shattered to think of anything else to do, and so constantly on edge worrying that at any moment this mini hiatus would be over and Drunk Mike would either come back again or just not come back at all, that my hands trembled much of the time. He, meanwhile, was so unwaveringly surly and distracted it was like living with a sulking toddler, dragging his feet along life's pavement. In the playground he often sat on his own on a bench on his phone, and at the beach he didn't go into the sea any more. He started having to pop here or there again, to get some water or chewing gum or I didn't know what.

It was the first week of July now, only one short, interminable week after his birthday, and the holiday to the Dolomites I'd *finally* booked for us a few weeks previously was now upon us.

Through some heady combination of extreme sleep deprivation and just bloody well wanting this adventure I'd dreamed of for over a year, we decided to see the trip through and get the hell out of the insufferable pressure cooker of Venice. I thought the fresh mountain air and change of scene would do us all good, and might lift Mike out of this more than usually bad patch. I still had no idea how much worse this 'bad patch' was than all the previous ones I'd seen. *Had* I, I might have realised that putting someone whose only thoughts are drink, wanting drink, needing drink and getting drink into a remote mountain village with nowhere to escape his mind or get hold of the thing he needed to numb it, was a really bad idea. For now, I just thought a holiday together might help, and he agreed. So off we went to Piazzale Roma, the big, bustling car and bus park where we'd first arrived in Venice, to rent a car and head off north for an hour or so, into the foothills of the mountains.

We were staying in a converted barn in an old rural hamlet looking out across fields towards the mountains. No pubs or bars for at least a mile or two, just a scattering of farms and houses, a village square with some scruffy grass, a broken bench and a dried-up fountain, and a collection of stray dogs. The owner was a lady called Adriana. She'd lived there all her life, had three grown-up children and was very much the Italian matriarch – kind but no-nonsense, and definitely the businesswoman and head of the family. She spoke almost no English but took an immediate shine to our daughter, taking her to the barn to see the baby chicks and play in the garden with the dog.

Things felt almost absurdly pleasant after the recent turmoil, and for the first two days we did all the things families on holiday do: we cycled to a village for coffee and pastries in the piazza, looked around the church and found a nice play area. We drove to the jagged Tre Cime mountains, swam in a lake so clear and turquoise it looked photoshopped, had lunch by a waterfall and talked about writing some travel features. Mike even took some photos to go with them, should it come to a commission.

The Insta-opps were everywhere: our beautiful child in a field among mountain flowers, me and her laughing together on the bike, all of us swimming in a river, me walking along a stark mountain ridge with my hair blowing in the wind. I think I wrote a caption about being 'wild, happy and free' or some shit like that. It all looked heavenly, and the comments came in: wow, you guys are having an amazing time, it looks AWESOME.

They were right, it did. And much of it was.

But every cropped, edited square was steeped in tension. There was nothing so beautiful or amazing that it couldn't be overshadowed by Mike's brooding, and little conflicts and sharp words bubbled up with the mountain storms. We'd argue bitterly in the car about needing to stop to find a toilet *again*, and why do you have to go ALL the time and for Christ's sake can't we just enjoy something for a second?, and then someone would hit their fist on the window or steering wheel and we'd carry on in tight silence.

I kept trying to suggest things, plan all the trips to places I'd waited a year to see, get the snacks and sun cream and nappies and maps and water bottles all packed for the day, make everyone HAPPY – but it was futile. Everything I did was crushed under an immoveable heaviness, and I found I got not only more and more tired but now also angrier by the hour, as all my efforts were destroyed by his inability to enjoy anything or contribute in any way to what was going on around him. I'd had more fun dragging my kids round a museum, but at least they weren't rude and thankless with it – and they were *kids*. He was supposed to be a man, and a father. Couldn't he help a bit? Be there a bit? Be *kind* to me a bit?

I was on constant alert for the next sharp retort, and I remember trying to hold his hand a few times but he found any contact too difficult or claustrophobic. He'd come along and join in as much as he could but that was all he could manage, and for the rest of the time he wanted to be in his closed-off little shell of unease.

I *still* didn't understand what was going on in Mike's head at all, or what torture it was for him to be out there when all he wanted to do was be drinking. Even over these last few years of his drinking bouts I'd barely been *initiated* into alcoholism yet. I thought he was just being a selfish prick who could easily stop being a selfish prick if he wanted to. I just wanted something nice for ME, for once. Why should his affliction have to ruin everything in *my* life?

As he was progressing – or rather regressing – through his stages of alcoholism so I was living through my own too, and was currently at Thoroughly Pissed Off.

Far from being able to even *see* the possibility that I had options, I held all my frustrations and anger in as much as I could, now double-parked by fear and anxiety and squeezed against the wall with nowhere to get out. I kept trying to play the Happy Families On Holiday game, hoping that if I kept this up he would suddenly come round and things would be OK again, as they'd been before.

I can only see *now*, with a lot of hindsight and understanding, how terrible it must have been for Mike out there. It wasn't at all a case of pulling his socks up and remembering to buy nappies for once, please. He had no control over his thoughts, and all his thoughts were of DRINK: how to get it and how to get away from everything with it. He was stuck in the middle of nowhere, with nowhere to go, nowhere to hide, no way of getting away from me and my incessant ideas and narks and complaints and attempts to make him do things he didn't want to do. Mostly, he had nowhere and no way to get away from himself.

On our third day of this Holiday from the Edges of Hell, good – but spectacularly poorly timed – news came in: someone in London emailed me to say she wanted to rent my flat with her two sons, for a last-minute getaway. And when I say 'last-minute', I mean … in two days' time. Renting the flat had always been a bit of a 'let's just see if we can do this occasionally to cover some of our costs' kind of a thing, and I'd never really expected it would happen, or happen so fast. I'd only listed it on a Facebook writers' group the week before, and we'd left Venice with no expectation at all that anyone would want to come and stay there. The kitchen and bathroom renovation had seriously dented my savings, so any rental income was now less a Christmas bonus and more of a financial lifesaver.

There was one minor problem with this good news: someone had to pop back to Venice immediately to clean and prepare the flat, and let the guests in the following morning.

That person had to be me: I was the only named driver on the rental car, and anyway it was my flat and I wanted to make sure things were done … properly. In any other relationship, this would have been a very simple case of, 'Off you go, honey, have a great time away on your own and treat yourself to a nice dinner – you deserve it'.

But living with an alcoholic spins the simplest 'simple thing' into a mesh of questions and problems, forcing us to wrestle our conscience, our sense of right and wrong, our principles and responsibilities to everyone, including ourselves. We have to weigh up risks we can't even measure, make judgements about things we can't fully judge and sometimes do things we're not entirely comfortable with because if we don't, we can't live at all.

The only question was what to do with our daughter. Taking her with me would be a total nightmare for both of us: I wouldn't manage to get even half of the work done that I needed to and I'd have to largely ignore her while I was trying to scrub, clean and sort everything out in the flat. Not only that but she hates car travel so she'd just cry all the way there and back, and it was scorching in Venice but lovely and cool up in the mountains. Here, there was a big garden, the dog, the chickens, the bike and lots of fun. In Venice there would be a roasting sweat-pit and a mother who was rushed off her feet with no time to play at all. It was almost a total no-brainer, bar one sticking point: Mike. How would he be, if I left him alone with her?

There are no definite answers to anything and all we can do is weigh up the risks, and decide what's right in each situation. Mike had never once let anything bad happen to her, even when he'd been drinking; he'd looked after her on his own plenty of times when I was out at work and he worshipped the air she breathed. If there had been any genuine concern in my mind about her well-being I would never have gone, and my gut instinct told me that, however bad he felt in himself, he would be fine with her, and it was safe for me to go on my own.

And if, in the worst-case scenario, there was any kind of emergency, I knew Adriana, the owner of the Airbnb, was there, and she'd handle everything just fine. So off I went.

Driving away felt unsettling at first, regardless of any concerns I might have had about Mike. Until now I'd only spent three nights apart from my daughter in her whole life, and it's something I've always found a bit of an unnatural wrench with all my children. But as the landscape opened up to the flatlands approaching Venice, I put the radio on and the countryside whizzed by, I relaxed and felt freer, more confident and stronger than I had for as long as I could remember. I suppose this really ought to have told me something about the effect on me of being with someone who made my life so difficult at times.

I got texts from Mike throughout the afternoon telling me how things were going back in the mountains, and everything seemed fine: a trip to the park on the bike, lunch, home to play. No dramas, no drink.

Being in the flat for a day and night on my own for the first time ever was both strange and blissful; all tension, bickering and aggression were gone, there was no worry of a door slam or any sudden vanishings, and nobody was slumped on the sofa asleep. I set about cleaning, tidying and organising my space, living my life for a brief period of time the way I can when I'm strong, happy and at ease. Still the messages came, saying everything was OK.

The humidity was still almost 100 per cent in Venice that day and the thermostat inside never dipped below 32 Celsius. Just walking about was like doing a HIIT workout wrapped in clingfilm in a rainforest, and by early evening the heat and toil of all the housework and organisation suddenly got to me. Mike's messages had slowed to a trickle over the last few hours, and a familiar, sickening anxiety had started tightening in my stomach. Just a little, but enough to make my heart beat faster, my breathing get shallower, my mouth become dry and my mind wander towards worry. My nervous system was already too primed for this now; it couldn't respond in any other way to the slightest flicker of a concern.

I messaged to ask how they were getting on now, and if he could please do one small thing for me, for the rental: could he write some short instructions of how to get from the airport to the flat and email it to me as soon as possible? I was up to my neck and the guests needed it today as they were leaving at the crack of dawn.

Sure, he said:

On it now

An hour and much sweating later, no email had come, nor any messages. I was properly angsty now, and also fairly peeved about the lack of help. It was *one* short email and would take 10 minutes to write at most – not even two episodes of *Peppa Pig*, if he needed some electronic child-minding. I've written *books* with a baby on my lap, surely one short email wasn't too difficult?

Long after our daughter's usual bedtime and with no call to ask me if I'd like to say goodnight to her, as was usual if either of us were out when she went to sleep, I asked again about those instructions. No response. I tried to keep my mind occupied by mopping all the floors but all I could think about was that house in the mountains, my child and Mike, the bizarre silence I was getting, and I couldn't stop the growing worry about what was going on. I felt sick, my breathing was shallow and I felt I had to pace and pace just to move away from the feeling of anxiety. What was he *doing*? At half past nine, with trembling fingers, I messaged him yet again to ask how things were, and where was the email, and how the hell was my *child*.

No reply. I tried again, breathless from worry now.

Mike? Are you awake? Wtf is happening there??

I watched the two WhatsApp ticks appear, waiting for them to go blue and show me he was there, and awake and able to talk, waiting for the *'Typing…'* in return, but neither happened. I slumped down onto the wet tiles, still holding the mop handle, and burst into tears. I was 100 kilometres away from my baby and couldn't contact the person responsible for her. The person with a drink problem, who'd promised to stay in touch. Again.

Shortly after ten o'clock my phone beeped.

Hey. Sorry. Been tidy the kitchen. I'm gonna go her in 6 as I reckon I'm on for a tough night. x

Panic is terrifying. It won't kill you but it comes pretty close to making you think it will. It happens when stress builds up in a person's nervous system and brain, like a pot of water being constantly heated by nervous, anxious energy. If it doesn't get calmed and allowed to cool again, it just gets hotter. My nerves had been at simmering point for so long, it took very little to make that water boil over.

I went through a period of having panic attacks in my thirties, when my children were very young. Everything would suddenly feel too bright, over-stimulating and fast, there was too much sky, too much space between me and safety, too much flickering of light and movement. For several years I couldn't use the London Underground, drive, or, at my worst, go into a shop without panicking about how far away it was from home, feeling dazzled by the strip-lights and claustrophobic at the checkout when I had to wait in line and couldn't leave. I still don't know exactly what caused it, but I had a course of CBT, I learned what panic was and how to breathe through it, and it all stopped eventually. But it was a Thing, and once you've had a Thing, your body knows how to have it again.

I should have just counted to a hundred, gone for a walk to the lagoon, tried to think rational thoughts about how Mike was probably just tired after a long day with a one-year-old and had gone to bed and fallen asleep straight away as any tired parent would. But Mike wasn't 'any tired parent', there's no 'should' in panic and there was no 'probably' in my mind – only immediate catastrophe: What if he'd passed out? What if my baby was crying and he couldn't hear her because he was so drunk a pneumatic drill to his kneecap wouldn't rouse him? What if she got up and choked on a piece of Lego or drank shampoo or —

I paced the flat, round and round the living room in that heat, hyperventilating, crying, feeling trapped and powerless, and unable to stop my mind whirling into further panic. Searching for any ideas my frantic mind could come up with to find out how Mike was, I realised I could send a message to Adriana through Airbnb and ask if she could please go and check on him. It was one of the weirdest messages I've ever sent a stranger, and I think I lied and said he hadn't been well that afternoon so I was worried in case he been taken ill and couldn't hear his phone. It took her more than 10 minutes of knocking on his door to wake him, she said, but he was there, he'd been asleep, and my baby was fine.

It was long after midnight before I got round to writing those instructions myself, so tired by that point from work and panic I couldn't even remember what the airport was called.

I stayed in Venice only as long as I needed to, to meet and greet my guests – a lovely lady called Zara, a writer like me, on holiday with her two sons, and it was hugely refreshing to have a normal conversation with someone who spoke my own language of motherhood, work and normal life. I felt happy, confident, at ease and proud of what I'd done to create a home out here in Venice and make this life for my family.

As I drove back to the hills that afternoon I thought about this a lot: who I was, what I wanted, how life could be without all the problems of alcoholism in it. I knew I was *choosing* to keep it in my life, and I didn't have to. But love and life aren't always about what we 'have to' do; they're about what feels right to us at the time, what we trust in our gut, and I still trusted in a life with Mike that could be happy for us all; I just wished we could find a way to make that possible again – and forever.

I arrived back in the Dolomites in the late afternoon, and something immediately felt, if not exactly *wrong*, then definitely not quite right. It's a sense you develop when you've been lied to enough times – you can't put a finger on what it is exactly, but it feels as if the air isn't sitting in itself properly. Something's amiss, but you can't see what, yet. Maybe I was oversensitive to strangeness by this stage, possibly even to the point of paranoia or imagination, or maybe my nerves were still so frayed from the panic I was ready to sense problems where there weren't any, I don't know, but there was something *odd* about the scene that greeted me. Or rather, didn't.

My daughter was playing happily with some little stones and a flowerpot in the courtyard and I ran straight to her for a big, relieving cuddle and a kiss, but Mike, who was leaning against the wall of the house, staring into a dead space somewhere between the three of us, didn't move. I got no 'hello, how are you?', no eye contact, no glimmer of being pleased to see me, no sorry for not writing the instructions email, nothing but a cold, unwelcoming shoulder. I sensed a ripeness for trouble even in the *way* he was standing; a cockiness about his face and stance, as if he owned the place. I just wanted a cuddle and a 'hello', like a normal family. Instead I felt I'd come home to a private event at which I wasn't welcome, and the let-down made my temper rise. Couldn't there just be some *niceness* around here? What was going on?

I clocked a half-empty bottle of non-alcoholic beer on the table and then noticed Mike was holding a cup of coffee. He almost never had a coffee at that time of day, and certainly not at the same time as a beer. Why was he doing this now, on the one day I wasn't there? Too many 'this is weird' buttons were being pressed too fast for me to hold, and without meaning or even wanting to I started quizzing him, agitated and angry all of a sudden, words and questions blurting out like automatic rifle-fire.

Where had he been this afternoon? What had he been doing? What had *she* been doing? Why hadn't he answered my calls earlier? Why didn't he answer me last night? Why hadn't he done the *one* thing I asked him to do? Was it *so* difficult? How come he fell asleep so early without so much as a goodnight? Why was he drinking coffee *and* beer just minutes before he knew I was arriving? Was he trying to hide the smell of drink? Is that what it was for?

The atmosphere was already loaded and cocked but I kept pushing, almost wanting a fight, wanting a sorry, wanting something I was never going to get.

I asked again.

'Have you had a drink, Mike?'

'*No.*'

'Have you taken her to a bar today?'

'No, of course not! Actually wait, we did go to one down the road but only so she could have an ice cream.'

Oh, I *see*; he didn't go to a bar … oh but wait, yes he did.

'And when did this "not going to a bar but actually going to a bar" take place?'

'Jesus, I don't know, about half an hour ago?'

'And you didn't remember *just* being there?'

'No, I guess I forgot. People forget things, Liz, it's not a crime.'

He *forgot*.

'Forgetting' was something Mike did a lot when he was caught out. He'd also get 'confused' or 'didn't mean' what he said or claimed I was stressing him out and making him say things that weren't true when *he* had done nothing wrong and I was *making* him lie. This shimmying and deflecting always made my mind spin, when *all* I wanted was one clear, honest answer – I didn't even care what the answer *was*, I just wanted *the truth*.

I should have let it go, I know I should. I think I even knew it then, too. This wasn't the time for a fight. But this *was* the time, and I wasn't letting it go at all. I'd had enough and I wanted more than being palmed off.

'Did you have a drink in that bar, Mike?'

'No.'

'Oh *for God's sake*, do you think I'm that stupid? Did. You. Have. A. Drink. In. That. Bar?'

He pushed himself away from the wall suddenly and banged his coffee cup down hard on the table.

Yes, he said, he had a drink. It was *one* drink, OK? He was an adult, and he'd been looking after a child for two days. 'You know, I was so happy until you got here. *You* do this to me. *You* make me angry.'

Everything escalated from there. He went into the house and I followed, knowing it was better to take whatever was about to be said out of range of tiny ears. How could he say *I* made him angry, when I did everything I could all the time to make this family happy, and he was the one lying – and drinking?

I started shouting torrents of *can't you just STOP* and *can't you tell the truth* and *can't you even be with your child and not drink?* We were in the bedroom now, he was swearing at me, the world, everything, throwing things into his rucksack, onto the floor and against the wall. Then he said he was leaving. He was going. We were done.

I couldn't bear it. Not *again*. I told him he couldn't do this to us, he couldn't just abandon us at will, he had to stop this madness, just *stop it*, but he told me to fuck off and get out of his way, said I was a nutter, he was leaving and he hated me. I was crying hard now, terrified of the prospect of being on my own again, out here in the middle of nowhere this time. How had things gone from so optimistic just a day ago to *this*?

He chucked his laptop into the rucksack and stormed through the kitchen towards the door. I followed, my face red from the shouting and crying.

Mike was outside now, striding past the car already and out onto the road. I shouted at him to come back, please, but he turned the corner and suddenly I couldn't see him any more. He was gone. He had no money, no charger and within an hour or so I'd have no way of contacting him.

I stood beside the car, shaking, breathless from the argument and shock, hand over my mouth to hold in any screaming that would upset my daughter, still playing happily in the courtyard a few yards from me. Look at her there. Look at me. Look at *us*. What *was happening*?

Before I could gather my thoughts, I received this message on my phone:

Fuck you, Liz. You're a joke. A fucking pathetic joke. You will never see me again. I'm done. You've ruined my life. I'm finished. I want to be dead.

If this was all happening today, I wouldn't have gone looking for him, and I wouldn't have called the police. I'd have let him do what he wanted, known there was nothing I could do to stop him, and that I can do everything I need to do without him. But right in the middle of the terrible Then, with nerves that worked of their own accord, emotions pumped high, everything operating on the boundaries of crazy, I was beside myself with panic again.

It was all so mad, I know, but in that second I just wanted to go and find him and bring him back safely.

I popped my daughter into the bike seat and started peddling towards the village. I had no idea where I was going, I was just going to look for Mike. We turned left, then right, past a park and into the deserted main square, me calling out his name as I pedalled furiously in the evening heat, sweat dripping down my forearms and shins already. Where would a broken man go if he didn't want to be found because he wanted to be dead? It was like those stomach-emptying moments when you lose your child in a department store and don't know whether to stay still, move, go left or right or round again. I just kept calling and calling, cycling and cycling. I needed a person, a police car, *anyone*. It was seven o'clock now, there was not a soul about and everything in the village was shutters-down closed – including, handily, the police station. There was a bell outside and I rang it. Again and again and again.

I can't remember what happened next. I can't remember if someone answered the phone or if I gave up and went back home. I can't even remember *getting* back home, or when the Carabinieri arrived. I just know that when they did I was sitting outside the house, the owner, Adriana, was sitting beside me and I was crying. Again, or still, I'm not sure. I'd changed my daughter into her pyjamas and wrapped her in a big blanket, and I was huddled on a chair with her, breastfeeding her to sleep and trying to calm myself. Adriana was saying nothing much, except that I should try to be *calma* and *tranquila*.

A little blue police car turned into the courtyard and crunched to a halt on the gravel, and two policemen emerged, trussed up in navy uniform, belts and a gun, and sauntered over casually like Tweedledum and TweedleGuido out for an evening stroll to the pub, hands in pockets.

'*Alora. Signora?*'

In my best, shaky Italian-English I started to describe what had happened, what Mike looked like, what he said when he left and how unwell he was. I was talking fast, and asking them to please go and start looking for him, like, *now*.

One of them was jotting a few scribbles in a scruffy notepad: *huomo, 35, barba...*

'Hmmm. *Alora.* Tell me, how long he is gone?'

'About an hour, I think.'

He laughed, put the pen down and looked at me as if I was a child whose ball had gone over the neighbour's fence.

'Signora. *Tranquila.* We wait. He come back. *Tutto bene!*'

'Tutto bene' literally means 'everything is fine', but *actually* means 'everything is fucked'. (Which, coincidentally, was the other suggested title for this book.)

They didn't seem to get it at all. Maybe all Italian men walk off in a rage saying they want to be dead, but for me, this situation was not very *bene* at all. Mike could have hitched a lift and be halfway to Venice or Florence or Christ knows where by now, be drinking or trying to hang himself. He was lying on the street comatose just two weeks before, saying he was off to Scotland. Tutto was not bene at all.

'*Please.* He is not OK. He is very depressed, and he drinks.' I started air-drinking my best pint of Tennent's. '*Molto molto, si? Per favore.* Please go and look? *Please?* Now!'

I started to shake and cry again.

They exchanged glances and sighed at this ludicrous English woman who clearly didn't understand a man's need for some quiet and a beer, folded themselves back into the car and went off in search of a Scotsman who wanted 700 beers and, no doubt, for *una birra* for themselves.

Half an hour later there were wheels on the gravel again and three men got out, in varying degrees of unrushed. Mike was smiling and completely wasted, making it almost as far as vertical before having to lean against the car for support. He saw me and broke immediately into a laugh – one of those puerile ones that sneak out when a situation is so shameful a laugh is all you can manage. Or because you're too pissed not to.

The local Carabinieri heroes had found him propping up the very first bar they'd looked in, and seemed to find it all rather splendid, this Scottish man, here in their little village, drinking wine with the locals. *Bravo!* Silly woman, making such a fuss. All *he* wanted was a little holiday peace and quiet, what was the big deal, Signora?

*Everything was the big fucking deal, Signor Policeman.
Everything.*

I was still sitting on the same chair I'd been in since they
went to look for Mike, a metal one with rigid, uncomfortable
armrests digging into my side and a baby still snuggled up into
me, while three men stood above me, not one of them even
acknowledging this mother, this woman who had just been
put through such an ordeal at the hands of her drunk partner,
amiably chatting and joshing about golf and Scotland and the
best local beers and why not fuck each other while you're
at it, lads?

I have never been as humiliated, insulted or disgusted by a
group of men as I was in those 20 minutes.

Or as far away from Mike.

Mike went to bed as soon as his new Carabinieri chums had
left, and fell immediately into deep drunk-sleep. I stayed outside,
holding our daughter close to me, feeling her breathing and
warmth. Adriana came out to water the plants before night, and
walked over to sit with me.

She asked if I was OK, and I said yes, and no, and I didn't
know. I didn't understand anything any more.

Then she spoke, gently, in broken English. She told me her son
had a drink problem. He got sad, she said, and he drank. Then he
drank a lot. He went away sometimes for a day, or a week, he'd
lost his job and his girlfriend, I can't remember if she said there
was a child too, but certainly it was all a bit of a sad mess. Then
she said it, just like any other word.

'*È un alcolizzato.*' He's an alcoholic.

I'd met her son the day we arrived. Mid-twenties, mountain-
handsome, strong and friendly, he worked in a town nearby,
helped his parents maintain the house and garden and was a really
nice, friendly bloke. How could *he* be an alcoholic? Can they
look so ... non-alcoholic?

I told her I was so sorry. But, I said, 'I think Mike is just
depressed.'

She put a wide, tanned arm on mine.

'No, he is alcoholic. I can see this. But you must not worry, for him. You must be *tranquila* for you, and the baby. You are the mamma, you must be *calma*. He can go, and he will come back, if he wants. *Non possiamo fare niente.*'

We can do nothing.

This is almost exactly what my therapist had said to me three months before. It's the key to surviving life with an alcoholic, and if I'd understood that yet and been able to live by it, as I am now, I think I would have avoided more problems that came to me than I will ever be able to count.

Said aloud, a word is given a shape and size. You can play with it in your mouth, in your ears and your head, feel it, practise saying it, get to know it and decide how to use it.

I sat outside on my own for a long time that evening, cuddling my sleeping baby in my arms, and saying it aloud. ALCOHOLIC. AL-CO-HO-LIC. *Mike is an alcoholic. Hello, I'm Liz. My partner is an alcoholic. This is my daughter; her daddy is an alcoholic.*

That one word gave Mike a whole new identity to me. And it gave me one too – one I didn't want, but at least I could start to live my life and make my plans with it. Mike was not a 'heavy drinker', a binge drinker when he was depressed.

Mike was an alcoholic, whether he was depressed or injured or happy or well. He was, and always would be, an alcoholic.

The next morning – now 6 July, in case you've got totally lost during this bonkers week or two, as lost as I was – I cycled to the local village before Mike woke up, and sat at a table outside a café on the piazza, under an umbrella with a Peroni advert on it. It was not even nine o'clock, but already hotter than England has ever been since records of hotness began, and I got myself a coffee and an iced water, and a croissant for my daughter. I tried to read her some books to keep my mind on anything other than screaming rows and humiliation, but I could barely focus on the letters so I started to breastfeed her and she fell asleep quickly, melting into my lap. It was a Saturday, and local families were out together, all talking over each other, waving their arms, smoking, laughing and gossiping the world to rights.

I thought about what had happened in that bedroom the day before. I could have broken every bone in my body during that argument, just by throwing myself at the walls.

We don't talk about anger in women very much. Boys scrap in the playground, young lads sleeve-roll outside pubs, even 'grown men' will throw the odd punch at a wall in frustration and nobody causes a fuss. It's not exactly condoned, but it's well within what we understand as 'normal'.

But if a woman hits, screams, kicks, lashes out, scratches, rips clothing or throws objects across a room she's unhinged, frightening and weird. *Problematic*. Women are not supposed to be angry, and definitely not violent. Doesn't she know she should meditate her way through unbearable frustration and mental torture? Can't she just be grateful she's allowed to speak at all?

Some people say anger comes from fear, others from sadness, and it probably comes from both, plus a fair helping of hormones and genetics. I was never angry as a child, and far more likely to cry or retreat than challenge or pick a fight of any kind. I don't remember feeling angry at all until I was at university, and even then it was a one-off and I was probably drunk after a night in the bar. I think any anger in me started towards the end of my thirties, perhaps as it had become clear that my marriage was beyond salvage and the realities of that were starting to sink in, my career went through some dips as careers often do, and my children had grown up a little and I didn't feel I had a voice or purpose in anything much any more. My anger comes from a sense of powerlessness or being imprisoned by words or circumstances, emotions or lack of clarity and truth. Gaslighting is pretty effective at causing all of that, and as Mike's lies had built up and my voice had been twisted and silenced, I couldn't always hold my frustrations in any more.

So yes, I sometimes lashed out – at him, at myself and at things. I wanted to smash the monster to bits, and get it out of our lives.

I wish it hadn't happened, but I'm not going to sit here now I'm out of the hellhole and sanctimoniously tell those who go through similar traumas or mental abuse that they should handle it more calmly, be better at detaching, be less hysterical or fucking *broken* by someone. When your mind is twisted until you can't even hear sense any more, even though you still KNOW sense when you hear it, you feel what you feel and you are allowed to feel it. If hitting out or kicking doors made me mad or bad or dangerous, then so be it. I think it just made me a woman who was pushed beyond her limit and couldn't take any more. And I don't feel guilty about it.

A year or so into his eventual sobriety, when Mike was finally able to speak about that terrible time, he told me that trip to the Dolomites was when he knew he had gone a bit mad. He'd held it at bay, tried to drink it away, wait for it to pass, hold on to some remaining shred of hope or wishful idea that he could keep going like this and it would somehow be OK again, but he couldn't any more and his brain just gave in.

Shortly after nine o'clock that morning, Mike started sending me a series of short, factual messages. He's out buying a phone charger in a supermarket. Now he's stopped to have a coffee and charge his phone. Now he's in another shop buying a phone charger. Now he's angry because he's got no charge. Then he says he'll come and meet me in 10 minutes and borrow mine. An hour later he's cycling to a village in the opposite direction and 20 kilometres away. He was so drunk, he didn't know what he was doing.

Then at 11.42 a.m. he announced he was leaving the country:

I'm going away for a few days. I'll come back now and get my things and passport, then go. You can't stop me. It's my choice.

He told me he was going to Edinburgh to stay with his brother. His flight was at 10 p.m. He had no return flight booked.

So that was that, then. He was going home. *Tutto bene.* Everything totally fucked.

I offered him a lift to the airport in Venice – he couldn't get there any other way as he'd drunk every penny I'd given him, and there was no way I was staying there in the mountains on my own at such a terrible time in my life – and he said:

Sure, whatever.

I cycled back to the Airbnb and packed everything up. Mike got back, didn't say anything, but stank of drink.

Just before we left, I found some paper in my bag and wrote a letter to him. I can't remember what I wrote, but I know it was the saddest, most heartfelt and heartbroken love letter I've ever written to anyone.

I don't know if he ever read it.

I remember nothing about the drive back except the feel of my hands on the steering wheel, the softness of the fake black leather, and how I gripped that curve all the way back. When we arrived at the car rental in Piazzale Roma, he went to the toilet and I took this little window in the chaos to google flight times to Edinburgh from Marco Polo airport. There weren't any.

When Mike came back to get his bags, unsteady on his feet and keen to get away from us as quickly as possible, I tried to get some clarity about where he was going before he left and I might not be able to contact him for a long time.

'Mike, where are you actually *going*?' I was quiet and calm.

'I TOLD you. Edinburgh.'

'Yes, I know, to stay with your brother.'

'Yes. *Fuck sake* I've told you all this. Just let me go, will you?' He was agitated and hot, and couldn't get away fast enough for this flight … in seven hours' time.

I told him there were no flights to Edinburgh from there, and he said yes there are because he's on one, dickhead. Could I see his boarding pass then, just to be sure he's in the right airport on the right day? He said his phone was dead, so I suggested we wait a few minutes and charge it from the car.

This ping-pong went on for a while, the two of us standing in this dusty car park in the heat, plastic bags, odd toys and books strewn about the car, our daughter eating some grissini I'd found in the glove compartment. People were staring. I would have too.

I tried one last time.

'Mike, you're running away to another country and that's fine, if you want to do that. But can you *please* tell me where you are going in case anything happens to your child, or me, or you? You're quite obviously not going to Edinburgh, and I just want to know what the hell is going on in my life now.'

'It's simple, Liz: I hate you and I want to get away from YOU. I'm going to Barcelona, OK? Happy now? I'm going to stay with a friend who actually gives a shit about me. Now fuck off.'

Barcelona? I was beyond even trying to understand what was going on any more.

He grabbed his rucksack and headed off into the bustle of Piazzale Roma, leaving me with everything else to carry on my own in this heat, and a baby. I watched him disappear, taking the ground with him.

There was so much heat and light, people buzzing about everywhere, looking at maps, pulling suitcases and arguing over which vaporetto to take. But there was no Mike. Everything was so loud and silent, and I didn't know where to go or what to do. All I could do was stand still. Someone was living in my apartment, and the place I'd just rented for our holiday was an hour away in the hills. I was here, now, in a car park.

It's weird what we do when we have to do something, and have no shame left.

I called Zara, the lady renting my flat, and left her a voice message. I told her everything. *Everything.* I think I cried. I asked if I could come by to collect some clean clothes for me and my baby, maybe grab a quick shower and then find somewhere to stay. I said I was so sorry, I never expected any of this. I was SO SORRY.

Even when I'd gone to Mia's house to get away from Mike in March, I hadn't said anything about him being an alcoholic, just that things were very bad at home and I needed a little space. But talking with Adriana in the Airbnb, giving the word alcoholic some air and form, normalising it a little, making it TRUE, meant I could say it.

It felt sad, hearing the truth. Really strange and sad, and I sat down on the hot, dirty pavement next to my beautiful little girl whose daddy had just left us to go to Barcelona, gave her some water and a cuddle, and cried again.

I heard nothing from Mike all day, and into the evening. You might think I was glad to be rid of him, glad to have such a nasty, drunk person away from me, glad for the rest from madness and fighting. Glad to be free. But I wasn't. I was heartbroken and empty, lost in Venice and lost without the man I loved so much, and I had no idea if I'd ever see or hear from him again.

Before his plane was due to leave that night, I sent him this:

Mike, I love you more than anyone has ever loved anybody. But if you want to go, you go. I will love you forever. I miss you so much I can't breathe. When the police brought you back yesterday and I knew you were alive, my whole world came together. Goodbye my love. I love you. Xx

―――――――――

They say when life gives you lemons you should make lemonade. Well, sometimes life gives you kindness, and you should take it, be forever grateful and find a way to be kind back one day. Zara had got back to me almost immediately, said she'd chatted with her sons and I should come and stay with them for a day or two, no problem at all, just come over, get clean and settled, and you'll be fine.

I was to be offered this kind of warmth and generosity many times from here on, now I finally felt able to speak out about Mike being an alcoholic, and the effects of it all on my life.

And it was *women*, especially, who came forward to offer help. Now, I have no sisters, I wasn't part of the girly gang at school, I don't do cocktail nights or 'gal pals' and that curious 'Sisterhood' thing was something I'd always been a little wary of, rather than felt part of.

But the next month changed all that as what started as a few friends and neighbours grew to become a wide support network of women, some I knew, most I didn't, and all of them ready to help me. Some I bumped into in parks, others I met on trains, sat next to on planes or connected with through social media. Some offered to look after my daughter for an hour so I could work, others offered me their homes to stay in, bicycles to use for a day or two, one lady from London, who'd rented my apartment in Venice for a few days, even brought my daughter's birth certificate and a pair of her dungarees all the way back in her hand luggage for me. These wonderful women let me cry on them, held me up when I couldn't stand any more and wove a safe little nest of words and love for me to lie in. I sat in it often, curled up, listening to them, trying to work out what I felt and wanted and should do. Many of them had also been touched by alcoholism, and it was shocking to learn how many people, people I'd *never* have guessed had this in their lives, had their childhoods stolen, had lost relatives, friends and colleagues, how many still lived with unresolved anger and regret, and just how kind they could be to others who shared this Thing. Without them, I don't know how I'd have got through it.

Venice was strange without Mike – almost a different place: *my* place. '*Ciao bambina!*' was now joined by '*Ciao* Liz!' and without any questions asked, everyone appeared to understand what had happened. Drunk, absent father; mother with baby. *Comprendo*. I was met with no judgement or scorn; everyone could see what I was shouldering under my skinny, scarred frame, and I suspected now that most had known for months anyway, having seen Mike in every bar in the vicinity.

It was also strange being back in the flat, sharing it with a family I didn't know but feeling more at home than I had for days. Zara and I stood in the kitchen cooking risotto, we ate together, talked about England and writing, motherhood and running. There was even a lot of laughter, which made a bloody nice change, and my daughter was so happy to be in her home, with her things, it was like watching a flower blossom.

We should have had this life, and on some level I think I knew already that it was going to come to an end far sooner than I'd hoped.

I can't remember what we did during those two days, where we went, what we ate, why I was still in Venice at all or where I planned to go from there. I remember trying to put a brave face on it all, see the positives, feel some liberation or independence or whatever Beyoncé would feel – but really I was exhausted, sad and heartbroken, and just trying to exist minute to minute, breathing to the next hour, the next feed, the next playground, the next hurdle. I wanted my friend back.

Mike was generally absent from all communication while he was in Barcelona, popping up only as and when it suited him, with chaotic, erratic messages that generally made little or no sense. There was some talk of getting arrested on a train but it wasn't their fault (two pissed Scots out on the lash in Barcelona – of *course* it wasn't their fault), then another whole day of silence and no replies, before popping up angrily to demand to speak to his daughter, hours after her usual bedtime so she was fast asleep, and then accusing me of not letting him speak with her.

I explained that the way parenthood works is you don't pick and choose when you want to be the doting, loving, involved dad and when you want to fuck off, get pissed, and be out of contact. He vanished again for most of the next day. The next time I heard from him, he informed me he was coming back to Venice. Tomorrow. He had no flight booked, as such, but he was 'trying to sort it'. So not tomorrow, then.

Chrissake, I'm doing my best here.

I pointed out that doing his best didn't seem to involve changing his daughter's nappy or getting up to settle her at 3 a.m. but *did* seem to involve being constantly pissed. I was told to fuck off and carry on being a 'superhero mum'.

He didn't come the next day, of course. He came the day after.

After the last two restorative days of calm and company away from the Maelstrom of Mike, I felt ready to leave Zara and her sons to enjoy the last few days of their holiday without a tear-stained woman and a pile of baby laundry, so I packed our bags, the buggy was loaded up again with all our flotsam, crumbs and bottles, and I trundled it all to a nearby hotel.

I didn't know how I felt about seeing Mike again, so soon. The man who'd left me in a car park to fuck off to Barcelona and get hammered for three days was hardly a dream catch, and I didn't know which version of Mike he would be turning up as, or what might happen when he did.

His opening line didn't exactly strike a note of much optimism or reconciliation:

I want to see her.

Great. I notice he didn't much want to see her while he was in a bar in Spain, not calling or answering any of my calls, though, did he?

Are you drunk?

Fuck sake, are you really going down that route? No, I'm not drunk. I stink. I need a shower. I'm exhausted.

Doing nothing was clearly far more tiring than I'd had time to realise, what with doing … everything. If we started a fight on the phone there was every chance he might vanish again for days and all I wanted was a bit of calm and to be able to talk about the future, so I said,

You can come and see her, but if you swear once or you're drunk, you have to leave.

Sure.

I'd be lying to myself as well as you if I didn't say that much of the reason I let Mike come back and see us so soon was for myself, I missed him and I wanted to try and help him *and* make things work for us all again. But the far greater reason for now was our daughter – for her to see her daddy, who, as far as she was concerned, was still just the daddy she loved, and for him to see her and remember what he stood to lose by carrying on drinking like this. A sort of cuddly lifeline in nappies.

He'd only been away for a few days but it was important to me to show him that I was never going to try and keep his child from him, for as long as it was safe. If you take all good things away from someone, it's almost impossible for them to pull themselves out of a terrible state. In some of my worst depressions and times of hopelessness, it was always my children, and the love I knew they needed from me, that got me back on my feet. I knew Mike needed his child's love to have any chance of mending, and in allowing their bond to remain strong I felt we all had the tiniest hope of keeping this little family together, in whatever shape it might take from here on.

It was 33 degrees Celsius outside but the air-con was pneumonia-cold, as it always is, so I had all the windows open to try and let a whisper of a breeze in. My daughter, chubby and blonde and sunshine beautiful, was sitting on the bed playing with some plastic jungle animals I'd bought from the local *tabaccheria*.

I've never heard such a faint knock on a door. Almost an anti-knock, to say 'I'm here but please don't let me in, I can't cope with existing'.

He came in nervously, like a tanned rabbit in the world's headlights, bringing a strange air in with him – hot and angry, edgy and nervous, an unnerving energy that could go anywhere at any moment. He reeked of booze, making the whole situation even more ugly, couldn't make eye contact, didn't seem to know where to put himself in the room and filled every corner with unease.

Damn, he looked good, though. Top off, summer-backpacking lean, deep-brown neck and forearms painting a naked white T-shirt on his torso, he looked broken, tired and beautiful. It must have been horrible for him seeing his little family again when he knew he'd just let us both down so much and I could see he was doing everything he could to hold this moment, make it work, not fuck it up and smash the place to pieces in despair. I *almost* felt sorry for him. He wanted to run to the nearest bar, I could tell, but he wanted to see his daughter more.

He sat down next to her but didn't seem to know what to say. I guess she might not understand 'Hi sweetie, sorry Daddy ran off to Catalonia to get pissed' just yet. They were a few feet apart but it might as well have been 10,000 miles, it looked so unnatural.

I remember hoping he wouldn't breathe on her, and bring that booze-smell into her existence. She held up a plastic tiger and he took it from her gently, almost touching her hand, but too sad to let himself feel it.

'Who's this, then?'

It was lovely to hear his voice, all gentle again. No shouting or swearing at me. I'd really missed it, and while I've no way of knowing if she'd missed it too, or even noticed it wasn't there, she was so young, she seemed very happy to hear it.

She started passing him the rest of her little toys, saying 'Tiger!', making 'raaarrgh' noises and smiling at him.

I know I should have been pleased to see her so happy, and I was, but it came with a surge of maternal resentment of this love for him. I didn't expect to feel that but it rose up in me like red mother-mist. *I* was the one doing all the work, *I* was the one getting none of the sleep, being exhausted and hurt by him, while he'd been hammered on drink largely paid for by me, bantering with a friend, going out to bars and sleeping until midday; *I* was the one caring for her and giving her everything, yet there she was, playing with him like some hero returned from battle.

I didn't understand yet that while I was in battle with him and his drinking, he was in a constant battle with *himself*. I didn't understand the illness yet, or what he was going through. I saw it all from my shattered perspective and I hated him in that moment for his weakness, his repeated selfish abandonment of us when it suited him to be on his own, and his ability to still be loved by the most beautiful little girl in the world.

It took digging very deep into my dwindling kindness bucket to push my resentments away for the duration of this visit, and give them this time together that I had no right to take away.

———

That first reconnection was short, calm and thankfully uneventful, and it may seem a little odd to you, but Mike stayed in my hotel room that night, on the sofa – very much the 'crashing extra guest', but he had nowhere else to stay, there was no reason for him *not* to stay as he wasn't drunk or nasty to me, and we really needed some time together to just *be*, regroup and stop the madness for a bit.

There followed a few days of bizarrely normal-looking family life. Zara had left my flat now so we moved back in, living together but still sleeping in separate rooms, co-parenting and co-hurting. If you look at my social media from that time – all there to 'keep face', as I felt I had to at the time, and keep my public persona successful and strong – you'd think everything was fabulous: bright, colourful photos of me and my daughter running through sparkling fountains, all of us having pizza together, Mike reading books to her, handstands on the beach, sunsets over Venice. It's amazing how this 'normality' could even be *pretended*, given the state we were in, and the thing it's very hard for me to explain is that even after such a dreadful few weeks, we did have some nice moments, we *did* chat and laugh as we'd used to – but it was such an obvious effort, a duty, almost, to try and resurrect this thing we had, and there were still snaps and swears, sulks and stormings-off to cool down for a minute. I *still* didn't understand the severity of this relapse. I *still* thought he might be about to come out of it any day.

God, I was such an alcoholism virgin.

I can't remember how many days this little hiatus lasted – maybe six, maybe as much as 10; it's all a big blur of happy moments and hurtful rows. He was definitely still drinking every day, if not drunk then very much not sober, he was mostly surly and still there was an anger just bubbling under his skin.

Those last days in Venice felt like a long, slow, sad, hot, unwanted but resigned goodbye. We really had tried but he was so deep into his drinking, I had start cutting myself again, and it was very clear that we were a disaster, Venice was a disastrous place for us to be, and we needed to be apart for longer than a few days.

We left Venice separately, me to Cambridge, him to Fife. Time out, back with our families, for whatever good that might do. Mike said he needed 'a bit of time to clear his head'. That had gone *so* well last time.

On our last night in the apartment, I wrote this message:

Mike, I hope this isn't the night we look back on one day as what was our last night, but we didn't know it at the time so we just let it go without kissing it goodbye. I could never have predicted this when we lay in the sunlight in Cambridge, in our little pool of light. I could never have known. I love you. X

He came to say goodbye to us at the vaporetto stop the next day. His flight was a few hours after ours – a few lost, beer hours. It was a heavy, heartbroken goodbye this time: no arguments or anger, just grim defeat and sadness.

Our boat pulled away across the water, away from our little patch in Sant'Elena, away from the cats and the greengrocer, from gelato at Gina's, the old women in the Co-op, the playground and our friends. Away from our home.

We had one carry-on bag each, and the buggy, and this was to be everything we lived out of for the next two months.

I watched Mike get smaller and smaller, standing under the trees in his red T-shirt and grey shorts, already walking away, head down, straight to a bar, no doubt. He sent me a message when I was in the departure lounge trying to keep a tired toddler happy, occupied, fed and awake until the flight.

Safe journey. I'm going to sort myself out. I just need a little time to get my head straight. I love you both x

I don't know if he was drunk or if he even meant it. He didn't know who he was or what he wanted any more.

———

Having left Cambridge nine months before to start a new, well-planned life, I was back where I started, this time on my own and with no idea what I was going to do next.

The set-up we had now was ridiculous; we had a lovely, newly renovated home in Venice but were both effectively homeless: we couldn't *be* in our home as Mike would drink himself to death over there, and there was no way I was going back into a sweltering furnace on my own with a baby, with no family or close friends around to help me more than the occasional five minutes here and there for me to weep into a macchiato.

I needed a solid, calm base in which to stop for a while, think and work out what to do now my best-laid plans had gang and got totally fucked up, and however much I'd been glad to get out of Cambridge, it was still the closest thing to anywhere I could call 'home' in the UK: my older children lived there, many of my mum friends and café friends were there, and it was a life and a structure I knew very well. It was also a good place for Mike to be, should he decide to come and live near us.

Cambridge in summer is an English paradise of picnics and parks, punting and Prosecco. It looks like all the films you see about Cambridge with added scorch marks on the grass from disposable barbeques, and it was lovely to be back. This was my university town, the place where I gave birth to all of my children and raised three of them, where I had a strong network of friends, had worked in many places over many years and I felt at home.

But it was now also a Cambridge I'd never known since I met Mike: a Cambridge without him. Cambridge was for *us*, not me on my own with our child, and it was heavy, almost grieving sadness to know his breath wasn't somewhere in the air near mine.

But here I was with a 20-month-old child, an absent, drunk partner and no idea what our future held. The time was not for sitting around grieving for what was lost, but to do everything I could to make my child happy and settled, and to make our life work.

I was lucky enough to be able to stay in a friend's father's house, but this time it was just me and my little girl, and instead of house-sitting on a family holiday it felt a bit like being given refuge. With my mind still a dizzying whir from the last few weeks of shock and emotional turmoil – actually *months*, really, with the exception of the brief respite in April and May – I was still worrying about where and how Mike was, what he was doing and what our now very rocky future held, but I did my best to try and make things as 'normal' as I could for my daughter; I took her back to our favourite playgrounds, bookshops and cafés, I found a couple of toddler groups so she could play with new toys and other children of her age, and I could finally chat with some other mums over a familiar English cup of instant coffee and a Digestive. I played with her, sang to her, taught her animal noises and the actions to Incy Wincy Spider, read her stories, changed, bathed and fed her, put her to bed, got up in the night if she woke and cried, settled her back to sleep and started it all over again at 6 a.m. every day. I don't expect a medal; it's called solo parenting and millions of people do it for *years*, not just a few months, so I know I was lucky to only do it for a short while. But it's back-breaking, tortuous, relentless, wearing, frustrating, exhausting, thankless and physically gruelling – and that's before you throw an alcoholic partner into the messy mix.

I also had to try and find some work. Now that it had become pretty clear I wasn't going to be in my home in Venice for a good few weeks, maybe longer, I had to think about bringing in some income to cover my living costs. I *had* hoped to be writing paid travel features with Mike, but now I needed a replacement source of income, and one I could do with a baby in tow. I sent word out on all my socials to let people know my flat was available to rent, and a few bookings came in pretty quickly, thank God. After all the local taxes and utility bills the actual income amounted to depressingly little, so I applied for various copy-editing jobs, translation work, proofreading and so on – anything I could do to keep my bank balance topped up. I missed out on most of these because I'd miss the application deadline what with trying to look after a child 24 hours a day, but I did manage to score one short-term contract writing social media posts for a Lithuanian road haulage company – my *exact* area of expertise. It was a relief, though, it gave me some confidence in myself again as a working woman, and it was refreshing to have something to do in my evenings that wasn't worry or cry.

After only a week away from Mike's exhausting lies and alcoholic mood swings, I was already getting a little stronger and more in control of my life and mind. Mike's stay in Scotland, meanwhile, was very hard to gauge; his communication was sporadic, vague and often contradictory. His phone kept suddenly dying, he'd lost it or left it somewhere or the reception was bad, and he noticeably never called or answered calls to say goodnight, so there was no way of knowing where he was in the evenings or what time he made it home – or not home – or in what state. He was relentlessly nasty in words and tone – *so* much swearing, contempt, self-pity and 'oh how nice for you to be with our daughter having a lovely time in a nice house and hanging out with friends' while he was suffering so much, doing ... nothing. By choice. He maintained throughout that week that now he was finally away from the nightmare of *me,* he wasn't drinking any more, 'but I will if you keep pushing me', and told me several times that our relationship was over and we couldn't be together any more.

He would disappear from communication for hours and then pop up again in yet another change of mood and tone, and the blatant lies about his whereabouts and what he was doing, followed by anger at me for asking, kept coming.

He told me a year later that he was almost permanently drunk while he was in Scotland for that week. When he said he was at his gran's, he was in the pub; when he said he was going for a walk along the beach and can't I just LEAVE HIM ALONE TO THINK PLEASE, he was in the golf-club bar, six pints under.

Knowing that now, I can see why nothing he said or did made any sense, but at the time it was very hard for me to try and keep anything clear or calm in my mind, and his manipulation of everything I said, twisting and turning of words and facts, insults and swearing, made doing everything I was already struggling to manage on my own even harder and my messages to him that week make for fairly distressing reading. I was SO tired, lost and confused, and above all, *still*, I was heartbroken. I didn't *want* to be alone. I wanted to be with *him*, and to find a way to bring 'him' back to us again.

There are thousands of small reasons why the big things happen in our lives, and we do what we do when we do it, because of how we felt *at the time*. I'm not here to defend any of my decisions or feelings in this story. I'm not going to say I should have done this, or shouldn't have done that, or anyone else should do the same or differently. Everyone's heart and mind are their own, and hindsight is a devilish thing to listen to. We live through life in the present, and the only people who need to understand, forgive or come to peace with why we did what we did at a particular time, are ourselves.

After a week or so back at home in Scotland, Mike messaged to say he was coming to Cambridge. He missed us, he said, and wanted to start again. He was ready to change, he said, and make amends. He would go to AA, he said, and start taking antidepressants again.

I watched our daughter go up and down the slide in the park, a bit like her dad and I were in our life, and thought about the prospect of Mike coming back, so soon.

It was very clear that this long-distance communicating was yielding no progress at all: his ability to vanish, lie and continue drinking every hour of the day and night while denying it to me made any trust – or mending of broken trust – totally impossible, and was also playing havoc with my anxiety, as every day brought fresh confusions or angry words that never got properly resolved by phone. Maybe being able to talk face to face, knowing where he *was*, knowing if he was sober or drunk, might be much better all round. Maybe coming back to a place of relative normality, seeing me and our child, remembering who he actually *was* and could be, was what he needed to get better. Maybe I was still searching for that Magic Answer that would fix him, or maybe my love for him and us as a family was still so strong it made me hang on to any reason I could to let him back in. I missed him a lot, and I also worried that the longer we were apart, the less my daughter saw her daddy, and at that young age a bond like that is very important, and can break fast. I didn't want that at all, if it was possible to avoid it.

So I decided I'd give it a go, and see how things went if Mike came back.

———

Nothing is simple when you share your life with an active alcoholic, and even something as extremely simple as getting an adult from the Pissed Kingdom of Fife to Cambridge was already a problem, largely because Mike had no money, despite managing to drink at least £40 of booze a day. Finding the means to buy the thing that has killed off all their means is just one of the many skills of an addict, and I will *never* understand quite how he managed it for so long. I said I wouldn't pay for his flight this time, what with having already shelled out for every holiday and train and taxi and bus and, oh, a house, and Christ knows what else for years and look where it had got me, and received a lovely reply to say thanks for no help at all, followed by a claim that his grandad had taken money out of his life insurance to buy a flight 'so I can see my own daughter, because some people actually *care*'.

Barely 12 hours later he said he couldn't come to Cambridge after all because he had no money for a flight. I pointed out that he *had* flights – remember, that thing you said about the life insurance and people who actually care? – and no, I was not about to transfer him the cash so he could go straight to the pub with it, but good try.

I was then told something about being a bitch and did I realise I was *making* him behave this way and why didn't I fuck off?

I took a deep breath, and reminded myself that he was a drunk alcoholic and didn't even know what he was saying or doing, and unless we got him out of the bottomless Scottish drink well we had no chance of ever changing this situation. Out came my debit card, and I bought the plane ticket for him. It was £77. It's weird, but in all the thousands I spent on his drunken chaos it's the small amounts I remember most. £42 on a hotel room. A £27 train fare from Edinburgh to Fife, several times, £15 on a taxi from the station, £10 for a pay-as-you-go mobile phone plus £20 of credit after he lost yet another one, and on and on. Over the years, it all adds up to a decent house deposit and I can't even bring myself to think about the far larger sums I spent on us as a family, and on the consequences of his drinking, or the amounts I lost because I was unable to work as I usually would. I know I'll never see any of it again, and after a year of bitter anger and resentment, I finally – *almost* – let it go. Dwelling on everything alcoholism costs us only wastes yet more of our life.

Mike's flight was at 6 a.m., from Edinburgh to Stansted. He said he was going to leave Fife the night before, take the train to Edinburgh, go straight to the airport on the bus and then sleep on a bench in the departures area until check-in time.

I'm sure that'll be loads of fun.

Edinburgh has almost as many pubs per capita as Venice, and for Mike it WAS where he drank – mind you, so was most of the northern hemisphere and that's only because he hadn't been south of the Equator yet – so getting out of there as fast as possible was a very wise move.

Around midday, he messaged to say he was on his way. This was 11 hours earlier than he'd said he would be, and a big change of plan like this was never good news. It generally meant he was firing on adrenaline, drink, anxiety or all three, and was about to go AWOL for an indeterminate amount of time, and I felt immediately anxious that everything was about to go very badly.

We spoke again when he arrived in Edinburgh, and he said he was at the station grabbing a quick coffee, then he was off to the airport and would call when he got there, in an hour.

Three hours went by.

This is the point where I should have put him out of my mind, known there was nothing I could do to alter his thoughts or actions and he would lie about it all anyway, focused on myself and my child and had a nice evening without worry. Unfortunately, I couldn't do that, because I was still deep in 'constant worry about my alcoholic partner' mode and hadn't learned yet how to switch thoughts of him off.

I called to ask how he was but he didn't answer it.

By 7 p.m. I'd called 14 times with no response. I was trying to cook my daughter some dinner and get her ready for bed, but my heart was pounding with worry and not a small amount of anger at yet another disappearance when he'd said all that stuff about trying again and wanting to do better, and because I hadn't even passed my Grade Two Alcoholism exam yet, I'd believed it. I just wanted to know what the hell was going on. Couldn't he just TELL me?

Three more nervous hours went by, my daughter was asleep in bed and I was pacing up and down the kitchen, mind whirring, breathing so fast you'd think I'd just sprinted for a bus, crying. There had now been eight hours of silence since he was having a 'quick coffee' at the station.

I went to bed, beaten by worry and tears, and cried myself briefly to sleep.

At 03.52 a.m., as if nothing at all out of the ordinary had happened, as if none of my calls or messages of worry had appeared on his phone, he sent me his first message since the afternoon:

I'm still in the airport

That was it. No clues as to what he'd been doing during the 10 silent, exhausting hours I'd just cried through. No apology. No how are you? No giving any fucks about anyone. Just a drunk man doing what a drunk man wants to do.

The game of 'Where Is Mike?' continued into the next day. Two hours after his flight landed that morning, he told me he was on a train to Cambridge. Given the station is inside the arrivals area, that's an impressively long time to walk 800 yards. An hour after the train he was *apparently* on should have arrived in Cambridge, there was no word. I called. Nothing. I messaged again. Nothing. I'd been up for four hours by this time, and had our child all ready and waiting to see him. Had he even got on a train? Should I be expecting him home, and keep waiting here to welcome him? Was he even in England?

An hour later I called again and he finally answered his phone.

His voice was low and tired, he said he was a disaster of a human, not worth anything and didn't know if he wanted to go on living any more. He said he was done. Then he hung up and disappeared offline. Perfect.

When someone has said more than once that they are 'done' or don't want to carry on, and has always returned in perfectly fine form, even telling those who panicked about them that they overreacted, it *can* be hard to know what to do. Is it another cry for help, a bluff, some garbage they're spouting because they're so angry or drunk or messed up they don't know they're saying it? If the last five times it was all just words spat out in a moment of desperation, should we ignore these ones – or is *this* time really an emergency? Do we ignore it or step in? Interfere or step back?

The number of suicides every year is horrifying, especially in young men and most especially where there's family break-up, financial problems or substance abuse, and as far as I'm concerned you take every single suicide threat seriously.

For all his talk of getting better and trying again, Mike's behaviour in the last 24 hours had been erratic in the extreme, and showed every sign of someone being very depressed and very drunk.

I called the police, explained the situation and asked if they could check Cambridge station just to see if he was there, or about to jump under a train. While I was trying to describe the exact position of Mike's tattoos, remember how tall he is and try to guess if the last time I'd spoken with him it sounded as if he had a beard or not, he phoned.

I switched calls and there he was. His voice. Broken. He talked, quietly.

'I'm drunk.'

I tried my best 'talking someone down off a bridge' tone, and asked how I could help.

'I just want to come home.'

I told the police, thanked them, hung up and burst into tears of relief, shock and overwhelming levels of tired.

Mike messaged from a taxi to say he needed to 'phase this booze out of my system to function' because he'd had about 12 pints a day all week, 'and the rest', and needed to have a drink in the next hour or so to steady the ship.

In case you needed any more explanation of just how little I knew about alcoholism at the time, I actually believed this might be true.

As this was clearly going to be a very un-sober reunion, I'd dropped my daughter off across the road with her older sisters and brother for an hour or so of much-loved sibling play, so I could deal with her drunk dad. When the taxi pulled up, a man in a burgundy sweatshirt fell out of the back seat, staggered to his feet and started walking towards the house I was staying in. He left the door open and didn't pay. He had somehow managed to pull off a strong Scottish look of tanned-but-also-lacking-all-vitamins and seemed to be having trouble finding his vertical. He stumbled into a few walls along the way towards the house, could hardly speak or see, and swayed about the pavement, head lolling, arms flopped by his side, sweating alcohol through his clothing. He was almost asleep on his feet and looked like a broken, but oddly also smiling, puppy. I picked up the rucksack he'd left on the ground, paid the driver and followed Mike into the house.

Using various items of furniture to steady himself, he made it the three feet across the front room and dropped onto the sofa like an assassinated potato. There had been no hello, no thank you and no how are you?, and he almost seemed to be enjoying his little one-man show of resignation from all care – especially for me. He just lay there, smiling into the middle distance. I asked where he'd been, and did he know I'd been very worried, and even called the police. He smirked again and muttered something about that being fucking stupid and not his problem.

I asked what happened to the money his grandparents gave him *from their life insurance*, leaving me to pay for his flight back.

'Drank it.'

And the money he said they'd given him to buy a present for his daughter?

'Drank it.'

It was so grotesque he laughed. I didn't.

'Is this the best parenting you can manage, Mike?'

His eyes rolled upwards into his skull as he lolled on the sofa like piped sausage meat. 'I'd happily look after her now, but you won't let me.'

Over the following five minutes of questioning, I learned that he was drinking all of the previous afternoon and evening until well after midnight, in various pubs in Edinburgh with his ex-girlfriend. I remember exactly how the room spun, just before I ran to the kitchen sink and threw up.

When I came back, cold and shaking from shock and vomiting, he lifted his blotchy red face to me, not smiling any more but defiant and hateful.

'*You* made this happen, Liz. You did this. Fuck you.' Then he fell asleep.

When I got back with our daughter an hour later he wasn't there any more, and he stayed out for the rest of the day, drinking.

Albert Einstein is said to have defined insanity as doing the same thing over and over again and expecting a different result. Whether anyone – Einstein or otherwise – actually said this or not, and whether I was sane or not over the following few weeks, I don't know, I just know that I wanted to keep trying and trying to get Mike in any way back on track, or even to find a track he could start to make his way back *onto*.

We had decided, or rather our inability not to break into argument and his inability not to be in some shape of drunk decided, that living together was not a good plan for now. It wasn't good for any of us to have such unpredictable moods and anger flare-ups; and I desperately needed any sleep or rest I could get, in a house without a pissed, often volatile man who still lied the entire time about what he was doing, where he was going, what time he'd be back and then often not coming back at all because he'd got too drunk to leave whichever pub he'd fallen asleep in.

He had plenty of people offering him a spare room or sofa to crash on – far easier when you're on your own than it is for a mother with a baby and all the clobber, noise, smell and generally being in everyone's way that brings – so off he went to stay with friends while I remained in our friend's dad's house, for now.

For the first week or so that we were in Cambridge together, as what now seemed like an interminable July neared its end, I remember feeling that despite all the recent awfulness, the relapses and the shocking change in Mike in the last month or two, there was *still* a chance of improvement in him and in our relationship. I reasoned that we hadn't been in a single situation where anything even *resembled* normal family life for almost a year, and it seemed to me that coming back to Cambridge, away from what had been so very hard to handle out in Italy, now back with people and things Mike knew and liked, places where we still had good memories together, where we'd met, where our child had been born, where he was near doctors and AA meetings, near my children and *his own daughter* again, he might pull out of his vortex pretty fast. I realise now that this was exactly what I'd thought when we were leaving Cambridge for the new joyful life in Venice. It was also 'if only this', 'if only that'. I just didn't see it at the time for the total displacement and denial it was.

This confusion, or delusion, I'm not sure which, was made harder by the fact that our time together in these next few weeks wasn't *all* terrible *all* of the time – at least to start with. Mike was still *capable* of niceness, had occasional flashes of what appeared to be remorse and self-awareness, and even expressed some recognition and gratitude for all I was doing while he was being so utterly useless and often very unkind to me, whether he meant to be or not.

He still *looked* a bit like Mike, too, and watching the way he moved, hearing his voice when it wasn't shouting abuse at me, sometimes sitting so close to him I could smell his skin, watching his eyes soften as he played with our daughter, now in that perfect stage of adorable-dom, there were moments of tender, almost mournful sadness between us – because at heart, we both still desperately wanted this family to be together.

But as so often, every glimmer of hope went out faster than a candle in a hairdryer. Mike's drinking, now almost constant for two months, never subsided for more than an hour or two, and as the days went by his mental health got worse at a staggeringly fast pace.

People sometimes ask me if Mike was just drunk all the time and my honest answer is I don't know. He could put away a lot without me knowing, he always had chewing gum or coffee or a can of Irn Bru to hand, so a lot of the beer smell was masked, and it gets almost meaningless to even describe an active alcoholic as 'drunk' after a while, because there is no sober, there's just steady drinking.

But steady drinking wrecks your brain, and Mike's was struggling to do anything normal at all. Regardless of how much he may or may not have had to drink, however nice he could be for an hour here or there, he was in a state of almost constant uncertainty, anxiety and confusion, and could only operate an hour or two at a time.

It had been hard enough to keep tabs on him when we'd lived together, but now that he was sofa-surfing and often not sure until late in the evening where his next bed for the night was, trying to hold him down to any arrangement or truth was like strapping an oiled, knife-wielding octopus into a buggy. He'd lie about where he was staying, who was there, what he'd been doing, what plans he had in place and what steps he was taking to get any better, until I got dizzy from trying to keep track of anything.

Trying to meet up with him was a tiring farce because he either didn't reply or turned up so late we were already leaving, and if all the stars did magically align and we found ourselves in the same place at the same time, it rarely took as much as three minutes before he was swearing at me and walking off.

Still, I tried.

I managed to get him to make an appointment with his old doctor, and even went all the way in with him like a teenager's chaperone – partly to make sure he actually went and told the truth when he was there, but also to listen to what the doctor said first-hand, as Mike would only lie about it to me otherwise. He was prescribed some different antidepressants – Citalopram, this time, which he had not taken previously, to see if this suited him better. Sometimes it takes a while to find the right medication for each individual, and maybe Mike's continued bouts of depression and drinking were because of this. Or, as is now patently obvious, because he was a raging alcoholic and was doing nothing at all to face it or stop it.

I paid for his prescription and even watched him put the packet into his jacket pocket. He lost it within two days, having taken no pills.

Yet another tack I tried was encouraging him – or rather pleading with him – to go to Alcoholics Anonymous meetings, but AA attendance is almost impossible to monitor, coming as it does with a fantastically helpful in-built dishonesty mechanism (ideal for people who live on dishonesty): it's anonymous. You can't bring anyone with you, there's no sign-in or register to say you've been and you can't take any photos in there as proof. It makes Fort Knox look like a 24-hour open-house party, and it makes lying about going laughably easy. To be fair to him, he *did* go to a few meetings and always looked a little bit more like 'Mike' afterwards: more centred in himself, calmer in his *soul* and much more reflective and empathetic towards me. But this brief, irregular attendance was more of a temporary blip in his non-attendance: he often went to the wrong place, or it was closed for the *first time ever* – amazing – or when he thought it said Tuesday it was actually Friday, and so on. After five meetings he announced that he'd given it a proper go this time and realised he didn't need it because he wasn't like 'those people'; he was just depressed, and the medication would help. (The medication he'd just lost, though I didn't know this at the time.)

This 'I don't *need* to go into any form of recovery programme' is classic denial from someone who wants to carry on drinking, and it's not unusual to have as many as 10 false or half-arsed starts before an addict finally admits they're completely powerless to get sober without shoving their addiction's massive ego into some kind of recovery plan that tells them to shut up, step up and start doing the work to become a humble human being.

Months later, he told me he usually had several beers before he went to an AA meeting and another straight after if I wasn't there to meet him.

As well as sobriety, medication, counselling and possibly a new liver, Mike needed a job. Without one he had no income, no structure to any part of his life, no purpose or drive and less than zero self-worth. And here we reach another of Life's bastard catch-22s: the people who really need a job in order to get their life back on track *can't* get a job easily because not having a job means they don't have half the things they need to get one. First of all, if you're sleeping on a mate's sofa you don't have an address.

The negative consequences of being address-less are astonishing, and most of us don't even think about it until it happens to us or someone we know. It's like being in a maze of dead ends with every step and you're basically fucked on arrival, and can't do any of the things that might start to improve your situation: you can't register with a GP, sign on for unemployment benefit, get on the electoral register, open a bank account, own a debit card or get a phone contract. You can't even *apply* for most jobs because they want to know where you live, and even if you use a friend's address you probably won't be living there for long so any mail arriving for you after a week or two will never reach you.

Even if you're lucky enough to have a mobile phone, just *charging* it is problematic without a house containing sockets, and if it's pay-as-you-go you might cobble together a few quid to top it up but if you're alcoholic you'd probably rather drink the cash. If you once *had* a contract, because you weren't always homeless and skint and drinking, you now can't keep up the payments because you have no income, thanks to having no job, thanks to having no address and also being drunk much of the time to numb the nightmare, so the phone provider cuts you off. Now no potential employers can contact you, even if they wanted to.

The only way you can now go online and search for jobs, or reply to an email from an application, is by jumping on some free Wi-Fi, and mostly this is available in a café, a shopping centre … or a pub. So there you are, with no home address, hopelessly looking for work online on a phone you can't pay for in a pub until your phone dies or you get so depressed you throw it under a bus.

To make matters worse, sofa-surfing often means you don't have anywhere safe to leave your belongings during the day so you have to lug them around with you, so going door-to-door to find work is bloody hard because you look like a travelling salesman, and chances are you have nowhere to wash and dry your clothes, or yourself, so you stink, you're filthy and you feel less respected than a pavement turd, and if you *do* get that blessed job interview you'll have to turn up in grubby clothes reeking of park bench piss.

All of this is hardly likely to make someone feel good about themselves, or their chances of ever breaking out of the constant cycle of misery, drink, and misery, and when you're at the bottom the relentless practical problems and emotional knock-backs can put out the most determined little flame of recovery. We have no idea how easy our lives are if the simplest things are in place and how impossible it becomes when they're gone. We can all get to that point very fast given just a few pieces of bad luck and poor decisions. Poor decisions made in anger or sadness tend to lead to more poor decisions made in desperation, until there are no decisions left to make.

Mike *did* get some work in little fits and starts, throughout the month of August, but yet another twist of unhelpful reality is that when you need a job immediately, because you've drunk all your money – and your girlfriend's money – cash-in-hand work is the easiest and fastest to come by. And what does an alcoholic want? Cash. Every job Mike managed to get was paid in cash, and he spent it on booze before it even hit his pocket. Not only this, but alcoholics are like homing pigeons for drink and every job either involved alcohol directly or gave ample opportunity for imbibing it: delivering beer to pubs, filling beer cans in a brewery (yes, *working in a brewery*), some gardening work where the odd tinny or five could be enjoyed over a quick prune of the rose bushes, and he even scored himself a weekend working at a music festival. I mean, why NOT hang out with 2,000 people who are all off their tits on drink and drugs, when you have a massive drinking problem?

I told him I really didn't think this was a good idea, but as ever when Mike had the chance to jet off for the weekend on his alcoholic flying carpet and I tried to convince him not to, he shouted something about me preventing him from trying to make money and get better, and anyway he would give me ALL the money when he got back.

In the end he quit the job halfway through and I never saw a penny of what he earned. I *did* see the scrawled tattoo of our daughter's name inked across his arm by a friend he was at the festival with. I think it's safe to assume neither of them was sober at the time.

The effect on a person's brain of constant intoxication topped up with depression and anxiety is as shocking as it is sad, and seeing Mike's confusion, paranoia and temper get worse throughout that horrific August was like watching a documentary about madness. He changed his mind and mood, plans and words every five minutes, didn't seem to know if we were together or not, even though he had ended the relationship several times by now in one text or another, always swiftly retracted, and said things that made no sense and which he clearly didn't mean, and could contradict himself five times in one sentence. He was given countless opportunities to come and see us but chose not to or turned up so late we'd already had to leave, or he suddenly had more pressing things to do – and *then* he'd claim I had tried to keep his daughter away from him. His messages were an almost unbroken tirade of

Fuck off. Just fuck off. You goad me into being like this.

You're a maniac. You are the worst thing for me.

You are a manipulative, self-serving narcissist and the world will find out about it. You leave destruction in your path, while you wander off with what you want. I have nothing left.

I'm like this because of YOU! Fuck you. I'm broken. I'm done with all of this. Goodbye. You caused this.

And so on. His blackouts now happened almost daily, and mid-conversation he'd often storm off, recall nothing of what had happened only hours before and then claim I was making it all up.

He seemed constantly uncomfortable in his clothes, on the chair he was sitting on, in the sunlight, near people walking down the street, even his own skin, and had to move all the time, away from one thing and towards another for no reason except moving. He'd jiggle his knees nervously up and down, he picked constantly at his beard, developed a nervous tic around his mouth, kept going to the toilet even though he'd just been or needing to go and buy food *immediately* when he'd just eaten, then saying he wasn't hungry.

He piled on nearly two stone of beer and pizza weight in a month, his face got swollen and puffy, his eyes sunk into black circles of hate, and even the colour of his irises appeared to have changed from a beautiful piercing blue to dead grey. On the rare occasions when he looked me in the eye – only ever when he was drunk or angry – I could see nothing I recognised as Mike at all, and it was horrifying, almost sickening, to see someone I'd known so well, found so knock-out gorgeous, kind and funny, now be such a nasty, aggressive, threatening man filled only with a desire to destroy everything and be as hurtful, damaging and cruel to me as possible.

As he slid further from depressed, sorrowful drunk to angry, vengeful, aggressive drunk, he even started trying to turn friends against me, painting a picture of a crazy woman who had taken his child and wasn't letting him see her. I don't know if anyone else had any idea how ill Mike was, because he was totally different in front of others than he was to me. But I do know that nobody in his friendship groups or family ever heard *my* side of the story, had any idea of what had happened with him in Venice, or the mountains, or before or since, and so with nothing else to go on, they – quite understandably perhaps – believed the one-sided bullshit he fed them.

I only came to know about this because he'd started telling me what others were saying about me, and none of it was based on truth, so I looked at his phone messages. You can roll your eyes in disgust, say it's outrageous to look at someone's private messages without them knowing, tell me I deserve everything I get for seeing things that hurt me or how I violated his privacy in some way, but I'll say my very *being* was violated by him every day and we're back to that thing about living with a liar and needing to know the truth, in case you have to protect yourself from some of these lies or prepare for their potential effects.

I'm not 'glad' I looked and still hate that I was put in a position to even think about it again, but it showed me things I needed to see. His correspondences with friends were a list of terrible things I'd done, how crazy I was, how he couldn't see his child because I kept her from him, and their replies of how terrible this was for Mike, and how I was 'batshit, mate', and he needed to 'get out of there'. One mutual friend even suggested a good *pro bono* lawyer she knew, in case he wanted to fight me over custody. I could hardly believe this spinning of the truth against me was going on, and how people believed it.

This is called triangulation, a powerful psychological technique where a third party is used, or rather manipulated, into taking a side, giving the person manipulating them – who is often a narcissist – some control over a situation, while reinforcing their own rightness or superiority.

To *me*, he denied any of this conspiring was happening at all, and the fact that I even suspected it was, he said, proof that I was crazy. Only by stepping out of his gaslighting could I know what I had to protect myself against.

The irony of him talking to people about how awful I was is that if he ever suspected or was told by someone that *I'd* dared to speak to anyone we know about what was going on with him and its effect on me, or even asked my own friends for some childcare help, I'd receive a raging barrage of: *Why the hell have I just received a message from so-and-so saying you've been in touch?? What business is our life of anyone else's? Why are you asking friends to help you? Are you trying to make me look shit? Do you realise you are making me drink? Do you know how pathetic this makes you look, and you're not doing yourself any favours?*

It was awful and it chipped and chipped away at what little fragments of armour I had left to protect me against falling apart completely.

And then he threatened to take me to court. A lawyer friend was helping him for free, he said, 'because actually he likes me, Liz, so I don't need any more of your pity money, thanks'.

I should have seen this for the hot air it was, and now I'd be able to do that, but I was so weakened by this point, so devoid of self-confidence or my own ability to stand up to anything, I saw it as a very real threat to my life with my daughter because some clever lawyer was going to say I wasn't fit to be a mum because I've had an eating disorder or I've cut myself or I'd shouted at Mike or *something*.

My brain was just too shattered to think rationally. I called a friend and wept down the phone at him, while he listened calmly and told me everything I needed to hear: that Mike was just trying to frighten me, there was no way he was taking me to court and anyway, it would be laughed out of any court because he was quite clearly incapable of doing any parenting at all right now. He said if it put my mind at rest I should maybe go and talk to a lawyer too, just so I knew where I stood.

I did go, and trembled and cried through an hour of grim talk about things I'd never had to think about before: shared parental responsibility (*responsibility*?), visitation arrangements, handing our child over from one parent to the other at an agreed, supervised place and so on. It was a bewildering, horrible, surreal conversation and I scribbled it all down and stared helplessly at the words on the pages. How was any of this in my life?

I came out of it tear-stained and £200 poorer, but at least bolstered by the knowledge that I wasn't about to 'lose' my child and I was in the stronger position, by far.

Mike made no legal moves, of course, and the court threat was just words from a place of fear in himself. But to me, at that time, it was yet another load of anxiety, another cost, and more exhaustion at an already blisteringly tiring time.

Chaos breeds chaos, and alcoholism, the epicentre of chaos, causes more mayhem than anything I've ever known. You find yourself living in a falling line of dominoes, you can't stop them crashing down on every aspect of your life and just when you think you have one thing sorted, another falls apart or gets broken: ideas, plans, dreams, phones, doors, laptops, windows, trust, careers, minds. In the space of the worst four months of his drinking, Mike lost or broke at least three phones, two chargers, one laptop, his wallet, a bike, numerous train tickets, several prescriptions, some of our furniture and half of his clothes. While I was trying to keep our family hanging together, he had trouble remembering why he'd thrown his phone in a bush – again.

All this chaos brought problem after problem for *me* as well: first, I was asked to leave the house I'd been staying in after an argument on the phone late at night caused a lot of shouting on my part, and the neighbours complained. So now, while Mike was sitting in a pub sending GIFs to his pals, I had to find somewhere else to live. Thank God, a friend of mine was off to America on their family summer holiday that week and she said I could go and stay there. More moving, more change, more exhaustion.

Then there was my work. It's almost impossible to stay on top of work, admin and any Adulting when your life is in constant turmoil, and I had hundreds of unanswered emails, utilities bills, invoices I needed to send, bookings enquiries I couldn't reply to so lost out on, an overdue tax return, the small matter of a book to finish the final edits on and the last bits of the copy-writing job I still had to do. It's quite hard to fill a 200-page Excel spreadsheet about EU Transport Laws and long-haul drivers' rights when you're constantly packing, unpacking, dashing here, trying to meet up there, building Lego towers with a toddler and crying throughout almost all of it, and the quality of my work dropped so low I was ashamed to even hand it in.

Paradoxically, the more I had to do the less I got done because I became paralysed by fear of all the things I hadn't done, and the less I got done the bigger the mountain of worry grew. I was late with payments, I lost things, forgot things, did things twice for no reason and was generally getting stretched to the very furthest end of my tether.

Looking at it now, the shift of 'power', or apparent shift of power between the two of us, was ridiculous: Mike, who had no strength or power at all, seemed only to be getting more forthright, dominating and intimidating, while I, who on paper held every card in the deck, crumpled into fear. I should have risen like a phoenix, shown him where to shove it, kept well away and left him to descend into his pit of drunken misery if he wanted to. I should have been in complete control, focused entirely on myself and my children, recognised all the good things I was doing and building on that without him pulling me down. I should have listened to Sofia and Adriana, been the lioness and the mamma, put my own life jacket on first and let him do what he wanted to do.

But I didn't. My mental strength and confidence was so shattered that instead of standing firm against his angers and attempts at controlling the truth, I tried to appease *him*, calm *him* and often adjusted my busy life with my daughter to fit around his timetable, which contained nothing of any consequence or urgency.

Physically, I also shrank in every way; I don't know when I'd last sat down at a table and eaten a home-cooked meal but it must have been quite a few weeks, and anyway, I was never hungry, had no desire to nurture or love or care for myself at all. All my care went to our daughter, and to Mike, and to hanging on to the threads of this family. I was very skinny by now, my elbows and knees jutted out like knots on a branch and I often sat with my knees pulled up to my chest, closed off, hunched and protective, eyes down, chewing away at my nails or fingers, sometimes scratching at the backs of my hands. My hair was lank and noticeably thinning from lack of nutrition and rest, my face was drawn and hollow and still had scratches and scars on it from a few months back, and I wore the same clothes almost every day for weeks: an old pair of soft, loose, black Zara trousers with a growing hole in the knee, a black vest, thin black jumper and black Converse. I wore it all like a safety blanket, nervous to wear anything different in case it made me less invisible or took my superstitious support structure away.

All this sameness was part of a framework of 'safety systems' I built around myself to hold on to, and I stuck to routine and familiarity, compulsive and unwavering repetitions, and even the simple rhythm of walking, pushing the buggy and singing was comforting, familiar and safe.

When I should have been stronger than ever, I was the weakest I had ever been in my life; I got more and more confused, swayed this way and that by the constant conflict between my own gut feelings, the bits of advice I got from friends and the incessant mind-bending from a man who only told me things to further break me down: I was a bitch, I was mad, I'd done this to him, he was perfectly happy on his own, we were over, I should fuck off, I was bad for my child.

He even started to make me question whether I *was* mad, *was* doing this to him and *was* a bad mother. I couldn't see that he was just an angry, self-hating alcoholic and I was an exhausted mother and had no strength left to see clearly.

I think things might have been very different for me had I not dealt with so much of everything that happened to me on my own. Sure, I had a few friends to call on and they were wonderful to me; we met up for coffee and chats, sometimes for a walk along the river or play in the park. One mum friend had my daughter round to play a few times so I could go for a quick, mentally restorative run; another lady I don't even know but was staying in my flat in Venice for a week brought some clothes back for my daughter that I'd left in a box somewhere, and we met up in London and drank Prosecco and I actually let *go* for a moment and laughed and felt happy. These things were all lovely little breathers of kindness, and really, I think that whole summer and autumn were pinned up on those moments. But in between them, the bad was very bad, and I *was* very alone.

One never knows how people will react to the arrival of alcoholism in a family: some are immediately sympathetic and do everything they can to help; others want to banish it forever. I understand this, and it's actually one of the main reasons I'm writing this book – to try and open more dialogue between the experiences of addicts and those whose lives they touch.

As a mother, I've asked myself many times what I would do if I saw one of my children being treated as I was and looking like I did as a result of it. What I would say to them, to what lengths I would go to try and separate them from the source of their suffering? How might I feel if they refused to do anything that might help them, but instead continued to support the person who was hurting them?

I imagine the frustration at being met with obstruction and rebuttal must become unbearable after a while, and there is also implicit guilt: if our child not only makes such a poor choice of partner, but also doesn't know how to look after themselves and get out of a bad situation, does it mean we've failed in some way as parents? I don't know, and I hope I'll never be faced with these questions, but I know that my own family only wanted to see *me* happy and well. When I arrived in Oxford for my daughter's graduation and they saw me for the first time in many months, now painfully thin and drawn, scratches on my skin and cut-marks occasionally flashing if my sleeve pulled itself up a little and with anxiety levels so high I'd scream if the microwave pinged, they were understandably fairly shocked and angry at anyone that could do this to me.

Mike had always been welcomed warmly into my family and he got on very well with my parents, but the door was now firmly shut to him, unless he could show signs of getting much better. These things are complicated, and now, with time to reflect and from a more stable place in my life, I can see it from their perspective. Mike himself says now that if anyone did this to *our* child he'd tell them to fuck off and never come back.

But at the time, it put me in a very difficult position: I never wanted Mike to be or even feel cut out, rejected, and treated as he already felt himself to be: done with. I always felt it was essential to anyone's recovery from a mentally dark, broken place to have a sense of belonging, to be given hope and a reason to carry on and get better. *I* also wanted to be supported and cared for without conditions or judgement – *even* with an alcoholic partner, *even* with scars down my arms, *even* with fear in my tired eyes.

Everyone shows love in different ways, and tough love is one. Maybe we just can't see it or deal with it when we're so tired we can't deal with anything at all.

Today I realised that this is my life. It's what I have and what I am. I'm one of those pointless, weak pricks, drinking at breakfast and not even caring. And you know what? I don't care, because this is all I can be. This is me.

I said 'apparent' shift of power, and it really was only that. In himself, Mike knew he had none at all, and had lost pretty much everything he'd ever cared about. As the little bits of work he'd got here and there came to an end and he had nowhere in particular to be and nothing in particular to do, he started spending his whole days in the pub in the early days of August, kicking things off in Wetherspoons at 8 a.m. drinking Strongbow next to the long-timers at the bar. He's told me since then that for the first few mornings he'd make up some excuse for being there – 'got the shakes after a big night, only place to get breakfast this early, just the one to set me up for a long day' – but by day three he didn't bother any more. He'd upgraded – or rather downgraded – to a person he despised, and now he knew he was one of them. So he gave up.

Giving up is blissful. Nothing matters any more, everything becomes *easy* and you can stop, breathe out all the weighty air and fall into warm abandonment. It's heroin for the tired of life, pain-free absolution of all stress, guilt, responsibility and worry, a deeply peaceful absence.

I've had enough of trying, fighting, fearing and failing a few times in my life; had enough of the exhaustion of addictive behaviour, counting calories, thinking about food, planning when to eat or not eat food, telling lies about eating, feeling shit about the lies, worrying about being found out for binging when I left careless piles of biscuit wrappers in my drawer, hating myself, being constantly depressed but having to pretend I wasn't. Addiction is eternally tiring, but there's a way out: you can give up on even trying not to be what you are.

You can resign yourself to it, embrace it, *be* the addict and wear the label. Labels explain and excuse things. When I was told I had an eating disorder I was given a ticket to starve and purge: if I lost weight it wasn't *my* fault, it was the anorexia. If I threw up it was the bulimia, not *me*.

There are only two ways to go, once you give up: to the end of living, or to a sweet spot where you give up on giving up and decide to change, when the dirt of addiction is more exhausting than the work needed to get clean – and that's the start of recovery.

As he sat in the pub looking at the drunks beside him, while the rest of the world took their kids to school and then went to work, Mike chose Option A. He gave up all fight to improve himself, any pretence at wanting to sober up, and channelled all his remaining energy into being a Professional Alcoholic. Blame, shame and guilt were all gone: he was a drinker, so he drank. He didn't need to care about anything or anyone any more, and could do what he wanted, destroy as much as he wanted because there was no consequence to him. In fact, it was *better* if he destroyed everything he cared about, because then there was nothing left to lose. And that included us.

One morning when I was in a toddler group with our daughter, Mike sent me a text to say he had something 'important' to tell me. I wondered if he'd had an epiphany at the bottom of his ninth pint of cider and was ready to apologise, and maybe decide to start pulling the remains of himself together.

Maybe he would cry, say sorry, hold my face gently in his hands and kiss me like he used to. Maybe harps would play and a unicorn would come trotting by, farting rose petals. Maybe he wouldn't come at all.

We agreed to meet by the Old Cavendish Labs in town; our old kissing corner. It was a stupid idea to meet there, I know, but it was very close to the centre of town and a stubbornly romantic part of me hoped some hot memories might be baked into the cobblestones, reigniting a long-dead love – as cobblestones are well known to do.

I arrived early and nervous, our baby asleep in her buggy after a long morning's playing. It was a proper hot English summer's day, limestone walls radiating heat and hope, and I stood in the sunny silence thinking back to our loved-up, horny days just a couple of years back. I couldn't imagine those two people were us.

Mike arrived late – doing nothing was clearly very time-consuming – and slowly, like a shadow licking along the pavement. It was strangely lovely to see him, this wreck of a man I loved, and I suddenly remembered how he used to run to me, right here, all covered in coffee and lust.

Today, he stopped a few metres short of me and leaned back against the wall, arms crossed, looking straight ahead at nothing. He looked dishevelled, tired, logged out, uncaring about the world – but still, to me, beautiful. A lovely, sad mess made of

Mike, in need of major repairs, and despite everything in the last months, my immediate reaction was to want to hug him tight, feel his shape against mine and smell his skin again – though what I could smell from three feet away gave a pretty clear indication of why he was this late, and how long it had been since he left the pub.

I didn't move. Neither did he. I said 'Hello', and his response was to suck some snot into the back of his mouth and spit it onto the ground. Then he spoke. Slowly and firmly, like a strangle.

'We are done. I don't want to see you again.'

I'm sure there are many women who would confidently have told Mike to fuck off at this point, and walked away happily into their own life, with their beautiful child, and without all this shit in it. But, for better or worse, rightly or wrongly, I'm not them. As his words punctured all hope, I felt the air from my lungs empty onto the street and the bones in my legs crumble. I would love to leave the next 10 pages of this book completely blank, so you could turn them slowly, and feel that empty, silent, dead pause.

This wasn't even heartbreak; it felt like grief. The falling away from everything I still wanted and loved, had tried to make work, and from all the oxygen it contained. If he could just *stop drinking* we could have all that back. I was right here. I could see it, feel it and until 10 seconds ago I could breathe it. Why couldn't he just *STOP*?

I moved towards him, instinctively, even pleaded a little for him to stop saying these terrible things, and we could try to make it work if he got some help and got well.

He pushed himself away from the wall with his foot, spat on the ground again and said, 'You have photos of me if you want to see me again. Now fuck off.'

And he left, down Free School Lane, where my world, now broken, had once been perfect.

I didn't see Mike for two days after that. He went away into his liquid sadness, and left me in a strange, airless place with no left or right, or way of deciding yet. I hated him. I missed him. I despised him. I *loved him.*

I carried on doing whatever it was I did in those weird, fast, interminably slow, dizzy days as August came nearer its end, and he did what he did: drank.

A few days later he sent me this message:

I'm so scared of losing everything I try to break it. I know I'm doing it and I don't want to, but it's what I do. When I want a hug I push you away, when I'm screaming inside to be closer I hurt as much as I can. I have no idea who I am right now. My mind is so fractured I don't recognise myself. I've destroyed something so innocent and beautiful, and it makes me want to burn the world. I can say sorry but I know it's meaningless. I want to be near you. Touch you. Speak to you. Hold you. Laugh with you. But I'm incapable. I'm pretty sure that's it. Over. I love you so much. I miss you. This is the worst period of my life.

We were now eight weeks into his meltdown, and Mike seemed to have decided to become almost dehumanised, both towards himself and me. I was the physical embodiment of everything he had lost and didn't have the strength to get back, a persistent reminder of everything he'd fucked up, and a final frustrating barrier to his alcoholic freedom. He wanted to be alone to drink himself to death, and any time we had contact, all of his anger and self-hate was directed at me. Exhausting and hurtful as it was, I continued to offer to meet up in town or in a park if he wanted to, to see his daughter and for her to see him and not forget who he was – but these meetings were always very short, and never went well. His verbal assaults were almost unstoppable within minutes of seeing me, he was aggressive and intimidating, swearing in my face, pushing me out of his way as he stormed off yet again, occasionally even lurching at me during heated conversation as if he was about to head-butt me. A few times I remember he pressed his forehead hard against mine, breathing obscenities quietly in my face, before smiling suddenly, swearing and walking off, bizarrely triumphant but hateful of the world.

He seemed to have completely stopped caring about potential consequences of his behaviour, or to even have any awareness of what people might say or do. During one of many unprompted outbursts in town, he spat in my face for the first time, straight into my eyes from an inch away. Being spat at doesn't hurt, but it's so puerile and animalistic, so removed from all civilised behaviour, it takes on a unique form of shocking and degrading.

And then there was the head bite.

It was early evening, still summer light, and I'd asked if he'd like to come round while our daughter had her dinner – just a simple gesture of kindness, and to keep her seeing him, and him in her life. He'd arrived very late, confrontational and clearly drunk, and when I pointed out that she had eaten over an hour ago and was now asleep in bed, he shouted something about taking his daughter away from him, kicked the wall and stormed outside again, almost breaking the front door.

I followed him outside, to calm him down a little so he didn't leave in such an angry state. It's quite a busy road at rush hour but now it was quiet, with no cars or people; almost like a stage. It was starting to spit with rain, and I remember Mike had a light grey shirt on, black drops marking it where they fell. He was pumped with anger, pale-faced and sweaty, and as I stood there asking him if he might like to try and just breathe a little and calm down, my own calmness only seemed to aggravate him more. He suddenly stepped forward to stand within a foot of me, and jabbed his finger towards my eyes.

'Stay away from me, Liz. Stay away or I swear to God, I'm going to knock the teeth right through the back of your head.'

Nobody had ever said anything like that to me before, and the words were so bizarre to me I almost didn't understand what he'd said.

'You're going to *knock my teeth through the back of my head*?'

'Yes. I mean it. Stay away.'

I tried again. 'Mike, this is not OK. When are you going to stop drinking?'

'Never.'

'When are you going to start taking your medication then?'

'Never.'

'For Christ's sake, Mike, do you *want* to be an alcoholic?'

'Yes, I want to die.'

'Do you want that for *your child*?'

That seemed to be one step too painful for him. He grabbed my face in his hands, shouted at me to 'GO AWAY' and then sank his teeth into my head; lower incisors in the middle of my forehead, upper teeth just above my hairline. I cried out and he pulled back, turned and stormed away into the rain.

I ran back into the house, sank to the floor of the living room, back against the wall, and started screaming into a cushion, kicking my feet against the wooden floor. I wanted my head to explode and everything to go away. I sat there for hours afterwards, exhausted, and with no idea what to do any more.

The bite mark was deep, and it went red for a day or two so I tried to cover it up with foundation and let my hair flop over my face a bit until the redness settled down a little.

I know I'm very lucky to have got as far as my early forties and never been physically assaulted by anyone, and now it had happened to me, I didn't even properly understand what it was, or meant.

I didn't know anything about personal boundaries and safety, or how to judge when enough really is *enough*, and I didn't have the language in me to understand what was happening. All I knew was that, for the first time since we'd met, I didn't feel safe near Mike. He didn't look like himself any more, act or speak like any Mike I recognised, and I no longer even felt sorry for him; I didn't want to be near him, or want him to be near us.

It was the very end of August now, two and a half relentlessly shattering months since his birthday meltdown in Venice. My nervous system was wrecked, and I couldn't manage any more.

I sent a message to my Swedish friend, Astrid. We'd met about 10 years before, had clicked from the start and kept up our friendship between Cambridge and London, meeting up once a year or so to pop to an art fair or drink wine by the canal before my train home, and I'd missed her since she moved back to Sweden. She'd often suggested I come over to visit her, swim in the local lake, eat fish and drink lots of wine, but I'd never had the right time to do it. *This* was exactly the right time.

She answered almost immediately. 'The spare room is ready, for you and your lovely girl. Come and rest.'

I booked flights for the next day. One way. I didn't know how long I was going for, where I would go after that, if I would see Mike again or what of him might be left if I did, but I knew I had to go. No progress or recovery was possible in this firepit of madness and pain. We both needed time to find ourselves again, and we needed time apart. Maybe forever.

PART FOUR

Scandinavia

If you ever need a place to escape chaos and find peace, I highly recommend Scandinavia. A haven of calm, it's an antidote to all disarray and pandemonium, and almost doesn't *allow* for crisis. Within minutes of our arrival in Copenhagen airport, clutching bags and trying to keep neither my child nor her blanket/milk bottle/fox toy/breadstick collection from falling out of the buggy as I negotiated more escalators, lifts and ticket machines, order descended: everything was clean, spacious, stylish and functional, trains ran to time, and every model-beautiful inhabitant was dressed to perfection in the permitted colour scheme of muted blue, muted grey, muted black and somehow even muted white. This quiet canvas of elegance was strayed from only occasionally by a carefully selected mustard yellow or navy, and the whole effect of this aesthetic bliss was like melting into a gigantic cuddle in a soft furnishings department of IKEA, complete with meatballs.

I also remember a lot of calming blues: light grey-and-white blues of the sky, green-blue of the sea, pale-blue houses, my thin, turquoise-blue anorak and the vibrant blue jumper my daughter wore almost every day. The sky here wasn't a saturated, gaudy Venetian azure but a pale, whispering September sapphire that didn't crush or dazzle but lifted my spirit and let me breathe.

I'd never intended to visit this shrine to pristine woollen outer garments and blisteringly expensive sandwiches, but it turned out to be the best place I could have gone, and marked a crucial turning point in my journey from someone who had all but ceased to exist separately from the problems and exhaustions of an alcoholic in meltdown to someone in my own right, with my own mind.

Away from Mike, unable to even try to meet up or be let down yet again when he didn't show, or did show and shouted abuse at me, I got my first taste of freedom from the near-constant turmoil, lies and tears of the last year. Here, on the shores of this windy, pastel peninsula, I started to disconnect from him, connect with others, and reconnect with myself.

Astrid's house was exactly like a Swedish house in a Swedish village with a Swedish bakery near a Swedish beach. A Moomin cocoon of unconditional love, every room seemed designed around the single, central purpose of being comfortable and safe. Soft sofas strewn with snuggly blankets and huggable cushions; strings of fairy lights, nice baskets of Nice Things That Looked Nice, and old candlesticks scarved in drippy wax telling of long summer evenings with wine and friends. Everything my life lacked, in fact. I hadn't seen her for at least seven years, but good friends pick up wherever they left off, need no explanation of anything and just get on with getting on well. 'We have a "good vibes only" policy in our home,' she told me when I arrived, haggard and thin, nerves like a fraying hem. 'All negativity is left at the door – just be at home, be calm and be loved. You'll see.'

Being 'calm and loved' is hard if you're not used to it any more, because 'awful' has become your normal. Waking up every morning dreading the day ahead; wasting hours of time and energy worrying, wondering, checking and being on constant high alert; living with almost daily shock, disappointment, lies, sadness and loneliness; going to bed crying, waking up crying, spending most of the day crying. This shouldn't be anyone's normal, but I had let it be mine to the point where I was so used to it, I barely even questioned it any more. I'd had almost no help or love for so long I was now an empty survival machine, waiting for the next angry message or drunken lie, and I couldn't manage to be at rest or feel in any way 'calm' for several days. But in these new, gentler surroundings, a new normal started to appear. Astrid gave me the perfect gift of total acceptance and zero judgement, criticism or responsibility other than to myself and my child, and my first taste of child-free *time* to stop, breathe and catch up on some of the mountains of piled-up work and problems I'd not been able to deal with on my own. She offered to have my daughter for an hour every day for me to 'do whatever you want: sleep, work, go for a run, have a bath – anything'. Most of all, she gave me kindness and safety, and slowly but surely my nervous system settled down, heart palpitations and shaking stopped, I uncurled and started to feel something resembling normal again.

I made a conscious effort to FEEL things; to stand barefoot on the dewy lawn every morning and focus on my feet planted firmly against planet Earth; to eat slowly and nourish my starved soul; to have no plan for the day except to be with my child and make her happy, to love this time together and to think about what our future might look like.

I have a photograph of myself on the day we arrived and one of a week later. The first is of a pale, frightened, cracked shell of a human, scratches on my lip, Mike's bite mark still visible on my forehead, sunken black circles under nervous eyes, pinched cheeks and a tight, leaden mouth. The second shows the beginnings of the emergence of a woman, under-eye shadows now smoothed by rest, scars healing and eyes with a little sign of a person inside them.

Our days in Sweden were simple; I cycled to the local town every morning, my daughter in a bike seat behind me babbling away, and we'd stop off for coffee and cinnamon buns before heading off to a windy little playground I found looking out across the choppy sea. In the afternoons we went to a sweet little library in town where I read *Maisy Mouse* books in Swedish and we laughed at the funny words Mummy couldn't say, we bounced together on the trampoline in Astrid's garden or went on little jaunts with her to some beautiful, hidden local beaches. There was no fear, there were no lies; we just *were*.

Aside from all the cycling and cinnamon-bun-eating, there was also a lot of work to do: copy-editing to complete, writing work overdue, my book's final edit to submit very soon, I had bills and admin to keep on top of back in Venice and I was behind on *all* of it. But now, with an extra pair of hands to help me even for only 20 minutes here and there, and with the benefit of some *rest*, I started getting things back into some kind of order. All the time and energy squandered on worrying, chasing, arguing, crying and trying to stop things falling apart could now go into the far more constructive business of *living*, and enjoying that life.

Astrid decided to host a 'crayfish party' one evening – a supremely Astrid and Swedish thing to do – and spent all afternoon decorating her porch with garlands of paper crayfish, crayfish balloons and crayfish napkins. She cooked a feast of salads, side dishes, relishes and mounds of ... crayfish. Her friends arrived bearing bottles of wine and Friday night dinner-party sparkle, and we sat on the porch in the candlelight until well after midnight, talking, drinking wine and laughing – not getting shit-faced, swearing at each other or lying about how much we'd actually had to drink. It was the first meal I'd had sitting at a table, off a plate, using cutlery and enjoying myself since June, and the whole evening was a taste of a life I'd missed for a very long time; a normal life of family and friends, laughs and *joie de vivre* and I bathed in every word, trying to soak it up and make it last. I lay in bed that night next to my daughter, listening to her slow breathing, so glad for her company in yet another lonely night in my life, and cried at how impossible an evening like that was to me now. But maybe it didn't need to be. Was this not just SO much better than living with a drunk liar? Would I not be much happier, healthier and more fulfilled in every way if I chose to go it alone?

—————

I remember very little of what Mike was up to during my two and a half weeks in Scandinavia, which, given how his every move and lie had dominated my life for so long, says a lot; it was the first time since we'd met that I'd felt, or was even *able* to feel, any kind of healthy disconnection from him at all, and it brought palpable respite and some settling of nerves. We did still communicate by WhatsApp most days, as and when he was contactable and coherent, so he and our daughter could see and hear each other, pull funny faces and have the little giggles they used to, and I sent him photos or videos every day of where she was and what she'd been up to. But between the two of *us*, any chat or interaction was still too raw and unpleasant.

Phone calls were off the cards as tones of voice were always misinterpreted or upsetting, and even hearing him shook me back to being with him in person, anxious and angry, worrying about where he was and what he was doing. I'd get upset when it was obvious he was lying or twisting my words, and then *he'd* get angry because he knew damn well he'd been in the pub all afternoon and probably the morning too, hated me for knowing it and himself for doing it, and it would all go very wrong very fast. Messaging was less fraught as I could switch my phone off if things got too heated, have an ice cream with my daughter and smell her sea-breeze hair. I tried to train myself to spend more time in this state of 'phone off' calm – not easy at first, if you're used to being in touch with someone, or checking to see if they've been in touch with you every five minutes – and after a few days of more frequent radio silence, the pneumatic drill of anxiety stopped digging up my brain.

I also started *talking*.

Now, I love a good rendition of Wind the Bobbin Up as much as the next knackered mum, but after weeks of being on my own with a toddler who couldn't speak and didn't seem up for many chats about psychological manipulation or bemoaning the absence of any sex in my life, I was desperate for adult company and conversation.

Now safely away from the fear of being reprimanded for speaking out or gaslit into believing I was making things up, I finally felt ready and able to open up, share and *tell* people the truth of why I was on my own, why I looked so tired, had cuts on my arms and cried so much.

So I did. I talked to mums in the playground, people next to me on the train, the hot-dog guy at the beach hut café, and the staff in the bookshop. People *listened*, kindly and with sympathy, and started sharing their own stories back, many of them also touched by addiction.

And then my Insta-family arrived. I'd been using Instagram for a while to share a heavily curated picture diary of our Venetian adventures; all drinks on the lagoon-front, sunlit bridges, cats in windows, our daughter being cute and the three of us having a ball. Recently, three had become two and there was no Venice any more, just a lot of travelling and upheaval, a lot of me and our daughter, and a lot of no Mike. A few people sent me direct messages to say 'Hi, your travels look amazing, but ... is everything OK?' and I started to answer cautiously, with a vague sort of 'Yeah, I'm with our daughter for a bit, everything's cool'.

I can't remember who I told first or how the open conversations about Mike's drinking started, but when they did a wave of love and support poured into my inbox from people all around the world who wanted to say something kind, and help me. And many, it turned out, knew a similar story all too well. Some had suffered at the hands of alcoholics, been physically assaulted or left husbands or wives because of alcoholism. Some had even attended the funeral of an ex-partner who'd been an addict. Others had been raised by alcoholic parents, or had to give up trying to help their addicted siblings after years of effort had made no difference. Some were addicts themselves and had been in recovery for years; others had no experience with alcoholism at all and were just sending good vibes my way, or were single parents who knew how brutal it is to pay all the bills and wipe all the tears, alone.

This online community of strangers gave me invaluable advice and counsel, and said everything Mike didn't say, or feared saying or couldn't admit. They told me I was strong and smart, doing brilliantly and could manage this. They taught me things I should have learned years before, like establishing personal boundaries, being able to say 'no, I'm not comfortable with that, thanks very much' and stepping away from things that damage me.

When your only point of reference is the very thing that's trying to break you down, you have no chance of breaking free. You can't see an alternative view through all the fear, and it's very easy to lose sight altogether of another you; the *real* you, strong, capable, clear-minded and able you.

The people I spoke to in those brief but healing September weeks in Scandinavia allowed the first green shoots of the confidence and self-belief I'd had crushed out of me to start pushing their way up. I started expressing things in my messages to Mike that I'd never dared to when I was with him. I told him to stop creating reasons to say sorry to me all the time, to go and ruin someone else's life if he couldn't change, and how I was sick of being treated like an idiot or an emotional punchbag. I started standing my ground in arguments, and instead of shouting at him in anger or frustration I could calmly switch my phone off for a few hours so I couldn't hear the angry, ranting beeps flying in and knocking the strength back out of me. I wasn't trying to be unkind, or to cut him out of my life, I was just allowing myself to exist for once, and it was well overdue.

While I was slowly but palpably becoming a little stronger, Mike seemed to be getting worse. Being without us had left him with nothing to look at all day but the spectacular disaster he had made of every aspect of his life and no target for his hate other than himself. His mind and moods seemed to be in a fairground unlucky dip and if I asked him the simplest question he'd reply by contradicting himself several times in one sentence or start a rant about how lucky I was to be on holiday, followed by, 'Fuck's sake, I was perfectly happy before communicating with YOU.'

At one point he announced he'd had an amazing revelation that he could't drink any more – *CONGRATULATIONS* – and then promptly went and got hammered for several days, resulting in lots of drunken messages, denial, blame, anger and insult – and then all the usual sorries. He played the put-upon, homeless victim card at every opportunity, reminding me frequently how lucky I was to be on holiday with his child, but it later transpired he'd actually been staying in some very nice hotels, paid for by various odds and sods who took pity on him, while running up massive bar tabs. 'Lucky me' was looking after a toddler all day, settling her back to sleep at night if she woke, and scrabbling around to finish my work in the evenings.

I didn't know this at the time, because I was given the Dishonest Director's Cut that he was applying for work and getting himself back into physical shape by running and eating better, but Mike was drinking constantly for the entire period I was away, and like all the best alcoholics, had successfully built his daily life around getting access to drink: he went to the pub with people who didn't know he shouldn't drink, hung out with mates who drank with him at home, and his brewery job enabled him to bring armfuls of full 'reject' cans of beer home every evening, which he'd drink before going to the pub. Again. He wasn't taking any medication or going to AA despite telling me that he was, and how he was working hard and 'turning his life around'.

Being collateral damage in the chaos of alcoholism can make us feel like a constant burden to everyone else: there's always a new problem, another weep-fest, another favour to ask, and another reason to feel ashamed, and after a week of Astrid's company and generosity, I suddenly felt I was in the way.

So I said my thank yous and goodbyes, and off we went again – buggy, rucksack, suitcase, changing bag, suitcase-crumpled clothes and the same six books and handful of Duplo we'd had for nearly two months. We took the short ferry crossing to Denmark and then a bus – on which my daughter threw her hotdog up into my lap – and finally arrived, like a travelling circus of disasters, in Tisvilde, on the blustery, beautiful north coast, where I'd been invited to stay for a few days with my friends Caroline and Anthony. We'd 'met' through social media a couple of years before, and I loved their whole vibe and outlook on life: self-motivated, self-employed, creative and hard-working, they'd successfully built a very comfortable, happy family life by having a dream, building it together and making it work.

Over the five days I stayed there, cycling to yet more windy beaches, playing in the forest, looking out to sea, thinking, watching how other people lived and interacted, I began to feel less 'free, wild and independent', and more alone, observing family life but not living it any more. In the evenings I'd stand in the kitchen while my friends cooked dinner for their kids, talked about work and stuff going on at nursery, and was struck by how they supported and respected each other, gave each other space, trusted each other, could say anything without fear of chastisement or blame and loved each other completely. It reminded me of something I'd lost so long ago I hardly recognised it any more: how two people can lift each other, not break each other down. It's amazing how fast we can become used to a sad, two-star existence when everything we do deserves a gleaming five, with champagne, and it made me realise how the hammering effects of Mike's alcoholism had made us the opposite of what a good couple should be.

I sat in that beautiful house one evening and became overwhelmed by a homesickness from *myself*, and I suddenly wanted to be on my own. Not with friends or people, noise or advice, however kind it was; I wanted to be with myself.

I had a quick look on Airbnb and found a one-room apartment just a couple of hours away, beside the sea near Helsingør, and off we went again, to another random place, another room, another bed.

———

In all the crazy travel that whole summer from early July right until these mid-September days, I remember that one room more clearly than anywhere else. Skandi-minimalist but cosy, it had an open-plan kitchen and a living area, one L-shaped sofa, a satisfyingly fluffy rug and one single bed, which I laid out as a mattress on the floor every night so we could sleep next to each other.

For a long time afterwards I tried to work out why I kept having such vivid, nostalgic flashbacks to this small, simple room with no emotional connection to anything, and then I realised that was exactly it: that room was the first place where it was just me and her. No memories, friends or talk, and nobody who knew anything about me, him or us. That disconnection from everything finally brought a sense of peace and connection to MYSELF. You can't *be* yourself when you live with an active addict. You can't grow, breathe, recover or flourish, because their behaviours crush you to a shadow of what you once were.

Only by getting away, from everyone and everything I knew, could I finally find a stillness and presence in myself, and know I would be fine. I wish I'd done it sooner.

Those last five days were blissful: my daughter and I spent 24 hours a day in only each other's company, a little band of two doing exactly what we wanted. I found a place to hire a bike in Helsingør, about six miles along the coast, and we cycled there every morning, smiling and laughing as we hurtled along beside blue sea under a clear late-summer sky. We'd find a little café where I could enjoy the world's most expensive coffee while feeding her, before setting off to explore. We walked around Hamlet's castle almost every day (he was never in), counted the white tips of the waves out at sea and waved across the water to Astrid and our Swedish playground; we went to an aquarium where I bought my daughter a little treasure chest of polished stones; we ate fish and chips in the harbour and ran around on the beach, watching the sea. On the way into town one windy morning, my jumper blew out of my bike basket and I bought a new, vibrant, burnt-orange one in a shop in town – it was the first thing I'd worn for months that wasn't black, and a bright sign that I was ready to stop hiding and come out to play again.

I Instagrammed the hell out of it all, with some suitably annoying 'We got this, baby' captions and loved all the messages of 'you go Liz, you're amazing' that came in. I didn't care how childish or validation-seeking it was: this was *my* time and I was sharing it with a group of supportive people who travelled with me in my pocket and made me feel GOOD.

The public show of support for me seemed to enrage Mike. He insulted and mocked the 'Liz Love-in' at every opportunity, told me they were all pathetic, I was a prick for thinking they cared, I wasn't doing myself any favours by showing the world how much *I* had failed at everything I'd set out to do, my friends in *real* life never cared about me anyway because they know how awful I am, and so on. I also got a lot of 'oh you're such a superhero mum, aren't you?' Yes actually, I was.

All the kindness shown to me only highlighted to Mike what a comprehensive disaster he was, while I, at least on the surface, was managing just fine. Around this time his communication dropped markedly, and he would disappear for whole days at a time, popping up only to tell me how busy he'd been and I'd taken his child away and everyone knew it. I even got a message from his grandfather at one point saying they'd been trying to contact him for three days, were very worried about him and did I know where he was?

No, I didn't, and I didn't really want to; any contact with Mike was like sticking my fingers in a socket.

I'd love to say my Scandinavia 'break' heralded some kind of Independence Epiphany, that I did a Bridget Jones-meets-Gloria Gaynor and realised I was happier on my own, ready to cut loose and Tinder the hell out of my remaining forties. But real lives don't work like a good script or lyric.

Despite all the good moments, I kept seeing fathers and daughters everywhere, walking hand-in-hand to school or playing in a park; every time I read *The Tiger Who Came to Tea* and 'Daddy came home', I had to stop and cry because my girl's daddy *didn't* come home and I worried she might wonder why not, or one day know it was because Daddy had left her when she was not even two years old, choosing alcohol instead. I didn't *want* Mike to live separately from his family and I didn't want my daughter to be without her dad. Oh, and I missed him. I missed the Mike I love very, very much. Every single day.

Getting advice from others is all very well, but knowing which bits fit with your *own* life and heart is difficult. It's tempting to construct an echo chamber of voices saying all the things we think we *should* want, and in all their noise and advice lose sight of who we actually are. All the bullish words and GO ME moments weren't really me at all. Not yet. They were still what I thought I was supposed to be saying, but didn't really feel.

You can't relearn your whole self-belief system in 18 days, however beautiful those days are in places, and my heart was still torn in all directions, as hearts in love are doomed to be.

I watched our little sunbeam throw pebbles into the sea, sang songs and played with her, noticed how fast she was changing, learning to talk now and getting used to her life without her daddy in it, and I felt sick with sadness that this could be happening. Anyone who actively chooses alcohol over a kiss with their own child is either a staggeringly awful human or desperately broken and messed up.

I knew all Mike's ranting was just anger, sadness, regret and fear, he was hurting terribly and wanted his family back too. He said as much towards the end of my time away, and his messages sounded softer, more self-critical, apologetic and empathetic towards my situation. They were aching words of regret for what had been lost to his depression and alcoholism, and promises for better times ahead. It's very hard to tell over the phone, of course, but he did *seem* to be gentler and ready to change. We had some late-night exchanges of photographs of us in our earliest days, kissing at a wedding, kissing in a pub, kissing on holiday. *So* much kissing. There were even words of horny longing, some sexting, declarations of deep love and a genuine lust for us that was still there when all the argument and hate stopped for a minute. Any hint of desire or love might seem truly bizarre next to the nastiness of only days before, but there was *always* something still there in us, that feeling we first had and could clearly still have, and maybe we were ready to give it another go after this little breather from the madness.

Loving an alcoholic is like living in a tumble drier and it means having to make decisions with very little concrete information. We only know what they tell us and we know that they lie a lot. But it's not *all* lies and I often had to base some fairly big decisions on a cocktail of second-guessing, hope and blind faith. Amazingly enough, given this fail-safe method of decision-making, it's easy to make mistakes, even though we felt it was right at the time.

In a plot twist even the world's worst scriptwriter couldn't dream up, serendipity had a stroke of inspiration – or possibly just a stroke – and delivered both Mike and me a reason to go back to Venice at the same time. He had managed to get himself a day's photography job in, of all places, Modena: home of balsamic vinegar, and only an hour from Venice. I needed to get back out there too, to sort out mounting Venetian admin, piles of mail, overdue bills that could only be paid in person locally, and now also the small matter of a front-door lock that one of my tenants had broken and it was proving near impossible to get mended without being there to hand-wave and swear at the right locksmith.

I wrestled with myself about what to do, and what I was truly thinking and feeling. Was I just trying to shoehorn a way to see him, when I could quite easily go a week or two later when he wasn't there? Was I so sexually starved by now I'd travel a thousand miles for some intimacy and urgent shagging with the one person I wanted to shag? Was it sensible to take this chance to reconnect in a place where we *had* both been happy until everything went so wrong – or was it beyond stupid? It hadn't exactly been the best of send-offs last time …

I listened carefully to the sound and tone of his voice on the phone in those last few days I was in Denmark, tried to hear who 'Mike' was right now and whether we were ready to be with each other in person again. He really did sound much calmer, kinder and more humble, more focused now he had some work lined up, and more … Mike – at least, when he was talking to me.

After nearly three weeks of big Skandi skies and restful blues, peace from all the arguments and head-messing, my nerves had cooled to a manageable tepid, my mind felt clearer and more settled, the mark on my forehead was almost gone and absence was doing its job to make our hearts grow fonder.

I had no idea what was the right or wrong thing to do, but as ever, I went with my gut. I thought of the good things we could all have if things did go well, and I decided to give it another go ...

PART FIVE

Shutting the Door

The plan was for us both to travel to Stansted – him from Cambridge and me from Copenhagen, as it was much cheaper that way than flying directly to Venice – stay one night in an airport hotel then Ryanair it to Venice together on the cheap, crack-of-dawn flight. It all felt fairly sensible and workable to me given the last few conversations we'd had.

And so we went back on the road/train/plane, arriving at Stansted at 7 p.m., both of us journey-crumpled, covered in scraps of food and spilled milk, and really rather ready for some *help*, please. Despite being weary beyond words, I remember feeling excited about seeing her little face light up when she saw Mike again, and his when he had his first cuddle with her for weeks.

I messaged him to say we'd arrived. There was no reply, but I assumed he couldn't hear his phone in the bustling airport terminal. I gave it 10, then called. No answer. I messaged again. Nothing.

Wearily, and now a little anxiously, I sat down on the floor in the arrivals area and fed my daughter the remaining bits of a sandwich I'd bought for her on the flight, and waited. And waited. Half an hour later, I received a message from Mike:

Hi. Won't be there for another few hours. Been really busy. Missed the train. I'll get the next one.

I'd been travelling for 10 hours with a toddler. This man had had nothing to do except get up and get himself to an airport less than 40 minutes away from his bed. Behold, the newly reformed Mike.

I told him how unbelievably shit this was for me, not to mention massively disappointing for her, having been told Daddy would be at the airport, to which he replied that it might come as a shock to me but:

> You're not the only one who's allowed to be busy, Liz. I have tons of stuff to sort out. Other people have lives too, you know.

To an outsider it might seem ridiculous, but I had expected Mike would be there on time, sober and friendly. I think he believed it too at the moment he said it. He hadn't sounded drunk or even remotely agitated. He'd been calm and full of intent to set a new precedent and do things right. But he couldn't hold that intent or feeling for more than an hour at most, before slipping straight back into drink mode. If indeed he ever came out of drink mode, which, I now know, he didn't.

I was livid at myself for being so stupid as to think anything would have changed, for still romanticising and dreaming about some fantastical, happy reconciliation and a night of passion.

As I waited at the bus station for the shuttle bus to the hotel, I stood beside a French woman about my age, with shiny hair and un-stained clothes and a French *je-ne-sais-quoi-but-I-want-some-of-that*. I looked a total mess. We talked for a few minutes, as people do when they're waiting for buses and one of them is in tears and has got used to sharing her life story with strangers, and the other one notices and is kind. Was it *right*, I asked her, not being met by one's partner at an airport, after nearly three weeks alone with his baby? Do normal people do this to each other?

She replied calmly, kindly, and perfectly Frenchly: 'You know,' she said, 'I've been with some assholes and I've learned one thing:

the only person in the world you can rely on is yourself. You're clearly a strong woman and a good mother. He's not worth a woman like you.'

By the time I arrived at the hotel and unpacked all of our things onto the least comfortable bed in Europe, it was well past my daughter's bedtime and Mike, now two hours late, still wasn't there. He messaged to say he was on the transfer bus to the hotel, so I waited downstairs in the lobby, which, like my fading energy, appeared to be suffocating under a thick, dusty carpet of neglect.

At last, just after 9.30 p.m. a bearded man carrying a large, dirty backpack and a lot more beer weight on his face than he had the last time I saw him, strode into the lobby, oozing unpleasant, stressed vibes. His opener was to tell me how tired he was, how heavy his bag was, and start blaming everything from the train to the bus to the weather to the moon phase for making him so late, before telling me he wanted to go to bed. Truly, it was hard to understand why anyone wouldn't want to marry him immediately.

I was so fucked off I couldn't even hide it, and told him I was disgusted he was this late, and had he not considered for one minute that I was maybe a *tad* more tired than him what with looking after a child on my own for weeks and perhaps he could have shifted his arse to be here on time? He was so drunk – or hungover, I couldn't tell which – he couldn't handle this sharp, justified taste of reality, and within less than 10 minutes of his joyful arrival he'd left again, back to the airport terminal, where he spent the night on a bench – not only conveniently close to all the bars but also giving the perfect reason to play his favourite 'oh poor me, while you're staying in a nice hotel, you lucky cow' card. Yes, lucky me alone again, having to get up, pack up and get myself and a toddler to the departure lounge by 4 a.m.

It takes years to heal a nervous system, and only a matter of seconds to go back to square one, and almost all the calm that had filtered into me in Sweden and Denmark was immediately removed that night.

It also takes years to come out of the kind of alcoholic vortex Mike was quite clearly still in, and far from this trip to Italy being his Big Comeback, it was more of a stage dive into oblivion.

———

After all the controlled cool of Scandinavia, the sudden rush of colour, heat, noise and unabashed vibrancy that hit us as we stepped onto the vaporetto and headed out across the water towards Venice was a very welcome blast of life. I'd forgotten how much I missed that energy and light and the little community I'd become a part of there, my apartment, my *home* where my little girl was so happy.

It was 19 September now and the air was a perfect late-summer pool of gentle warmth, not the furnace we'd left in July. After nearly three weeks in Scandinavia, I looked and felt so much better than when I'd left that awful day in such distress. Mike, by contrast, who had barely spoken to me since he boarded the flight and ordered his first two cans of Heineken, seemed to have returned to his Venetian watering hole even further into his whirlpool than ever.

He seemed lost in mental fog half the time, then he'd suddenly click back into focus and become engaged, chatty and 'normal' before drifting away again, and he could go from 'want a cup of tea?' to 'oh, piss off' within a breath. Having told me he'd been taking his antidepressant medication for three weeks, it transpired that of the 28 pills he was given there were 27 left. I'm not great at maths but I'm pretty sure 28 minus three weeks' worth isn't 27. When I asked about this, he shouted something about how the fuck should he know and can't I just give him a break?

I now know, of course, that it was madness for us to go back to Venice together and think it could go anything other than wrong. Mike associated it with nothing but drinking and depression, and he stood no chance there of getting anything but worse.

He repacked his bag and left for Modena the same afternoon we arrived, which was a blessing, given how tense things had been in the short space of time we were together. By the time he got there he'd completely changed tone and vibe, sounding upbeat and confident, and looking forward to the shoot. It was actually very nice to hear. This was a Mike I knew, and I loved seeing him impassioned by his work, getting some recognition and success for what he produced. By evening, though, his tone in messages and when we talked briefly had changed again, and he was now noticeably less caring or interested in anything that was going on at home, what we'd been doing, how his daughter was and so on. It was as if he'd just cut off into his working life, and was far happier with these nice, fun people who didn't nag at him all the time. We had an argument on the phone about whether he'd been drinking at dinner – he sounded as if he had, not in a drunk way but a mood-change way – and I was told actually no, he hadn't had a drink, and didn't I know that all my questions just made him want to drink when he was doing so well on his own, thank you? It wasn't for another year or so that he told me he'd been drinking not only at dinner, but also at lunchtime on the shoot, and before he came home the next day.

When he got back to Venice, he seemed in good spirits again, buoyed by the work – and the wine I didn't know about – and I have photos of us over the next two days looking … sort of happy, I'd say. We went out for a pizza in the evening, walked home together and waved a cheery 'Ciao, buona serrata' to people we passed. Anyone would have thought we were just a normal family.

I didn't feel this at the time, but I think now we must have just been playing at it, really, hoping or wondering if we could do it, and if forcing ourselves to try and do normal things might make normality seep back into us by osmosis. But it was wishful, tired fantasy. Having lived apart since July, suddenly sharing a house and a bathroom and space and breath for the first time in months was all terribly strained, Mike was so changeable and distant it was impossible to feel at ease and I was constantly worried he might get angry and walk off again on the turn of a word. His eyes still had that 'blank' look they always did when he was drinking and away in himself, as if they contained an infinite pool of blackness that could flood out at any moment. I had no idea how close they were to doing just that.

Nothing especially dramatic prompted it. It was early evening and our daughter was all tucked up in bed and asleep after her bath and bedtime stories. Everything had been pretty calm that day, and I think we were both hoping to have a drama-free evening of TV and bed, but a little argument started, just a trivial, tit-for-tat exchange about something Mike had or hadn't done when he'd been in Cambridge, and on which I wanted some clarity – always very likely you're going to get clarity from someone who has no idea what actually happened because they were pissed at the time, and they're a compulsive liar.

I know I should have waited for my anger to pass, gone for a walk and then talked calmly and rationally when things were less reactive. I'm sure there are lots of things we 'should' do in many tricky situations in life, if given time to reflect, introspect and retrospect. But people are just people, and we're not the best we can be when we're emotionally smashed to pulp. Seeing Mike again now, exactly as he had been for months after so much time and opportunity to get better, having *told* me he was getting better, going to AA and taking his meds, and even sounding as if he *was* getting a little better, made me so angry with myself at believing it and his continued inability to stop drinking and lying and ruining everything for one damn day that I couldn't take his shit any more.

We were standing in our bedroom a few feet apart, me shooting questions at him, while self-contradictory replies and a cascade of lies kept falling from his mouth like acid rain, corroding any chance of reconciliation, and the heat rose fast as I pursued my cross-examination, irritated and aggravated further by every fresh deflection, inconsistency and twisting of reality, a geyser of FUCK YOU bubbling in me.

I argued with myself for months afterwards about whether I might have contributed to what happened next in some way. I'd play it over and over in my mind, pushing myself to be honest about whether I could have reacted better, if my inability to contain my anger and frustration any more sparked something in Mike, if I 'caused' it or even if I was to blame in some way. Many victims of abuse of one kind or another are prone to this kind of warped, self-critical thinking; with so little self-confidence left, so gaslit and blamed by their abuser, they can even find a reason to blame themselves when that abuser hurts or threatens them.

It's almost crazy-thinking, but it's very common until some distance can be found in which to recalibrate one's mind, to hear a different view – often from a friend or a psychologist, or a place of refuge – and get the confidence to stand up to terrible treatment and not be afraid. I didn't have any of that in that moment; I had only me, what had already happened to me and what was happening around me now. For his part, Mike was so saturated by alcohol, self-loathing and anxiety he was constantly on the verge of a panic attack; nervous, wired, aggressive and primed to snap, and his mental health was so wrecked he was in no place to be challenged on anything at all, however deserved or justified it might be.

He needed calm, to stop the 'blah blah blah, you are shit you are shit you are shit' flying out of my mouth on repeat, to stop me saying all the things he couldn't bear to hear, and just get some damn *quiet*. It was just like the hot evening back in June on the night before his birthday, right here in this flat, when he'd pushed me away from him because I was banging on about this and that and he just wanted to STOP the noise screaming in his brain.

He stepped forward and pushed my head with the palm of his hand, with no pause to think what it might do to me; just to stop the talking for a second. I staggered backwards into the door of the wardrobe, barely even registering what was happening before he leaned in, pressed his sweaty forehead against mine, beer-stained breath panting into my face, teeth clenched, and whispered, '*I FUCKING HATE YOU*. I want to stab you right now. I do. I want to stab you with knives.'

I didn't say or do anything. I just stood there looking straight into his eyes. I don't remember feeling frightened, exactly, but the sheer insanity of this scene, the fact that *we*, me and Scottish barista, photographer, funny and lovely Mike – could be in this situation at all, was too much for me to understand. He took a step back again, threw a pillow across the room, said he was leaving and started packing his bag, ramming in any clothes he could grab from his wardrobe and throwing the rest onto the floor. A few minutes later, he was gone.

Right there, against that wardrobe, in that room with the thin, white curtain blowing in the breeze, I decided that this was it for me. Mike could never live with me and my daughter again – unless he was completely and utterly, permanently sober. And that choice was entirely up to him to make.

Mike's fall from here into the next new low in the progression of his disease happened faster than a beer goes flat, and almost nothing from this point until his eventual sobriety is likely to be either comprehensible, forgivable or possibly even believable at times to anyone who wasn't there – and this is already a very heavily condensed and sanitised version of the actual events.

He was an angry island of hate unto himself, and it was one of the strangest and saddest things I've ever witnessed. Mike was a dead man smashing his grim way to the end, didn't know who he was any more and didn't care about anything. Now sprinting headlong down the final straight of drinking, which lasted another month or so, he seemed to be playing a grotesque game, messing about with the world to see how far he could push it, what madness and havoc he could wreak before he left. Constantly bordering on manic, he flitted and crashed about each day, hell-bent on being as hideous as possible, made ever more frequent threats and developed a bizarre new air of glee about his awfulness, almost revelling in his impressively ghoulish cruelty. I knew all the way through it that he didn't *want* to be like this, he didn't mean to be like this, he was just so ill now he wasn't there, but my role in this last act of our long, exhausting dance was now only as a mother, there to look after my child and myself, and get my life in order.

It didn't matter any more *why* Mike did what he did, what had 'made him' do it, whether it was drink or depression, mania or panic, whether it was even 'him' any more or some version of him in a stupor of mental breakdown: I couldn't have that in my life. Even if I loved him, even if I wanted to help him, even if I was desperately sorry for him and wanted him to come back to me and be who I knew he could be.

For a while at least, I had to close the door on this man. I had his house key, and he had no way of getting in unless I let him in. And that's exactly how it had to be.

Within two hours of leaving my flat, Mike messaged to say he was 'mortified at his behaviour' and 'so so sorry', it was the adjustment to being with us that he found hard and he would like to come back and try again. This was followed less than an hour later by a stream of:

I'm going to the pub. Best tell your pals.

I don't have any money for the pub.

I'm perfectly calm. Can I come back now.

Fuck this, I hope you're happy in your house.

I'm too weak. Liz, seriously it's passed. I'm fine now to come back.

At 8 p.m. he asked me to leave him some warm clothing on the window sill as he was clearly going to be spending the night outside because I was being so unkind as to not invite him in for tea, and when he came to collect it, he shouted through the window that I was a bitch and spat on the wall outside.

Just after midnight he was back on the messages again, asking to come back in, said he'd only had four double vodkas, five Spritz, three beers and wine and then passed out mid-sentence.

At 4 a.m., my doorbell started ringing.

Venice has very attention-seeking doorbells: a kind of buzzer-cum-fire-alarm, they emit one of the loudest, most grating sounds in the city, and at 4 a.m. in a high-ceilinged, tile-floored, sparsely furnished apartment in a street so quiet you can hear a piece of dry penne drop, it's the loudest sound there is.

It rang again. And again, longer this time, like a caffeinated woodpecker hammer-drilling into my skull. I ignored it, and him, and waited for him to stop.

More ringing.

After half an hour of head-splitting noise I caved and messaged him to stop ringing the bell please, it was going to wake everyone, including our child. He told me to open the door. I didn't.

The ringing continued for the next hour, punctuated only by more messages of 'let me in now' and 'open the door', and finally:

Thanks family. Fuck you. I won't be here. I'm not drunk. Bye.

Just before 6 a.m. the bell-cacophony started yet again. With the sun now up and daylight making things feel a little safer, and with Mike quite clearly not giving up any time soon, I told him he could come in to get some clean clothes but *only* if my front door stayed wide open the whole time. Without a hello or thank you, he went straight to the bathroom, had a shower, changed into clean clothes and then told me *I* had made him drink like this and to be anywhere near me he needed to be annihilated. He then informed me that we were officially separated and instructed me to throw the rest of his belongings away. I asked what his plans were exactly, as regards his daughter, now he was apparently leaving us yet again, and he said, 'I won't see her again. Now fuck off.'

That was the last time he was ever in that apartment.

My daughter was up now, padding about the flat in her pink pyjamas and heavenly morning wake-warmth. I made her some breakfast and we sat on the fluffy white rug in our living room playing, sun now streaming in through the high windows, making the whole apartment glow. I was so exhausted I couldn't even manage a jigsaw puzzle for two-year-olds, but these little moments were glorious medicine for me and I tried to soak up every drop. The familiar morning shout of '*A posto!*' came echoing in from the street as the bin men took the daily refuse away, and she scrabbled up over the sofa to her favourite window ledge and waved to them. She was so used to all these little routines and Venetian ways, the sounds and smells that filled so much of this formative year of her life. I still saw her as a Little Venetian, and wanted this simple, calm life for her, but it was becoming increasingly clear that it might have all come to an end now. I didn't want to be here on my own, and Mike had effectively already gone.

Within an hour of his theatrical exit he messaged to say he'd bought a flight to Scotland for that afternoon, immediately followed by:

> Come and have a drink with me. I'm willing to make this my last day of drinking if you do it with me.

Everything was so utterly absurd, broken and confusing now that a drink in the middle of the morning with the paralytic father of my child seemed no less bizarre or reasonable than anything else on offer at the time.

I pushed the buggy along the waterfront and carried it over two big bridges to Angio's, a café on the promenade where we'd enjoyed many coffees together back in the good times. Mike was already there, deep into another Spritz, and could hardly speak, he was so pissed. I asked him, just out of curiosity, how he was paying for all this drink, and he casually explained that he'd just walk out of a bar before he was charged. He seemed to find this amusing and extremely clever. He then launched into some garbled, grandiose ramblings about how he was going to make a good life for himself now, me never having helped him out once except to make myself feel virtuous, and how irritated I must be to have lost so much of my money to someone who didn't even need it: 'And you'll never see any of that money back.'

I sat there quietly, watching his mouth as he talked, his hands on the glass and his body hunched and purposeless, listening to his horrible, hurtful, gleeful words, spoken from a place of such eternal emptiness no light could get in or come out. There was no point saying anything back, he could barely even hear or think.

He then stood up, steadying himself against the table, and announced that he was leaving now. He left like a drunk rat towards the nearest alleyway, and disappeared from sight.

I took my daughter to the cool and calm of the nearby library, and read her a few *Peppa Pig* books. I noticed Daddy Pig wasn't hammered or insulting Mummy Pig.

At midday, So Long And Goodbye Mike was back on the phone again, this time asking if I wanted to have sex with him. I *somehow* managed to decline this fabulous offer. An hour later, by which time he ought to have been well on the way to the airport, I got home to find him asleep in the communal hallway. He was lying across the stone floor, arms crossed on his chest like a dead, sunburned hero lying in state, sweating, eyes closed and smiling. I needed to get him to stand up immediately and get out of the way, because any neighbours trying to get into their apartments would have to step over him, and most of them were well into their seventies and usually pulling a trolley. I knew shouting wouldn't help, so I bent down and talked to him quietly. Would he like some water or coffee, or maybe to come to the beach? (Internal dialogue: would you maybe like to fuck off and stop being such a revolting disgrace?) He just lay there, laughing, with his eyes closed.

'Mike, please. What are you doing?'

'I want to sleep.'

'I thought you were going to Scotland.'

'I am. I'm drunk. I'm happy now.'

I remember looking at him, watching his deep, slow breathing, thinking how weird it was that this body was Mike, how lovely he had been, and could be when he wasn't so unwell, and how finished you must be with life to be happy in this state. It didn't matter who he was now, what he had done or could do, separate to all that I still felt very sorry for him for being so messed up and so unwell. I tried one more time to get him to move.

'Mike, come on. How is this helping anything?'

'It's not. I'm an alcoholic. I like it actually.'

Right, OK.

This was clearly pointless and I was never going to get through to him or manage to move him out of the way, so I left him there and went to make some lunch for my daughter and work out what the rest of my life might look like.

At some point Mike must have managed to get up and stagger back out, because incoherent messages started arriving in my phone about him being in a bar and did I know this was all my fault?

Then at 3 p.m. he asked if I'd like to have dinner together. He'd downloaded *Peaky Blinders* and did I fancy it?

I can be there by 4.

Two hours later he messaged again to say he'd had loads to drink but anyway he wasn't drunk, he was fine, and could he come round now?

I said no.

I was called a bitch and told to fuck off, and was informed that only *I* was stopping him from coming home.

It was evening now, and my daughter was fed, bathed and asleep in her cot. I could hear rain falling in the back garden and the temperature had dropped significantly, giving a first hint of the approaching end of Venetian summer.

While I was tidying the flat for the night, a 'clearly not on a plane to Scotland' Mike reappeared on my phone, asking if he could please sleep in my basement. Tough guy didn't like rain, it seemed.

I won't bother you. I'll go straight down there and sleep. I'll make changes and start again tomorrow.

Is there, I wondered, a number of tomorrows that is too many tomorrows? Because if there is, I think we may have passed it.

Goddamn it, though. How can you leave someone you actually love, and who you know to be very unwell, out in the rain and the cold? Did I really want to tell my child one day that I made her dad contract pneumonia on a park bench in Venice, where he died in a pool of Aperol?

My conflict with this was twofold: first, I knew what it was like to behave in ways we didn't mean or want to when we are mentally unwell, and to regret it all and never be able to forgive ourselves.

But second were stories I'd heard a few times over the years, of people thrown out by their family because of their drugs or alcohol problems, and who died, either through overdose or not long after. I thought about these stories often, in Mike's last, dreadful drinking months, and knew I never wanted that to happen to him, especially not as a result of me throwing him out. I always wanted there to be a lifeline for him, a hand to take hold of if he chose to, a sign of hope at all times.

I told Mike he could come into the building and sleep in my basement. This wouldn't require him coming into my flat at all, just through the communal hallway and then down the stairs. There was still a big wooden door and a brand-new lock and safety chain between me and him, so I felt very sure he wouldn't be able to come into my flat. I popped down to the basement quickly to unlock it for him and leave a bottle of water, a banana and a clean sheet for the mattress. A few minutes later I heard him stumble heavily across the hallway and down the stone stairs and slam the basement door.

Five minutes later he messaged to ask if he could have a front-door key because he was:

Gonna go out to get some bread

I pointed out that he'd only just arrived and no, he couldn't have a key to my house any more when he was this drunk and horrendous, obviously.

Yeah well, I'm going out again. It's shit here and I'm hungry.

Gosh, if only someone kind had just left him a banana in case he was hungry. I heard him stamp back up the stairs and into the hall, and I opened my door a fraction, keeping the safety chain on, just to see what kind of state he was in. The stench of alcohol was so strong it was enough to make the granny upstairs paralytic. He was standing in the middle of the hallway now, navy peacoat collar pulled up around his face, hands deep in his pockets, a lazy smile scrawled on his drunken face.

'Nice in there in your cosy house?'

'Mike, you're slaughtered and you *stink* of booze. Jesus. I'm sorry but I can't have you in *any* part of this building if you smell like this – it's totally unacceptable for everyone else. Go for a walk in the fresh air, get some coffee or whatever works and come back if you can become any less shit-faced and reeking.'

He swayed back and forth on his heavy brown boots – a pair of Red Wings I'd bought for him four years ago on a fun day out in London.

'If you can let me sleep on a bare mattress in a mouldy basement I'd really appreciate it,' he said, sarcasm oozing between the ethanol fumes.

I said I'd appreciate not being lied to or having an alcoholic, abusive partner.

He laughed loudly, clearly enjoying this macabre stand-up show more than his one audience member was.

'You throwing me out?'

'No, you are throwing *yourself* out, Mike, and you know why it has to be this way.'

'Yes, I do.' He slid his boot slowly across the dusty floor, and smiled. 'Because you're a *bitch*, Liz. You really are a piece of shit, though, you know that? I want to stab you.'

'Jesus, Mike, just stop with all that, OK?'

He took a step towards my door. 'I might try to. I don't know. I *might* hurt you.'

I told him he'd better go now and he clomped slowly down the steps to the main door. Holding it open, he turned to face me.

'You could have stopped this, Liz, you know? You are making me go out and drink. This is all on you.'

The night wasn't quite over yet.

An hour after he left, joy of joys, the doorbell started ringing. I was in bed now, and I got up and went to look out of the window. Mike was standing in the middle of the dark *calle*, looking straight at me from this silent, stony stage.

'I want to come and get our child.'

'Mike, please go away.'

'You're a piece of shit. Let me in.'

I said if he rang the bell again I'd call the police. I had no idea what the emergency number was in Venice and my last encounter with the Carabinieri hadn't exactly gone well, but I meant it.

He didn't care.

'If you don't open the door and let me into your basement again, I'll make this a problem for you. I'll ring the bell all night, and you'll be awake until five o'clock in the morning again. It'll be hell for you.'

'Mike, are you actually *threatening* me?'

'Yeah, I am. Let me in.'

I pulled my head back into my room and shut the window. What was I supposed to do now? I couldn't let him in, drunk and saying he might stab me, but keeping him out meant he was going to wake half the street, and probably my child as well, with his incessant bell-ringing. Why couldn't he just GO AWAY, and while he was at it, STOP DRINKING?

The doorbell started up again before I'd even reached my bed. Ring, ring, ring, riiing every few seconds. He kept it up so relentlessly I got up again, went into the living room, stood on the first thing I came to – very helpfully this was my daughter's toy Scottie dog on wheels, called Dougal – and smashed the bell to pieces by jabbing a broom handle at it. Silence descended like a welcome last breath.

I went back to the window and looked out. Mike was leaning against the wall as if it needed him to hold it up, still pressing the bell next to the nameplate I'd put in there the day we arrived: 'Fraser-Sim'. Now, it seemed, just Fraser.

I leaned out and spoke slowly, calmly and clearly.

'Mike, listen to me carefully. You may not come into my house, my basement or any other part of this building. You are frightening me and threatening me, you are drunk and I have asked you to go away.'

'Basement.'

'Do you understand? I've asked you to go away until you are sober.'

'Basement.'

He carried on repeating it over and over again, 'basement, basement, let me in, basement' until I couldn't take any more. I ripped at the necklace holding my engagement ring so hard the clasp broke, and lashed it against the wall, bending it completely out of shape, and shouted out of the window:

'*Just get away from us, Mike*! GO AWAY! *You are DRUNK!*'

He looked at the ground, and I heard him laugh. 'See you later. You're a bitch. Leave my things outside.'

At 1 a.m. I dropped a bag containing some of Mike's warm clothes onto the ground below my window, went back to bed for the last time and recorded this into my phone so I would never forget it:

'I think this marks the end for me. I don't want to stay here another night. Mike has completely lost the plot, and I'm exhausted. I think this whole Venice adventure is completely over now.'

———

Mike was out all of the next day, I've no idea where. Everything felt numb, lonely and unmanageable and I was so far beyond sad I don't even know the word for it. I tried to keep things as light-hearted and normal as possible for my daughter, while my head and body ached with grief, loss and uncertainty. We went to the park via the arched walkway where she had watched him skateboarding back in May: '*When you think your daddy is the best thing ever – and you're right.*'

This whole year had been a disaster. So had most of the year before, if I was honest, and the year before. Drink drink drink, always coming back, always wrecking more. I looked at the sea, I looked at her playing with some yellow leaves as they swirled into piles of early autumn, I looked at what had become of me and couldn't take any more.

I booked flights to the UK that night. There was nothing left for us here. Mike was out there somewhere, drinking himself into oblivion, and had spent the night I don't know where. He sent a barrage of nasty, self-pitying, accusatory messages throughout the next day but I didn't respond and I heard nothing more from him before I got onto the vaporetto that evening.

We pulled away from the shore at 5.30 p.m., almost exactly a year since we'd arrived. The evening sky was bleeding from orange into deep night blue, the trees of Sant'Elena stood black against the sunset and the lagoon gleamed silvery-white and gentle tonight, to say goodbye.

I sent a last message just before my little corner of Paradise slipped out of view:

Mike, my love, you have completely broken my life. I have done everything I possibly could to try and help you, but it has proved impossible. I'm leaving you in the most beautiful city in the world, where I tried to make us the life we both wanted, a city I love and where our baby was so happy. Drinking has ruined it all. As a final goodbye you've just called me a bitch again and told me this is my decision. It is not my decision, Mike. It is *yours*, and you have given me no choice. I love you.

That was the last time we would ever be on the island at the same time.

PART SIX

The Eternal Chaos of the Broken Mind

And so, while Mike was drifting somewhere in Venice, I arrived, yet again, in Cambridge – heading in my own direction this time, not lost in someone else's pandemonium. A lifeline with us was always there for him to take if he chose to, and I did everything I could to enable any recovery he might want to make, but not to my own detriment any more.

I'd booked a room in a hotel in town, very close to my children's house and all the parks, and with a 24-hour concierge who could stop any unwanted, possibly not entirely sober or friendly visitors who might decide to show up. It's strange how we have to think when we don't feel entirely safe any more. Within only a matter of hours a lovely sense of quiet normality descended, as we revisited our familiar spaces, hung out with my older children and met up with a few friends in one café or another, and I started straight away to think of some clear, solid plans for my future: where I would live, what work I would do, how my daughter would be brought up and how, if at all, Mike might fit into it.

Step One, I decided, was to go to Oxford as soon as possible: my parents were on holiday and said I could stay in their house while they were away, and I could use that time to find somewhere more permanent to live there. My middle daughter would be back at university there soon, so I'd have happy company, and all round it was a good, sensible plan.

While I was focusing on these plans, catching up on overdue admin and trying to get a lot of the awfulness of the last week or so out of my blood, Mike sent a steady canal flow of woeful messages about what a terrible time he was having in Venice, how he was hungry, dirty, covered in mosquito bites, sunburnt, stinking, cold, hot, sweaty and miserable, and how lucky I was. The self-pity radiating out of my phone could have powered most of Europe.

It turned out months later that for all these tales of misery and woe, while he *had* spent one night on a bench, he was then put up by a very wealthy friend in one of the most glamorous parts of town, with a very comfortable bed and free food. He was still drinking all day every day, on his magical cash supply of stealing or begging, and continued flipping from 'I'm going to Scotland' to 'I have no money so I can't get home' to 'You've ruined my life', every few hours. I pretty much ignored it all, as he'd brought all of this upon himself and I had enough to be getting on with, what with looking after our child and trying to build a stable future for her.

A mere three days after I left, Groundhog Drunk-day dawned: Mike had decided he was coming to Cambridge, 'to make this all better'. Or rather, he had run out of places to get drink and not pay.

And so the Prodigal Drunk returned. And with him, the chaos: at 9 a.m. he arrived at Stansted airport, which turned out to be Gatwick airport because he forgot where he was, then fell asleep at a bar in King's Cross for three hours, emerging only to ask me to book him a room in a Travelodge because he had no data on his phone. Nice to have you back, honey.

To be honest, it *was* nice to have him back a bit, if only to know that he hadn't drowned in a lagoon. He was so clearly extremely unwell and I worried about him, and though I didn't want him in my house, I didn't exactly want him dead either. Being in the same city meant we might have the chance to talk face to face about what was going to happen from here, instead of relying on text messages from a thousand miles away. If trying to keep *track* of someone who's drinking themselves into a grave is hard, attempting any form of adult conversation about financial contributions, living arrangements or workable plans is almost impossible, but there was a child and her future – not to mention maybe ours – in the mix, and however difficult it was going to be, there were conversations I felt needed to be had.

We met in a Caffè Nero the next morning, the day before I was leaving for Oxford. We used to have coffee here when we first got together, and before we'd even ordered we'd be kissing in the queue. Today he was a nervous dog, hunched in the far corner upstairs, sunglasses on, blending in like a Kalashnikov in a kids' nativity play. He told me he was off the drink as of today, and was on his way to a pawn shop to sell his camera so he could pay me back for the room he'd just stayed in. For a photographer, getting rid of a favourite camera is like flogging a kidney, so I offered to buy it off him and look after it until he was in a position to buy it back one day.

I was told to 'piss off, I don't want your pity money', followed by 'OK, sure, have it'. He then told me he wouldn't be coming to Oxford, and left without a thank you or goodbye. He didn't look at me once in the whole exchange.

An hour later he messaged to say he *did* want to come to Oxford with us, he'd stay in a hostel there and go to AA, and get a new doctor, and he was sorry for everything he'd done, and he didn't mean to do these things and he wanted to start again.

Right.

A further hour later he started message-ranting about how he had no life and *I* had done this to him and I should stay away from him or he might hit me and he shouldn't come to Oxford tomorrow after all.

I could almost see the pints being sunk, sliding his moods up and down the Drink Graph. Sorry as I was for him, my sympathy was running a little on the low side now.

It was the last day of September, and a big autumnal storm was brewing above Cambridge. The sky was rage black, leaves were being ripped off trees and whipped around wildly like the thoughts of a drinker. I'd said goodbye to my children after dinner and fought my way back to the hotel, battling the buggy against the violent gusts and heavy rain. This was my last night in Cambridge, and I was cuddled up in bed now, with my sleeping girl in my arms, hot and limp, trusting and at peace. She was beautiful beyond words, and we lay together in warm silence for a while, safe in our little bubble, the wind outside gusting branches against the window. Mike's own tornado seemed only to be strengthening too, and just as I was thinking I might finally catch up on some desperately needed sleep, he wrote to say that tonight was his final straw and he should be put down. He said he was walking around outside, shouldn't be near people, and had to force himself not to throw all his bags into the river:

I can't do this life. I don't want to get better. Tell the fucking world. I hate myself. I'm going to hospital.

Reading through the drifting moods and words of a drinking alcoholic and trying to translate their true meaning correctly into Sober-speak is very difficult, but Mike had never said he was going to hospital before, and now I was worried.

I called, but it went straight to voicemail. Damn you, Mike. Damn it all, and damn you, Liz for still caring so much.

I got dressed, wrapped my daughter in blankets and tucked her into the buggy, still fast asleep, and set out to find him. Bus shelters were rattling and bits of shop signs were blowing all over the road. I didn't even get a hundred yards before I saw him, huddled into his down jacket, pacing up and down the pavement, left and right like a fallen branch. The pavement was covered in shards of smashed glass and bits of metal from his phone, which looked like it had been bludgeoned by an ice pick for an hour.

I shouted hello towards him into the wind from a few metres away, but even when he looked straight at me he didn't seem to recognise me. I walked up to him and put my arm through his to try and ground him a little, but he shook me off and told me to get away from him. I asked if he wanted to come for a walk just to move a bit and centre himself, and he said something about how I should probably fuck off, and stormed away.

Sometimes, when we've tried our very best for others and there's nothing more we can do, we just want to do what *we* bloody well want, and in that moment, in that storm, what I just bloody well wanted was a last drink in Cambridge. Just for me. To say goodbye.

I pushed the buggy across the park and into the first bar I came to, settled myself at a table in the window, parked the buggy beside me and ordered a glass of champagne. The world felt immediately better.

It was smart in here, all dark-green velvet, a brass and marble bar, and chandeliers, and I felt quite the grown-up for a change.

Before I'd even taken my first sip, Mike walked in, like a dog after its owner – though it had felt rather the other way around for quite some time. I'm assuming he'd just followed me and decided to come along, as he had nobody else's evening to ruin.

He sat at the adjacent table, turned the chair around and leaned over the back of it like a menacing Catherine Keener, staring at me, smiling, coat still fully done up.

Those smiles he'd started over that summer always unnerved me. Anger I can understand, but this weird, sinister leering thing seemed to rise out from evil I'd never felt in myself so I couldn't understand or 'read' it. It seemed to give him some kind of Creepy Asshole Pass that let him do anything and get away with it.

He cocked his head to one side, chin nestled into his folded arms, and asked if I was enjoying my drink.

I didn't want a scene so I played along.

'Yes, thank you. Remind me – why are you here?'

'I thought I'd like a nice night with you. It's fun.'

I took a slow, deep breath. There were another 15 or so people dotted about the bar area, a few waiters and some classical music

I couldn't make out, and I felt pretty secure to go along with this little charade he seemed to want to play out.

'Mike, what do you *want*?'

'I want to spit in your face.'

'Right, OK. That's a little … unusual.' I looked him in the eyes. He stared back at me, still smiling. 'What's *happened* to you, do you think?'

'You. You've happened. I want to destroy you, you see?'

He said it as if he was chatting about his next holiday plans. I took a sip of champagne to wet my mouth.

'Can I ask you honestly, Mike, do you think that's a sane thing to say?'

'No.'

'Do you think you're OK?'

'No, I'm not.'

Being perfectly comfortable about being 'not OK' was almost worse than having no awareness of it.

To anyone watching, we'd have looked like two friends having a private conversation in a bar, and I remember feeling we were in a room within a room, and nobody could see or hear us. If I'd screamed or had to call for help, nobody would have heard me, and even if they had, he would have just kept up his charade, kept smiling, said he didn't know what on earth was the matter with me and he was sorry for the disturbance, and they'd have thought *I* was crazy. For all the surface pretence I found this whole situation very strange and unnerving, and my breathing had got so shallow you could drown a heartbeat in it. All I could do was keep playing and not let the tension combust into argument.

'You said you were going to take yourself to hospital. Maybe you should?'

'Maybe you should fuck off.'

'You're being awful, do you know that?'

'I *am* awful. I'm a terrible, horrible person. I'm an alcoholic piece of shit. An abusive cunt.' He was so composed and measured it was like watching someone performing a play.

'You really need some help.'

'And you need to piss off.'

I paused for a moment to check on our daughter. She was still sleeping beautifully and peacefully. I wanted to know peace like that.

Mike was still staring straight at me. He didn't even look at her. I'm not sure he could bear that pain.

'Why do you want to destroy me, anyway, Mike? I'm the mother of your child.'

'I don't.'

'You just said you did.'

'I know. I say things like that because I'm not very well, remember?' He smirked like the cat that got *all* the cream, with sprinkles on.

'Do you think I feel safe sitting opposite someone who tells me that?'

'I don't know.'

'Do you think I feel safe with someone who changes what they say every two minutes and can't even remember what they just said, even if it's that they want to destroy me?'

'I think you'd be right to feel scared.'

'Should I feel scared of you?'

'Yes, I think you should.'

That was enough now. I told him calmly and clearly that I was asking him to go away. NOW.

He stood up and laughed. 'Sure. Bye now. Enjoy having my child.'

Ten minutes after he left, he sent me an email – thanks to the latest smashed phone, the only way he could communicate with me now was on his laptop, when he had Wi-Fi and battery – to say he was sorry, and could hardly remember being in the bar with me at all. He said as soon as he walked outside he felt like he'd been in a trance and didn't even know how he'd got there:

You have been the love of my life, Liz, and I still love you beyond words. You have been nothing but brilliant throughout this nightmare, but I will continue to push you away until you're safe from me. I look into your eyes when I say these awful things and I'm breaking inside because I don't WANT to be saying them, but it's all I am capable of. I love you. I'm going to leave town tomorrow, and not come back.

By morning, under a clear late-autumn sky, swept clean by the rain of last night, Mike's mind had done another flip and he'd decided to come with us to Oxford after all. On the way to the station he changed his mind four times, kicked several walls and stormed off twice, while I waited for him to return. When we finally arrived, now with only five minutes before our train left, I dashed to buy our tickets and some food for the journey, and when I got back he said he wasn't coming after all.

He was sitting on a bench outside the same pub where he'd fallen asleep back in July, after that awful night of drinking for 10 hours in Edinburgh. He was holding his head in his hands, body hunched over, and looked as if he wanted to sit there forever in a little ball of defeat. If I left him, he might very well do that.

I sat next to him, not so close as to crowd or irritate him but just to offer some emotional closeness.

'Come on, Mike. The two of us are going, and you should come. *She* will be there, there are jobs there, there's AA there, you like it there and you can build on all that. There's nothing for you here and no good will come from staying. You'll know it one day. Come on, let's catch that train.'

───────

There's a phenomenon called the 'surge before death' or 'terminal lucidity', or, as I prefer, 'What the fuck is going on NOW? syndrome', which happens in the days or even hours before someone dies. A sudden, elated rush of energy, a bit like 'nesting' in the last weeks of a pregnancy when you start manically scrubbing kitchen cupboards and arranging all your books into colour groups despite being almost unable to breathe you're so stuffed with baby. It's as if a soul senses it's approaching the final stop and decides to pop up for a last dance before The End, and Mike's was quite the Danse Macabre.

These final three weeks in Oxford were a Pollock-splattering of attempts at progress, moments of hope, arguments, apology, insults, despair, chaos, and finally a goodbye. Mike was absolutely awful to me, but he was also awful to himself. When alcoholism gets its dirty hands around depression so tight it can't breathe, a sufferer has almost no chance, and I don't want to paint an unfair picture of a useless drunk who can't get his shit together and isn't even trying.

He had little flashes of clarity as his brain flipped and switched, crackled and spun and could see how horrible it was, but he just didn't seem able to reach the person inside him who wanted it to stop, instead saying and doing the opposite of what he thought or wanted.

It might *almost* have been fascinating to watch this final episode of the Netflix-worthy Breakdown Horror Show, had it not been so exhausting for me. I'd be in the middle of trying to finish some copy-editing work to pay for the next month's nursery fees, while long, yoyo-ing reams of word-spew were pouring into my phone from various Oxford drinking stations: begging for help, vicious accusations, apologies and declarations of love. It was all just crazy ranting out of guilt, shame and self-hate, and the more he did it, the more he hated himself – and the more he drank.

I found his awareness of his own behaviour, in such opposition to what he wanted, very hard to bear at times. He'd write things like, 'I refuse a hug when it's all I want, and scream at you when I want to whisper and be held tight. I'd love to get better and feel better, but I know I won't.'

And I felt very sorry for him – but for now, there was nothing more I could do.

My main focus had to be on building my new life here, in all the ways that required: childcare, work and somewhere to live

more permanently. I had three weeks left to stay at my parents'
house while they were away, and my daughter now had a place
in a nursery three mornings a week, giving me some TIME, at
last, to function like a person without a smaller person attached
to their leg/hip/breast.

I tried to focus my attention on *myself* and do all the things
I've read we're supposed to do when we 'move on': I got my
lank hair cut into a choppy, sexy bob, I painted my nails their
once-trademark black for the first time in years, and I started
wearing the clothes I used to love before my confidence got put
in a blender with 17 pints of wine. Mike, meanwhile, was making
some personal progress too, now some semblance of stability and
order had been put in place, and there were a reasonable few days
where things looked slightly optimistic: he was living in a nice
hostel in town with clean showers, a spacious kitchen and his
own private room, and this seemed to give him some hope and
will for a better future. He went to AA meetings every day, got
a sponsor and started looking for work, and he sounded a little
more settled and clear-minded at times, as if he might be pulling
himself together. We met up in the park a few times and talked
civilly, almost as friends again, while our daughter climbed trees
or fed the ducks.

He was still drinking every day, though he told me he wasn't,
and at the time I either didn't know or didn't think he was:
he never smelled of drink – chewing gum and coffee helped –
and he could conceal at least four pints without me knowing.
Anyway, it had been so long since I'd seen him sober, I couldn't
even remember what he was like without booze sloshing about
in him, and I doubt he could either.

As the days went by he had his first moments of humble
lucidity for months, and seemed to be readying himself for
change: 'I've always lied to myself about my situation,' he
wrote to me one evening. 'If I was drinking at 11 a.m. in a pub,
looking at the drunks and wasters around me, I told myself I
wasn't one of them. Even lying on the street wasted? That's ok,
it's just a one-off. I need to stop these pathetic excuses and the

"my life is shit" nonsense and turn that around. I want to. But I still don't know how.'

Fact was, neither of us did. We were both clueless about sobriety, how to get there, the enormity of it, the hurdles it would keep throwing in our path and the lifelong commitment, effort and strength it takes on both parts. We were infants in this journey, bumbling about and toppling over.

Of course, he wasn't 'pulling through', I can see that *now*. He was an alcoholic still fathoms deep in addiction, any positive signs in those first few days were never going to last and defeat was as inevitable as it was imminent.

A build-up of frustrations, resentments and disappointments, a few spats of angry words and irritations sparked by his continued despondency that he hadn't got a fabulously exciting and respected job or become a self-made millionaire overnight – patience is not a virtue of the addicted – brought him down again very fast, and his treatment of me in those last two weeks of October was some of the worst in the entire two years.

His messages quickly returned to a familiar, confused bullet-shower of:

I'm in the pub because of you

I'm dying, let me live with you

I have taken my meds today

I'm in a bar, I'm 4 beers, 3 tequilas and 2 double vodkas down

I don't know what to do

Then often a final:

I love you

To further his self-improvement he started smoking for the first time since before I'd even known him – yet more expense which he somehow managed to beg, borrow or steal – delighting in throwing his cigarette butts on the ground to accentuate how few fucks he now gave, and he started burping loudly, picking his nose and flicking whatever he found up there onto the ground, and was almost constantly pissed. He didn't even look like Mike to me any more; newly clean-shaven, he'd had his hair cut into what I can only describe as 'Victorian orphan trying to get into a nightclub', he was pale and angry, wired and ugly from the nastiness of his entire being, and quite honestly the whole get-up was tragic.

With this descent into not caring or functioning, the chaos came back with a vengeance too – the night before we were due to go to an interview I'd managed to secure for a writing job for me *and* a photography job for him – through no small effort or risk to my own job, but I really wanted to try and give him some purpose again – he left all of his camera equipment behind a bar in town because he had no money for his tab, thus losing us both the job; he'd lose his wallet every five minutes then find it again on a bar stool somewhere, and he never turned up on time to any rendezvous we'd arranged for him to see our daughter.

He asked me every day if he could come and pick our daughter up from nursery, quite happily informing me that he'd had anything from 'seven pints and a large vodka and tonic so far' to 'five pints and about two-thirds of a bottle of wine' to drink that morning, and when his request was inevitably declined, he had an immediate and self-created reason to feel downtrodden and miserable, and thus the perfect excuse to go drinking for the rest of the day.

He started going to the pub by nine o'clock in the morning most days, because he was 'shaking and sweating really badly and needed to steady the ship', and when asked he often had no idea how much he'd had to drink, but he was 'pretty sure it was lots'.

His moods were now changing like a chameleon sprinting over a zebra crossing and a typical day would contain everything from he wants to kill himself, he's poison, I should call his gran and tell her he's never coming back, followed immediately by strangely pedestrian claims that he's very calm, thank you, 'I just need to find my wallet.' Then back to, 'You did all this. Fact. I'm off to the pub because of you. I have taken my meds.' And after the twelfth Pint of Woe the tone would finally slide into: 'I loved you so much. You're an incredible woman. You should be treated as such. I've lost a battle I was never going to win and never will. X' By next morning it was back to insults.

We were back to arguing every time we saw each other, and the rows were sharp, vicious and worse every time; I was called a bitch, a twat, a saggy old wench and some words I don't even know but it's fair to say they were not entirely complimentary Fife-isms, objects were often thrown and kicked, I was told he hated me and ordered to move out of his way or he'd hit me. In one bizarre episode he accused me of getting him kicked out of the hostel – 'you fucking moron, they threw all my things out because of you' – when in fact he'd checked himself out, left some things in his room and they'd kindly put them in a box in the office for him to collect.

When I suggested he call his sponsor, I was told AA could fuck off and he actually liked being an alcoholic.

I found it all extremely harrowing: the arguments and constant chaos, the exhausting stress and uncertainty, the sadness and loss of so much love and hope, and I remember crying a lot during those weeks. I'd lie awake at night reliving every angry word he'd spouted at me, every twist of truth, every insult and threat, my body hot and aching from anger and mental strain. I remember wanting to break my skull open and scrape out all the words and memories, get them *out of my brain*, and be rid of it all.

I was so tired, so sad, so worried about where I was going to live and what I was going to do – and, always present in my worries, what was going to happen to Mike.

I can't explain it to anyone else, but I still missed him terribly. I missed my lover, my daughter's father, my *friend*.

Alcoholism had destroyed almost everything we were and had, but somewhere inside, deep beneath all the fear and sadness, *we* were still there.

Somewhat incredibly, given the current state of him, Mike got a job – and not just any job, a good one setting up and managing a new café they were opening. I can only assume he'd decided not to mention the fact that he'd been pissed out of his skull for the best part of a year, with brief gaps of sobriety. The position came with responsibilities, a decent salary and, as a bonus, some impressive delusions of grandeur. Oh, and one other thing: did I mention the café was in a pub? Yes, the only coffee machine in Oxford next to a beer tap. He didn't see any problem with this at all, proclaiming proudly that he would turn up sober and ready for business in two days' time. Shame he couldn't have managed this for his own child, I remember thinking.

Caffeine Mogul Mike also claimed he was going to co-own the place and get a fifty-fifty cut of all profits, while I, no longer required as a fount of cash for him to drink/gamble/lose/waste, was suddenly dispensable:

I don't need you and your charity, Liz. I'm fine on my own.
This *job* is going to save me, not you.

With only two weeks left before I had to vacate my parents' house I was now desperately searching for places to live, and very urgently needed to pin Mike down to talk practicalities: I didn't even know how many bedrooms I should be trying to rent – just for me and our daughter, or potentially for all three of us if he pulled a miracle, sobered up, became less of a prick in six months' time and we tried to make it work? Always that door open, should it be possible to step through it …

We met in the King's Arms, a traditional Oxford drinking haunt frequented largely by students. (Wait, correction, we met in Waterstones first but he walked off almost immediately and when I messaged him 10 minutes later to ask if we could please finish the talk we hadn't managed to even start in Waterstones, he had no recollection of having been there, and he was already in a pub. That is actually how it went.) He was in the back room by a fire, sinking a pint of lager. There was an empty beside it already.

He looked bullish and barely took his eyes off mine, like an animal tiring out its prey. I asked about his plans for being a parent to our daughter and he said she's 'not mine any more'. He might as well have been talking about an old T-shirt.

I remember sitting there looking at him, trying to work out what it must be like to be in a head like that, to have such fucked-up chemistry and psychology you have no control over what you're saying, or thinking, and it made me very sad. This man was once Mike, so bright and engaging, funny and loving. Now he was utterly revolting and hateable.

With his pint finished, he stood, said he was going to set up a direct debit to contribute towards his daughter's maintenance – I did query this alleged direct debit and was told 'if you want my bloody money then trust me' – then said he'd better go because he wanted to stab me, and he hoped I would have a nice day. I was left to pay for the drinks.

That night he messaged from a pub to say he was beyond fucked and claustrophobic in his own body:

I want to rip everything to pieces. I want to be sober. I can't stop shaking. Anyway, I'm starting work at 9 a.m.

Mike didn't turn up to work; he went to the pub and got pissed. The direct debit he'd promised to set up was cancelled before a single penny was ever transferred or made, and he'd drunk the one chance he had – and he knew it.

The first I knew of this was when he sent me a message an hour after he'd been due to start work. Heaven only knows how many pints down already:

I love you. Always have from the moment I saw you. I'm sorry I've been so awful. Tell my little girl how much I loved her. Goodbye.

He'd never told me to say goodbye to her before. This, on top of screwing up such a great work opportunity and facing the reality that he'd fucked up yet again, really did sound very bleak, even for Mike.

I called him immediately and, for once, he answered.

'Take me to hospital,' he said. I think he was crying. 'Please. Now. I'm dying.'

He said he was in Nando's – a good place for a last supper if you're into the idea of veganism – and I told him to stay there, I was on my way.

I made it halfway and saw him leaning against a wall, swaying like a windsock, bags all over the pavement. He couldn't focus enough to look at me, and I instinctively gave him a hug and told him everything was going to be OK.

He went calm and sad for a moment, then, while I was calling a taxi to take us to the hospital, he suddenly started bobbing up and down like a boxer, trying to pick a fight with random passers-by. He was too weak and drunk to even raise his hands properly but here he was trying to lamp shoppers on a Tuesday afternoon. It was ludicrous. Before he decked a granny he declared that he was starving and wanted a burrito. We were waiting for a taxi anyway and he didn't appear to be 'dying' any more, and anyway, food was probably a good idea to soak up some of the litres of methanol in his blood, so I said OK and we went to a Mexican takeaway just yards away, me carrying all his bags. In the five minutes we were in there he indulged in loud, excruciatingly embarrassing banter with the staff, dropped half of his food on his crotch and then announced that he needed a drink.

I said I thought he didn't.

'I do. Let's go to the Four Candles. Last one. You and me. Like we used to.'

Fuck it. Fuck it. Fuck it all. FINE. Let's do it, the taxi was still 10 minutes away and I was about to take my partner/fiancé/father of my child/ex/WHAT-THE-HELL-EVER to hospital. Mike had a double vodka, and so did I. The taxi arrived, I paid the bar tab and Mike sauntered out like a King on the way to see his People, now in such jovial, larky mood he asked the driver if we could stop for another drink – 'last last one?' – on the way to A&E. We didn't.

I'd never taken an alcoholic to hospital before and I'm not sure exactly what I was expecting would happen. Would they send him to a psychiatric ward, check him into some rehab facility or send him home and tell him to grow up? How 'emergency' was it, anyway – was he *actually* dying, did he just need his stomach pumped or was he in need of urgent, life-saving medical attention? Did he need to be sectioned, and how does being sectioned even work? Is it all *One Flew Over The Cuckoo's Nest* and straitjackets? I would *love* to know what he said to the receptionist on arrival, while I was putting all his bags on a plastic chair across in the waiting area: 'Hi, I'm an alcoholic and an hour ago I thought I was dying but my girlfriend has kindly dropped everything to save me and now I've had a burrito and some vodka I feel terrific, but while I'm here I'd like some free NHS care from a team of your highly trained medical staff please.'

Once checked in, he settled himself down and launched into a one-man A&E Comedy Show, recounting stories to anyone who would listen. I asked him how he was feeling but was completely ignored, now that my 'urgent help' wasn't required, and I remember getting quite angry at that point; it was all so humiliating and insulting, painfully reminiscent of that awful evening in Belluno with the Carabinieri, him ignoring me after I'd busted a gut to try and help him, and I thought he was an unbearable prick, to be honest.

He was called through by a nurse, I think, and I have a photo of him sitting in the assessment room, slumped in the chair, looking at the floor, suddenly broken and quiet; resigned, ashamed and very tired. She took his pulse, blood pressure and sugar levels – all perfectly normal and not immediately dying – gave him some high-dose vitamins, which I remember thinking I could have done with too, thank you, and told us the waiting time for an assessment by the psychological services was at least four hours.

I don't know if Mike thought they were going to give him a back massage and a big cuddle, but the words 'psychological services' seemed to change everything. The sudden reality of being referred to a team of mental health experts, who might not only tell him he had a problem, which he did, but would also prevent him from having any more drink, which he feared more than death itself, made him almost bolt for the door.

'Fuck this, I can't be arsed to wait. This place is shit. I'll come back another day.'

After such good, free medical care by kind staff, I was so disgusted by his lack of gratitude I nearly left him there. We left and started walking back towards town, me helping to carry some of his heavy bags, and halfway there he suddenly took them from me, said he didn't want to be anywhere near me and sauntered away. I was left standing like a worm in the road. I don't know what I shouted at him, but I remember I shouted at him a LOT as he walked away. And then I cried and I cried and I cried.

———

At 9 a.m. on 18 October, Mike told me he'd been throwing up since 6 a.m., he was going back to Scotland that day and was on his way to buy a toothbrush because his mouth stank. I took our daughter to her nursery with a fresh packed lunch and a big kiss, and then cycled into town to meet Mike and say goodbye. He kept his rucksack on the whole time I was there, didn't look at me once, wasn't apologetic, sympathetic, empathetic or any other kind of 'etic' apart from pathetic. It took all of four minutes and we were done. The last thing he said to me before he got up and walked away was, 'You're a *dick*, Liz. I'm going home now to be with the people who *actually* care about me.' I thought I was going to be sick.

I watched him go, small, weak and lost, off into the street full of shoppers going about their lives, now just a stranger among strangers.

Mike drifted oddly away over the day, and I saw him sink into each pint through his jumble of messages, and I let him and his madness go.

I'm so glad I have all of our correspondence from that time. They're a perfect, unedited picture of a disease that slowly got such a stranglehold on someone, he couldn't breathe any more.

11.58 I'm getting the 12.39 train. I hope you realise I don't want to do this at all. I'm going to sober up then come back and look for work.

12.24 I don't want to go to Scotland.

12.38 I didn't get on the train.

13.39 I have no idea what the fuck I am doing. I've fucked everything so badly.

14.19 I'm going to Scotland this afternoon, and coming back on Sunday. I'm going to come back, work and get fucking better. They said I can have my job back if I want it. I will make it work. I will go to AA. You are right, I'll have the support I need in Oxford.

16.53 My mind is a total train-wreck. Please don't take my daughter away from me.

20.09 I can't stop crying. Everything felt good. It was so clear. I've broken everything.

That evening I went back to the King's Arms for a pub dinner with my middle daughter and her little sister. We had sausages and chips, and nobody threatened to stab me. I looked out through the old windows onto Broad Street, pink in the evening light, a few bikes gliding by, couples hand in hand, heading out for drinks or dinner, not sneaking off for a seventh pint, and suddenly became breathlessly overwhelmed with the emotions of the last months.

I asked if I could quickly step outside for a few minutes on my own, and I walked round the corner to New College Lane to the Bridge of Sighs, Oxford's homage to Venice, with the Sheldonian Theatre behind me glowing pink in the last of the sun. I'd watched my eldest daughter graduate there in a proud river of black and white just two messy months ago. I walked on, to the Radcliffe Camera square, like a deserted Venetian campo without the Spritz, sat on the steps to the Bodleian Library, put my head on my knees and watched my tears drop onto the cobblestones.

Mike was gone, again. I was home, again. But this time, to stay.

———

A year after I moved my life to Venice in a van, I was about to move it all back. There were two small problems: first, I had to do the entire road trip across Europe without Mike, and even if I *did* somehow manage to pack up my whole flat and load it onto trolleys and then onto a boat and into a van and drive it 1,000 miles with a now 23-month-old baby, I'd have nowhere to put it all when I got back because I *still* hadn't found a place to live yet. Renting as a self-employed, solo mum had turned out to be much harder than expected, and despite my constant searches and enquiries, many places were off limits because toddlers apparently spend all day doing nothing but drawing on walls and eating carpets, and some landlords didn't seem to want to rent to a Bad Single Mother on principle because this is obviously still the Middle Ages. Even if I *did* find a place for someone as morally reprehensible as me, getting references from my 'boss' was impossible because my boss is me, and a few random copy-editing gigs didn't exactly cut it in terms of guaranteed, regular income.

Hard as it was to do all this Emergency Life Management by myself, it was a bloody relief to *get shit done* without Mike and his alcoholism dragging me down, and I found I had an amazing amount of strength still in me that could now come out at last, and help me get through this next challenge, or rather set of challenges. There was a new headache in Venice thanks to the Italian gas supplier switching my gas supply off with no warning, and despite calling and emailing them every day I'd not managed to get a clear answer as to why, or how to get it back on, and the only solution was quite clearly to be there in person and swear in Venetian. I now had only a matter of days until I had to vacate my parents' house, and I needed to get to Venice, pack my home, get my heating fixed and drive back to a home I didn't have yet.

I needed an emergency saviour – ideally one who could drive a van, had a large supply of elastic bands and packing tape, and was completely bonkers.

I messaged Marta, who'd come out to Venice when we arrived and drove our van back for us. Did she, maybe … fancy doing it again, the other way around?

I'm sometimes not sure if Marta is even *human*, she's so incredible, but without her immediate reply of 'Sure, when do you need me?' I would never have managed it. She was allowed a maximum of five days off work, so the whole trip had to be kept very tight; two days for the drive from Cambridge to Venice, with an overnight stay with a friend in Germany, one day to help me pack my flat up, and the remaining two days to drive back with me, empty the van into my house in Oxford – which I hadn't found yet – and get herself back to Cambridge. There was almost no wriggle-room at all for this timetable, but all we could do was try our best. There were no other options for me at this stage.

In the week that followed I booked flights to Venice for me and my daughter, a transit van from Cambridge, the Shuttle crossings from Folkestone to Calais and back, a hotel for my first night in Venice because in late October I couldn't stay in my flat while it still had no hot water or heating, an appointment with the gas engineers to fix the boiler the day after I got there, a boat to transport my luggage round to the car park when it came to leaving day, and two people with trolleys and strong arms to help carry everything out of my flat on to that boat. I also viewed six rental properties in Oxford, all of which were so rank I wouldn't keep a hamster in them let alone my child, and cried down the phone to a lot of letting agents.

The day before I left, I visited one last house. It looked a bit run-down in the photos, but I was so desperate I'd have viewed a shed if it was all there was left to live in.

I didn't get further than the entrance hall before I knew this was the place for me and her. And maybe all of us, one day, who knew? It was small, simple, open-plan downstairs, welcoming and homely, and I had the same feeling as the first time I set foot in my apartment in Venice, and in the room in Denmark I'd rented, where I'd been so at peace and happy.

There was a nice garden out the back, a bedroom for me, one for my daughter and a spare room for my older children to come and stay. It was *perfect*. There were three other people interested in the house and I was told I'd have to wait a week for all the checks to go through. I explained that I needed it in seven days from now, and I had a very young child, and I was doing all of this on my own, and I had to go to Venice tomorrow to … oh never mind, it was complicated, but I really needed to rent the house. They said they would do their best.

On 25 October, I flew to Venice with my daughter to pack up our dreams and bring our life back home – with no confirmation yet of where 'home' would be. It was dusk when we landed, still holiday-warm, and as our vaporetto chugged across the water and the sky faded from night-blue into squid-ink black, I held my little Venetian girl up to the window and smelled her hot, sweaty neck. You can't really tell with such young children, but I am certain that she knew exactly where we were, and she looked very happy to be back.

By the time we pulled up at Lido, where we were staying for the night, it was pitch-dark and the lights along the main drag were all on, locals and a few late-autumn tourists were out having a *passeggiata* and a natter. I was high on late-summer-night heat, and a strange mixture of sadness and elation to be back, and I bought my daughter an ice cream at our favourite gelateria for old time's sake. I have a lovely video of her dancing on the pavement in her little green dress with foxes on it, as she had so often in the June heatwave, when her daddy was lying on the street or in a bar somewhere, paralytic.

No news had come in from the letting agent in Oxford yet.

She was getting tired now, so I popped my dancing girl into her buggy and started walking towards our hotel, singing to her all the way and watching her huge, amazed eyes gaze up into the darkness at the swaying palm trees and oleanders, the crickets and the moon keeping us company all the way. I slept more deeply and peacefully than I had for weeks.

The next day was postcard glorious – but this wasn't a holiday, and all the hard, sad work had to start now. It was to be a very difficult last few days, emotionally and practically, with a lot of drunken ends to tie up.

At almost every café and bar I passed, where we'd always had a friendly rapport with the owners, I was now greeted with an unusually cold shoulder and a brusque 'Ciao', often followed by an unpaid bar tab from Mike's bender back in September – €40 here, €25 there. It came to over €200 in total. I settled it all, said I was so sorry, explained a little about how Mike wasn't well and got nods of understanding and a few sad details about which chair he'd fallen asleep on and for how long. They all knew, and they were all sorry for me and my daughter, I think.

My beautiful home, meanwhile, was a mess of piping, wires, tools and sweaty people replacing miles of ancient plumbing so they could get the gas supply turned back on. This seemed to require much drilling through walls, making it so noisy I could hardly think, and covering the whole place in dust. It was like the previous January all over again, when the renovations had started and Mike was pissed with his baby while I was in IKEA buying everything for our new kitchen and bathroom.

I tried to start packing some things into bags and boxes, but kept crying and having to stop until I could face it again. Every plate was a meal we'd once shared, every book was one I'd sat next to him on the sofa reading, every surface and piece of furniture a part of a story that had gone so wrong, and it hurt too much to see remnants of the happy times we *had* shared. It was also borderline impossible with all the drilling going on and making sure my daughter didn't swallow a screw or chat up a Moldovan electrician.

A cold snap came blasting down from the Alps the next afternoon, whipping across the lagoon and stripping Venice of all her colour and welcome, leaving a grey sea, grey sky, grey rain and a grey heart. The reality of what had happened, how many dreams and plans had been lost, the memories of our happy start here, evening walks, bike rides along the waterfront in the sun, discovering all the corners and views, the drunken descent and the terrible end all came flooding in, drowning the last little shreds of adventure and excitement. This was the dirty, shutters-down end of a happy dream, shattered entirely by alcoholism. I'd lived on adrenaline for so long, but suddenly on this cold day, with nothing more to look forward to here but goodbyes, I felt infinitely weary and lost.

The boiler was now fixed and there was a huge amount of cleaning up to be done, plus all the packing and sorting the final logistics for the journey back, and it all had to happen in small chunks broken up by visits to the park for some run-around time for my daughter. I bumped into a friend while I was in the Co-op on Via Garibaldi, a street filled with dreadful memories of throwing Mike out of a bar, drunken arguments and so on back in that cold, mad, Carnevale February and March. It was cold again now, grey and rainy, and somehow almost worse for being sad, not just angry any more. We grabbed a coffee and huddled under an awning trying to keep warm. I told her everything that had happened. It was strange, sad but freeing, being this open and honest where previously I'd kept face and nobody had known how difficult things were behind the façade. It didn't give me any *pleasure* to be telling people the truth but it brought me a sense of relief not to have to pretend any more. I don't think anybody understood why I could still be so sad about losing Mike, and why I could even consider the possibility of a life with him in the future, and I don't think there was a single person who didn't think I should leave him and move on.

That was always the hardest thing for me – to reach my *own* conclusion about whether he should stay or go. If I should try again, or if there was no going back EVER after such terrible things had happened. These are the choices we make individually, the ones we judge are right for us, for our own reasons that only we know.

For now, I still wasn't sure and wasn't even able to think about it much – there was enough to be getting on with and I was there to end this bad chapter, and not think about the next.

The next two days felt like constantly stirring an enormous admin risotto; paying all my utility bills, opening piles of letters in Italian that I couldn't understand, taking overdue books back to the library and paying the fines, queuing in the post office to buy one stamp for a letter I had to send to a municipality office in town because just emailing them would be far too easy here.

I went across to Lido to transfer my bank account there as it was far closer than traipsing all the way to Rialto every time over Christ knows how many bridges, and spent two hours in there while my daughter helpfully polished the floor with her coat and sour-faced old ladies stood obediently to attention behind *la linea rossa* tutting at me, and *then* it transpired that I didn't have some Official Banking Code or other and I couldn't get it because they have to text it to you and I didn't have the right kind of Italian phone or it was a full moon or BECAUSE VENICE. I remember wanting to tell them all to shove their banking codes and puffer jackets and their rude attitude up their Venetian backsides and maybe try to think what it might be like to be doing what I was clearly falling apart trying to do.

When I emerged, tears of exasperation streaming down my cheeks, pushing a buggy with one hand and carrying a wriggling toddler in the other, I bumped into two friends out for a walk and a Spritz (it *was* 11 a.m., after all) and judging by their somewhat aghast expressions, I must have looked a state.

I was informed that I looked terrible, and needed a break. NOW.

'Go to the beach, Liz, have a walk, swim in the sea if you like. We will take your little *piccolina* for a walk and a sleep – she'll be fine, OK? *Vai!*'

The beach was bleak and cold, the wind now so strong it blasted wet sand up my nostrils and into my eyes. Nobody else was mad enough to swim in such Baltic conditions by local standards, so it was just me, alone for the first time in weeks. I swam out into the choppy Adriatic, all the pain and sadness deadened by the cold, floated on my back and looked towards the shore. Washed of all her colour and warmth, washed of us and our story, there was nothing I recognised or wanted to see. Venice wasn't mine any more, and it was time to say *grazie* ... and go home.

Mike, meanwhile, was looking out over the choppy waters off the shore of Fife, and appeared to be sifting through the flotsam from his havoc-wreaking; he'd started sending occasional photos and messages, asking how we were, how our daughter was, and telling me how much he wished he could help with everything I was having to do. It was all I could do not to tell him to go shove it and have a nice time playing golf while I was clearing up the horrific mess he'd made of my life. I was so angry at being left alone in a shattering position yet again, with not ONE BAG packed by the person who had caused all this chaos, or one euro being contributed to help cover the huge costs of this move back home that I'd never intended to make. Maybe he *did* wish he could help, but I wished none of this was happening at all.

I wanted to be here all together as we had talked about and planned.

But here I was, putting it all to bed, alone.

The day before we left, now 30 October, Marta arrived. I went all the way to Piazzale Roma with my daughter to meet her, exactly where I'd watched Mike walk away from me when he went to Barcelona four shattering months before, and when I saw her striding towards us through the throngs of newly arriving tourists, bearing gifts of flat-packed cardboard boxes, string, plastic ties and a smile, I cried. I cried most of the time, to be honest. Now she was here and all my admin was finished, the packing itself could start in earnest.

As I had no idea what my future held, I had to leave my apartment in a state in which I could rent it out if I had to, or even move back into if we ever decided to do that, so all the big furniture, kitchen equipment, all bedding, rugs, books, wardrobes and so on had to stay. Everything else was packed to come back. There was still no confirmed news from the letting agent in Oxford, so I had no idea where I would be living when we arrived.

Two of my friends came to help us pack, allowing me to do all my mummy tasks in between bouts of shirt-folding and ornament-packing, but mainly to put away all of Mike's things for me. Every time I saw or smelled his clothes I'd burst into tears, so I was ordered to go out and get some air and leave it to those who didn't still love the person who had put her in this horrible situation. An impressive collection of cans and bottles was unearthed from almost all of his jacket pockets and drawers.

I put a few of my favourite items of his clothing into a little bag in my suitcase, along with his aftershave. There was the T-shirt he was wearing when we found out I was pregnant, the jumper he wore when he proposed, and his old, worn blue sweatshirt I'd carried with me on all of my travels, and even occasionally worn in photos I posted on social media, just to show him I was still here, and I still thought about him. Some of it stank of stale sweat and dirt mixed with a hint of Mike, and I loved that most of all.

Just as we were sealing the last boxes with brown tape, I received an email from the letting agents. My references had been accepted, and the little house in Oxford was ready for me to move into. There were yet more tears.

At 3 p.m. on 31 October, everything was ready to go.

Boxes started being loaded onto the trolleys and pulled to the boat, already waiting for us in the nearest canal. It was very sad to see it all there again, just as it had been a year before, heading in the other direction.

When the boat was completely full there remained eight black bin bags containing only Mike's belongings, piled in the hallway. The hallway where he'd called me a bitch just a few weeks before. There was also his set of golf clubs.

'Come on, Liz, leave it. We can't fit it in, you don't have time to bring the boat back again and get it, and he doesn't deserve it anyway. He's lucky we haven't thrown it all in the lagoon!'

They didn't understand why I couldn't think like they were thinking, cut Mike off and chuck him out of my life, why I still cared about him or any of his things. How could anyone care about a person who'd done all this to them, and wasn't even here to help? *I* understood. I understood very clearly how a disease can make us who we're not. And I still believed that disease could be brought under control, and allow Mike to come back one day.

I looked at the pile of 'Mike in bags' and knew I had no right to throw it away, so I said no, we would take the boat all the way around the island to the car park, unpack everything into the van, and come back for another round trip, just for his things.

When everything was finished, Marta took a photo of me and my daughter on the steps outside my flat. I have an almost identical photo from the day we'd arrived a year before, all three of us standing there, so happy; now only two were here to leave.

All that remained of our adventure was the brass nameplate beside the buzzer Mike had rung all night, to 'make this a problem' for me.

We left Venice at 6 p.m., over the bridge to the mainland in the dark, away from the lights of Venezia. We crossed the Italian and Swiss Alps on exactly the same stretch of road as I'd driven with Mike on the way to start our new life, this time shrouded in a fog so thick we could barely see the next hairpin bend, and then down into France at dawn. We had to do this journey as quickly as we safely could, to get Marta back to work in two days' time and to cover as much ground as possible while my daughter was asleep, and it really was quite the epic journey.

Torrential rain hammered down on the Autoroute all the way, making driving dangerous and tiring, and we had to keep stopping to grab half an hour of shut-eye in a car park, give my daughter some food, a nappy change and a little run around, then pile back into the van for another four-hour stint.

By late afternoon, 22 hours after we had set off from Venice, we were now halfway through France and had to find an IKEA to stop at, for me to buy everything I needed to set up home, now I'd had to leave everything I'd already bought a year ago, in Venice. Amazingly enough, in all the chaos we had somehow neglected to realise that it was All Saints' Day and almost everything in France closes for the day.

Frantic googling revealed *one* IKEA in Reims that didn't seem to care all that much about Saints, so we took a small detour and spent three hectic hours loading four gigantic trolleys with furniture, bedding, sheets, towels, crockery, nice things for my daughter's bedroom, tea lights (obviously) and the same mustard-yellow armchair I had often sat in to feed her or to read to her in Venice, so she would feel at home in our new house. All in all, including an essential portion of meatballs and chips, I spent more than £2,000 on things I should never have had to buy again.

With the van stuffed to the roof, we were so tired we'd started to lose our sense of humour, but we were now on the final slog to the end of the marathon. We reached Calais so late we'd missed both our original Shuttle booking and two more I'd rebooked by phone along the way, and the lady at the ticket kiosk said we couldn't use our ticket because it was now after midnight. We had been travelling for 31 hours at this point, my debit card was a wreck and I couldn't take any more.

I looked at her, I looked at my daughter and I pointed to the back of the van.

'Mademoiselle, we've just driven all the way from Venice, this is my baby, her father is an alcoholic and has left us, this is my friend Marta who drove all the way to help me, and this is my whole life in a van. Please.'

She moved our booking on to the next crossing, at 4 a.m.

At 7 a.m. on 1 November 2019, our heavy, tired van pulled into Oxford. I collected the house keys as soon as the estate agent opened, by 11 a.m. we had unloaded everything into my new house, and by mid-afternoon we'd unpacked all the furniture, assembled a table, a bench, my daughter's bed and the mustard yellow armchair, put cutlery in drawers, plates in cupboards, books on shelves and cuddly toys on my daughter's new rug.

Marta left that afternoon. There were more tears. Looking back, I'm really not sure how we did it, and I can only put it down to having no choice, a determination to see this thing through together, and being tough as *all* the nails.

By early evening, my daughter was all tucked up and asleep under her new duvet in her new bed in her new room in her new house. I kissed her goodnight, went downstairs and sat on the living room floor. The only sound was the humming of the fridge. No rushing, packing, driving, carrying, decision-making, fighting, phoning, talking, arguing, messaging, sorting or crying. Just TOTAL STOP. I sat there for an hour, just *being* in that room, feeling it and making friends with its shape and air. We made an agreement that night, me and that house, to get along, to be happy and to have Astrid's 'good vibes only' rule. It's been the rule in that house ever since that first evening.

I *almost* stuck to it.

PART SEVEN

Rock Bottom

I hope you never have to experience an illness that costs you everything. THIS is my rock bottom.

It's hard to know how to start this part of the story. I *want* to say it marked the beginning of the best days of my life: a new start, new home, new job, new wardrobe, new hair, maybe a new relationship, freedom from all the damage of living with alcoholism, and all power to me for having survived it all. I want to paint you a montage of my daughter and me making pizzas in our new kitchen and not caring that the whole place is doused in flour and I have lovely new friends round for dinner and I do yoga in the garden and I sleep well and drink wine in the bath and love my life because I'm SO HAPPY.

I'd like to say all that.

But you don't emerge from years of loneliness, fear, loss, shock and threats, and just make pizza. It takes a long time of slow healing, gently allowing yourself to trust anything again, embarking on the long process of working out who you are now, what you feel about a lot of things, what you want and how to achieve that, what you are prepared to live with, what you can come to forgive, what you can dare to let in and love, and what you can find the strength to live without.

Recovery is gradual, non-linear and at times very frustrating, and just as addicts remain sober one day at a time, so we who live, or have lived, with them go forward one day, one wobble, one relapse, one post-trauma-fuelled argument at a time – and one success at a time.

I had a refreshingly *normal* first week in Oxford, that first week of November. I had breakfast with my happy little Oxford girl every morning, made her packed lunch, dropped her off at nursery, worked as fast as I could while she was there, picked her up at lunchtime in a new running buggy I'd got so I could do some exercise at *last*, and in the evenings I'd have a relaxing bath, do some stretches and breathing in the living room, and go to bed calmly and early. No arguments. No fear. Just quiet recovering, and blissful, drama-free ordinariness.

As I slept more and argued less my skin started to look younger and smoother, my eyes brightened, my mind was clearer and I felt a focused, calm strength coming back, and I did start the process of getting on with the new life, new job, new routines and new hair. And yes, in those early few days I thought about the possibility of a new relationship, but as a solo mum I wasn't exactly free to go on dates or have a wild social life – and I didn't want that anyway.

I wanted the man I loved.

I still talked to my daughter about her daddy every day, always kindly; I showed her photos of him and always told her he was coming to see her soon. Despite all the hate I'd felt towards him, I *still* believed in our family, in Mike, in the love we first had and still had for each other and in the ability of humans to mend even when they're so broken they almost don't exist any more. I still knew he was just ill, and if he could find a way to get better, get some treatment and commit himself to wanting to change, we might be able to come together again.

Meanwhile, Mike, who was still staying with one of his brothers back home in Fife, was now in touch most days to ask how we were getting on and give me a few vague details as to what he was doing and how he was, and as with every single previous excursion to the place, where there was very little structure and very much booze, he didn't seem to have got a whole lot better since he'd gone there on that terrible day after the hospital visit, still only two and a half weeks before, but given the crazy amount of things that had happened in my life in that time, it felt more like three months to me. He was still mentally all over the shop, and seemed unable when questioned to take any responsibility for the fact that his situation was entirely the consequence of his own actions, while my now-improved position was entirely the consequence of my own hard work *despite* his actions.

He appeared to still be oblivious to anything and anyone other than his own wants and needs, and was almost never available to have phone calls when it suited his child's timetable but only when it fitted into his fantastically busy schedule of doing nothing except drinking. We did have some calmer, more 'normal' chats both by message and on the phone, but he was still emotionally very changeable and could become angry and paranoid very quickly, convinced I was trying to take his child away and ruin his life. He seemed to flip between two states: bitter, angry, self-pitying and aggressive, or sad, regretful and desperate to see us.

As usual, he still seemed perfectly able to fake civility and sobriety in front of others, popping round to his grandparents' house for tea most days, helping his brother do up his new house and garden and going for walks with his friends along the beach – but to me he was often, though not exclusively, pretty unpleasant and irritated. I was the only person who saw right through him, challenged his drinking behaviour, refused to forgive it any more and was quite clearly living a better, happier life than the one he was choosing – the life he actually *wanted*, but was powerless to get back.

For all his 'fuck you I don't need you anyway' words towards me, he was inches from the end of what he could bear, and his messages got noticeably and rapidly sadder over that week.

He started to say he didn't feel like a dad any more, he'd lost everything and had nothing to live for, he was lonely and sad:

> ... a desperate, pathetic alcoholic, a terrible parent, and I don't feel like she's even my daughter any more

He said he just wanted to be with us and wanted his life back again.

It might be easy to read all this and think, 'Yeah, but he has said that a hundred times before. Why is it different now?' and the answer is that there's no way of knowing if someone has changed until you give them a chance to show that change.

All the way through Mike's entire alcoholic breakdown, I *knew* what he meant and what was bullshit, because I KNOW him, and when he said he wanted his family and his life, and he wanted to be better, he meant it more than anything else he ever said. All the rest, all the insults, the 'I don't need you', the 'fuck off and leave me alone', the shoves and the eventual madness, was just anger at himself, resentment of things he had done, and *self*-hate – and eventually a mind that didn't even work.

I also knew that for as long as Mike was in a place with no proper support network, where he could do what he wanted unchecked and unchallenged, and was separated from the things he loved and needed to love him back, he had zero chance of getting any better, and a strong chance of reaching his end.

Maybe being in my own home and having some calm made me let my guard down, or maybe I'm just a sap or I'm stupid or too kind or I don't know what, but I offered him another chance. Not to live with me for now, but at least to be in a better location for him, and maybe for us to start to get to know each other a little again and start to mend. But that was down the line. For now, yet again, I set out some simple rules and boundaries:

1. He attends AA every day.
2. *He* buys a breathalyser and takes a test every time he's with us. If it's positive, he leaves. This was a condition of

seeing his daughter and it was up to him to provide it if he wanted to.

3. He takes his antidepressant medication every day, in front of me.
4. He registers with a GP in Oxford and gets some counselling.
5. If he swears at me, he has to leave.
6. If he's aggressive, verbally or physically abusive, he has to leave.

I know we'd agreed to some of these before and had both completely failed to stick to them, but things really were different now: I had my own home, the only key to the front door, and a confidence I'd never had before. If he wanted to be any part of our life, that was now totally up to him.

———

Mike arrived in Oxford on 7 November. He'd found himself a room to rent – I didn't even ask who was paying for it this time – in a nice house about two miles away; a safe distance from me, but close enough to pop by.

There were still verbal scuffles and tensions almost every time we spoke on the phone but he did sound upbeat and positive about coming back, and ready to try and improve himself and his life.

We arranged to meet in town when he got off the train, while our daughter was still at nursery so we could have a calm, undisturbed hello and I could see how he was doing. I remember I really made an effort to look nice for that meeting: favourite blue jumper, silver DMs, a white shirt, and painted nails. I know this display was largely to show him how happy and well I was on my own, but it was also a not even subtle bid to make him fancy me again. I am, after all, a girl who loves a boy, and wanted him to love me back.

I needn't have bothered with any of it; Mike was so drunk he didn't come up to meet me at all.

He DID manage to meet me the following morning, so I could decide whether he might be able to see his daughter that day, but he arrived late, reeking of alcohol and stormy-eyed. I said I'd like to breathalyse him, as he'd agreed to buy one and be tested, remember, and was told to fuck off if I thought he was going to be breathalysed 'like some prick', and anyway he hadn't bought one because he had no money. Except all the money he'd just drunk. I heard nothing more all day or evening.

The next day was the same.

Scoff or laugh at me if you want to but I truly didn't think it would happen exactly the same again. I thought that now, with his child in a nursery, me in my own home and him with his own space to live in and find some peace and calm in himself, *now* things might be different, and better, because they *were*. I thought the hospital and throwing away his chance at a stable, good job had been his rock bottom, he'd been away to think about it and he could now see it as the worst day of his life, and start to come back up now.

Our daughter developed a rash that afternoon, and I took her to the emergency doctor. They said it was probably nothing to worry about but I should keep a close eye on her in case it got any worse.

I now faced a dilemma: my rules said Mike wasn't allowed near us if he was drinking, and given his state that morning he clearly had been. But keeping someone away from their unwell child didn't feel right to me at all; what if she became very ill suddenly, maybe even had to be rushed to hospital and he'd not be able to see her? I decided I had to tell him and, naturally worried, he asked if he could come and see her that evening.

I thought about this for a moment. What was really so terrible about letting him into my house to see his child? What did I honestly think he was going to do? There was not even the slightest worry in my mind that Mike would do anything other than come and see his daughter, and be fine.

I also thought about the breathalyser. See, the thing with that was not that it would change anything in particular, but it would give me some proof that he'd been drinking, and an indisputable reason for telling him if I didn't want him near me, or her. When you live with a liar, or a gaslighter, anything that can provide proof, evidence, clarity and fact becomes a bit of a mental saviour and some armour against the bullshit.

I was annoyed that yet again it seemed to have fallen to me to pay for something that was only necessary because of him, but on balance I'd far rather have the damn proof, and be able to show it to him.

It was another £137 gone – but it proved to be one of the best things I ever bought.

When I got back to the house in the rain, there were wet footprints on my doorstep. I was a few minutes early, and they couldn't have been there for more than a minute or two as they were still fresh-wet. Instead of waiting those two whole minutes until I brought his daughter to him, Mike had grabbed that miniscule window to run to the pub up the road and get another drink in him.

Ten minutes later, there was a knock at the door, and I let him into my home.

He sort of slunk in, rather than arrived, nervous and awkward, and went straight over to say hello to his little girl. It was lovely to see them together, and so much of what I'd hung in there for, for so long.

I've never seen anyone use a breathalyser before, nor knew how to use one until I'd read the instructions. I felt like a prison officer asking him to use it, but he was very calm and understood why he had to do it. Almost as soon as he blew into the plastic mouthpiece, the screen blushed red. I checked the reading, and it was so high he was either dead or had had a drink within the last few minutes. That would be the pub dash, then.

This small, white piece of plastic with its irrefutable electronic display of truth played a significant part in prompting Mike's eventual recovery, I'm sure of it. It was such a simple representation of his illness, a visible measure of his inability to stop, and for me, it was a tiny bit of power in my hands: he couldn't lie when the truth was there to see in red, and he knew his bullshit time was up. For £137, that's not bad.

Mike stayed for an hour that first time, and left without incident. I'd broken at least three of my rules, but it was a big, positive sign from me of what he could have if he wanted it, and that I wasn't to be walked all over any more.

We met six times over the next three days and I have a photo of each test result: red, red, red, five times over the limit, three times over, five times over again. Where our first meeting had been quiet and calm, largely because he was so desperate to see our daughter when she wasn't well, the next were far less so, and he walked away from every one in a hail-shower of swearing and insults, enraged with himself that he STILL couldn't change and that screen was still red, and he was just a failure after failure after failure.

His first green test result, the first *clean* one, was such a shock I almost couldn't believe it: Mike had no alcohol in his blood. I doubt that had been the case since July, at least, but here was the first little 'Green for Go' sign that he *might* be ready to stop.

It took one more day to hit the bottom.

———

What made Mike stop, in the end? What caused that moment of clarity, and the decision to stop giving up and start starting to live?

I'm asked this often, by desperate people who want their partner or son, sister or friend to get better, and my frustrating answer is that I don't know what made him stop, and he doesn't either. He'd just ... *had enough*. This search for the Turning Point, the fabled Rock Bottom and the sudden CLICK to turn a life around is exhausting. We can't force it or do anything to make it happen, but when it comes, it comes, and that's all there is to it.

We were all in my house, it was the afternoon of 11 November 2019, and Mike's breath test on arrival had been clean. Things were going well and calmly.

I don't know what happened then, I really don't. I don't know if it was just that his body and mind couldn't cope without having drink in them, or if I said something he didn't like in a tone he didn't like or in a way that suggested to his paranoid, sobering up, freaked-out mind that it meant something else, but he suddenly flipped mood, like a firework going off, and started swearing at me. I told him calmly that he had to leave the house now, and he told me in return to fuck off with my fucking rules, that I must be loving this power trip and I'd wanted this all along. He started throwing things: books, a cushion, anything he could grab, he kicked the wall and punched a kitchen cupboard as he stormed towards the back door. As he stepped outside, he turned.

'Fuck you both. You've ruined my life.'

He spent that evening in a pub, drinking.

That night, the worst storm for 75 years hit Venice. The whole city was flooded under metres of water and the wind whipped the lagoon into waves so strong they lifted 10-tonne vaporettos up onto the shore, smashing stone walkways and splintering the wooden vaporetto stops. The beautiful stone balustrade where Mike had taken a photograph of me against a sunset on the day we decided to move there was smashed down by the water and many of the trees in Sant'Elena came crashing down. It was a sign from the world saying this was it now. The old life was gone. It was clear-up time.

The next morning, Mike sent me his first message from his start of sobriety:

I've been crying all night. What I said yesterday is unforgivable. I can't take it back, it's just another horrible thing I've done.

I'm too tired of saying sorry, and you're too tired of hearing it. I want to be a Dad so badly, yet I'm the worst parent I've ever known. I don't know how to be a partner any more either. I'm utterly exhausted by existing. I hope you never have to experience an illness that costs you everything. THIS is my rock bottom.

An hour later he went to an Alcoholics Anonymous meeting, and at the time of writing this, he's been going three times a week, and has been sober for a year and a half.

PART EIGHT

Sobriety

I found it very hard to know how to write this section of the book. There were so many things going on at the same time, all intertwined, similar but different, and they each followed their own path, changing pace and direction all the time.

Really, there were not one but *three* recoveries going on at the same time: his from alcoholism, mine from his alcoholism and mine from my own addictions and mental health issues, which hadn't even come to the fore again yet.

I can't write about how it felt for him to go through his recovery, and anyway that's not why I'm here; I'm just here to tell my story of how it was to live with someone going through recovery, having been with him during his terrible times.

That last bit proved to be a very big challenge for us: I wasn't a new partner who met someone already in recovery; I was the partner who had lived with him throughout his drinking, had suffered at the hands of his addiction, and carried enormous scars and pain as a result. This would have been bad enough, but another complicating factor was that, after the first month or so, we lived together throughout his recovery, and into mine. Recovery very often happens alone because a couple has split up, or someone goes into rehab, or a family member doesn't live at home any more. The addict has space and time to focus entirely on themselves, which is exactly what they need. Those affected by it all have peace and space to slowly begin to understand and unpick the traumas they've endured, they can slowly detach from the pain and anger, and their own recovery journey can begin too.

For us, this time and space didn't happen because we were in the same house every day – and not only this but most of our first recovery year was spent in lockdown during the COVID pandemic, so we were almost constantly in each other's company. Two damaged, tired, angry, sad people trying to mend individually and as a couple, while sharing the same space. What could possibly go wrong?

To make matters even better, I was living with the *source* of my pain, so every day I could see, hear and remember what he'd done to me, and it triggered my PTSD almost constantly. He, meanwhile, was living with the person he'd destroyed, and seeing my ragged face, anxiety-fuelled panics and fears, and how little self-confidence and happiness was left in this girl who had once glowed with health and vitality was enough to make him hate himself so much he could hardly bear it at times.

Both of us needed love and support, and neither of us was in a place to give it to the other yet, and for the first year or so it was like asking a leaky ship to rescue you from drowning.

It may seem from the outside that we were crazy to do it this way and it would have been far easier to get over some of our pains on our own, healing separately, and in our own time; I'm sure there's something to be said for that, but we'd lived apart so much in the last year, it certainly brought us closer together and both of us wanted our family back as soon as we could make that happen. If we carried on living separately for very much longer, there might be nothing to try and get back *to*. So, for better or worse, we fought our individual and mutual demons under the same roof at the same time, trying to co-parent and re-love. It was a bloody hard battle, with many defeats and a lot of tears, but we fought it hard – and, at the time of writing this, we are still very much together, and a testament to the way we did it, and to our love.

I should say something about the state *I* was in when Mike entered sobriety, because it affected our recoveries a lot. Put simply, I was an emotional and mental wreck. Sure, I carried on working, I paid the rent on time, did the shopping, took my daughter to the library, the swimming pool and the park – but I was shattered to my core and my PTSD rattled my veins 24 hours a day.

Post-traumatic stress disorder is not some vague term for 'I'm a snowflake' that people make up to get some attention; it's a very serious anxiety disorder caused by distressing events, or a traumatic experience. Symptoms often include high anxiety, low self-esteem, depression, confusion, fear, distressing flashbacks, social withdrawal, loneliness, difficulty concentrating, memory problems, insomnia, chronic physical pain and fatigue. Not much, then. PTSD bypasses all cognitive thought, and when triggered, our reactions can be so hard-wired they're almost reflex. I had no control over my responses to certain triggers for at least the first year, and one word could cause a full-blown panic attack.

These triggers were everywhere and could pop up at any time: a smell, a taste, a colour, a scene in a film, the name of a person or a town. Even writing this book and having to go over everything that happened, I started having night sweats that soaked the whole bed again, I had terrible insomnia, I couldn't concentrate, my bones and joints hurt, I suffered blinding headaches, I trembled a lot and I had paranoid thoughts and insecurities about the tiniest things. All of this was triggered and maintained by exposure to the sources of this distress, or even just the memories of it.

Psychological damage is often harder and slower to recover from than physical injury, and you can't see it, wrap it in a bandage or measure if it's getting better; it just sits there inside us until we find a way to heal it. It doesn't matter whether you are 'predisposed' to breakdown, or have had psychological problems of one kind or another in your life, the effects on a person's mental well-being of living with an addict can be catastrophic and lifelong and they need to be recognised and supported.

There is so much fascinating research about trauma I could be here all year writing about it, but one thing I found most helpful when I started reading about PTSD is how trauma memories are stored in our brains as if they're in a locked box. Most other memories are in more accessible, 'malleable' bits of the brain, developing and changing over time as we tell stories about events, embellish them a little, add a touch of exaggeration here and there until we can even come to 'remember' things differently to how they happened.

Trauma memories are very different; they remain fixed, almost frozen in their memory box, and when we're triggered back to the event that caused them we relive and re-experience everything EXACTLY as it happened – and our reactions remain exactly as if we were in that moment.

Even months after Mike was sober, if I saw a photo of Venice or if Instagram helpfully sent me a 'two years ago today!' reminder of what looked like a happy afternoon punting in Cambridge but in reality I'd been on my own for weeks and Mike had sworn at me several times that day, my pulse would go up significantly, my breathing would tighten and I'd often burst into tears or suddenly have the urge to hurt myself to get the pain away.

Oddly, anniversaries or memories of our *good* times were almost worse: 'happy' reminders of all the loss of what had been, could have been, and perhaps never would be again, and I cried many tears of grief, almost mourning, for so much beauty and happiness lost.

Some theories of trauma recovery suggest we can 'move' traumatic memories out of their 'box' and into a different part of the brain, where neural pathways can be altered and ultimately replaced by new, un-traumatised ones, and we do this by verbalising the trauma: speaking our pain, talking about how we feel, describing it in as much detail as we can manage. It's like bringing the fears and memories into the room, looking at them and deciding not to be hurt by them any more.

This was exactly what I needed: to get it all out and find some closure and reconciliation, peace and mending. I wanted Mike to let me ask him about things that still didn't make sense to me, to explain and admit to some of the lies and give me the truths I needed to hear to be granted freedom from it all. I wanted to go over the same old pains again and again, hate him again, hear him say sorry until all the memory scars were healed by his remorse and admission, and I needed to say it all to *him* because *he* did it to me so I needed *him* to heal every wound he caused me.

But for almost a full year Mike couldn't let me speak to him about any of what had happened, because he was far too early in his own recovery to be able to deal with it well. If I was upset he'd say I was stressing him out, then I'd go into reflex mode and become frightened, tearful and sometimes angry and this made *him* angrier because he couldn't cope with all the emotions flying around everywhere. I can understand that now, but this silencing greatly prolonged and worsened my symptoms, and heightened my anxiety even further, and the whole thing was a bit of a mess for at least the first six months, if I'm honest.

Oddly, what upset me most – and still I struggle with this quite often – was seeing old photos of myself looking young and happy, glowing and confident. Photos where I looked ... *pretty*. I couldn't bear to see how happy I'd been, how lovely my skin was, how much healthier I looked and how filled with excitement and dreams I was. I really didn't believe I would ever, EVER, be that happy again and I wanted to scream 'LOOK WHAT YOU DID TO ME!' – and I often did, in fact. Still now, I cry sometimes to remember the years I lost and the damage to me. I know I've aged faster than I would have without all the tears and exhaustion. But there's nothing I can do, except go forward from here trying to mend as much as I can.

Just as I'd known nothing about alcoholism, it turned out I was clueless about recovery as well: what it takes, what it involves, what a bloody nightmare it is at times and the fact that it goes on for life. I thought sobriety would be the answer to all of our miseries, and after the world's most horrific hangover for a week, lying in bed feeling sorry for himself, Mike would then get up, make a strong coffee, get some counselling and go back to being the Mike I loved and had hung in there for all this time, within a month or so. And why not? I'd seen him turn around pretty quickly quite a few times before, and things had only got terrible again when he'd started drinking – so surely, I reasoned, when the drink was gone, and *stayed* gone, all the problems would go away and stay away too. It was just logical.

This was as sensible as expecting an anorexic person on death's door to eat a few pies, return to a healthy weight and develop a fabulous relationship with food by the weekend, because **NEWSFLASH: mental health problems are not logical, and not drinking doesn't mean you're not an alcoholic; you're just an alcoholic who doesn't drink.**

The reality is that you don't just 'dry out': you dry out and then wake up into a world you barely recognise or know how to operate in. You have to meet yourself again and you might not like who you are, and now there's no alcohol to take the edge off all the jarring emotions. Things Mike had hidden from or slunk through blindly in a depressed, drunken stupor were now almost unbearably clear to him, and he almost didn't know how to BE. I was wanting to get on with our lives; he was trying to work out what living even WAS and how to do it, and far from becoming nicer and calmer when he stopped drinking, what actually happened was more like taking all the toys and Ritalin away from an already angry baby.

The list of things I didn't know just kept coming and coming throughout the whole of the first year: the emotional effects of withdrawal, the appearance of the Dry Drunk, the mood swings, paranoia, sudden flashes of new 'feelings' a person in recovery can experience as they're coming clean and facing the world through non-drunk eyes and brain, throwing them into a spin for days or even weeks.

I didn't know about recovery programmes, what the Twelve Steps are, how AA actually works, what sponsors do or what Step Work is. I didn't know he'd be thrown into periods of painful internal struggle, pulling him away from me yet again as he faced things he'd done while drunk, learned to self-criticise, apologise and make amends, and tried to work out who exactly he is.

I also didn't know in how many ways it would affect *me*: how much *more* work it would take from me to support him in this next stage, the ugly resentment and jealousy I would feel about his recovery and the 24/7 free support network lavished on him, the rifts and arguments it would cause if I challenged any aspect of his recovery, the debilitating extent of my PTSD, the sudden relapses to Drink Thinking and behaviours or the emotional crash I was to have when I finally stopped being everything to everyone and let go a bit.

I didn't know long it would take, how many false starts and bumps there were going to be along the way. I didn't know *anything*, and having just got a First Class degree in Addiction, I found myself forced to sign up for a Master's in Recovery – both his, and mine.

They talk about recovery being non-linear, and whoever 'they' are, they're not wrong; if Mike's descent was a zigzag heading towards the ground, his gradual climb out of the abyss had more dips and troughs than a stock market crash, and the first month was as brutal as it was unexpected.

For the first few weeks he was in Oxford, Mike was still living separately to me, renting a room in a house nearby, and it was a very good way to start this slow reconnection; it gave me a little distance from him, some calm in my evenings and a door I could close if required. It also gave him some space and time to work on his early sobriety, which, understandably, was a very difficult adjustment for him indeed, chemically and emotionally. As November reached its middle, we started spending a little time together out and about: we had some daytime park meet-ups, went to see the Winter Lights display in town, had Sunday morning sausage baps in a café, and even a few afternoon home visits, which went fine. We played in the garden on the trampoline with our daughter, he read her some stories and she showed him her new chalk board and doctor's kit.

On 19 November, Mike had his first evening meal with us for months. He cooked, I played with our daughter, and it was the first time since June that year I'd had anyone cook for me while I had a moment to play with her on my own.

I found it very emotional, that first dinner; seeing the three of us sitting at a table like a family, listening to my little girl chatting away with him, watching the way he held his fork and leaned his shoulders in before every mouthful, every action and sound that was so familiar to me, and had become so estranged.

That night, after he'd left to go back to his room again, I searched for 'Hey Laura It's Me' on YouTube and played it on my phone, holding my daughter in my arms, dancing with her in the lounge. I remembered Mike singing it to her when she was only a few days old, how he'd adored her so much, how she looked up at him and that bond they had that no drink, yet, had broken. I listened to that song knowing it would make me cry like a baby, and knowing it would make me want us to be a family again.

The next morning, I opened the fridge and there was a bottle of Irn Bru standing in the door. Just like those cans of beer I'd found hidden in his drawer, it was so much more than just a bottle: it was a sign, a little hello, a fizzy request to keep trying, and a little piece of Mike in my home. I think I might have cried again.

These happier moments, healing and welcome as they were, were only fleeting to begin with, and far from melting into gentleness, Mike's anger and volatility seemed only to increase in the first week or two of his sobriety. He was easily agitated and irritated, his mind seemed occupied all the time with I didn't know what and his mood swings were strong and unpredictable.

I didn't understand it. Why was he still so unpleasant, withdrawn and angry, when he wasn't drinking? I'd seen him sober for days, even weeks, many times before but he was never like *this*. The reason I didn't understand it was because I'd never met a dry drunk before.

The term 'dry drunk' isn't loved by many alcoholics, who quite rightly don't want to be labelled as someone who is in some way a 'drunk', whether sober or not. This is very understandable, but I'm using it here because it's a very clear description of what it is. From what I have witnessed myself, and from many accounts from others, a dry drunk is almost the same as a drunk drunk, but without booze: they still have all the same drink-thinking patterns, symptoms of drinking and behaviours as drunk drunks, but now they have neither the thing they crave to ease their unease, nor the excuse of being so pissed and weakened by drink they can't manage any better.

You might ask why this doesn't happen every time an alcoholic stops drinking for a while, and actually, to a far lesser extent it probably does, as frustrations, anxieties and cravings play havoc with a brain that needs booze and doesn't have it. But when an alcoholic truly goes *into sobriety*, not for a week or a month, but, they hope, forever, and when this change happens after a long period of very heavy drinking, it's an entirely different, thirsty beast.

Their entire physiology and psychology, brain chemistry and personality are being asked to change out of almost all recognition, and many alcoholics experience post-acute withdrawal syndrome, or PAWS, as they fully enter sobriety.

From dizziness to slow reflexes, problems with balance and coordination, physical withdrawal pains, passing out and vomiting to delusions, angry outbursts, sweating, memory problems and paranoia, many horrible, sometimes agonising side effects can wreak utter havoc on a person who's trying to do something every atom of their being doesn't want them to. It takes huge courage and strength, and an adjustment to every aspect of their being, and it can take months, even years, to fully come out of. If anyone can manage that and be angelic, I'd like to meet them.

In his first month of sobriety Mike was often almost indistinguishable from when he was drinking, except he wasn't. He went into rages, kicked walls and swore at me, forgot things, once threw his bike into a hedge on a walk home from nursery and then disappeared for hours, returning like a totally different person, quiet and humble, ashamed and tired; he'd get up and leave us in the middle of the park for no apparent reason and we'd not see him until the next day, or longer, and he'd change his mind constantly about whether he was coming round or not, whether he wanted to stay for dinner, he'd be late for meetings, then get angry, then say sorry, then walk off, and so on.

He didn't *mean* to be this way, and he talks about it now as a terrible time in his mind and body, where nothing he felt or did was as intended. I really did feel sorry for him going through this painful transition into a man he didn't like or want to be, but it was a very difficult few months for me too, filled with yet more aloneness, anxiety, tears, changes, uncertainty and being on the receiving end of some horrible bouts of anger, blame and near constant exhaustion again.

I *had* hoped my life was about to get easier, what with Mike around to help with some parenting now, maybe put the bin out for me once in a while, or even talk a bit, you know, *reconnect* and try to do something involving Not Being Awful, and while there were those fleeting moments of niceness, the dinners, the tentative laughs and even a little hand-hold or a smile, they were baby steps taken cautiously. I did ask myself a lot in these first, hard weeks, which made me very tired and made my anxiety go up again, that if this was Mike sober, then who even *was* he now?

Addiction is the most narcissistic, selfish little motherfucker I've ever known, even in recovery. In fact, maybe *especially* in recovery. Having dominated every part of my existence for its own wants and needs for drinking, it now wanted me to give it everything it required for recovery. Even with the best, most compassionate, patient and generous will in the world, it was very hard to Keep Absorbing And Carry On, to be honest, and one of the biggest things I had to adjust to was sharing my life with AA.

AA is recovery Marmite: people seem to either dedicate the rest of their lives to its workings – literally, as it's saving their life every day – or decide it's absolutely not going on their sobriety toast, thank you. All the stuff about finding your 'higher power' is a bit 'woo-woo' for me, and the God bit puts a lot of people off, which is a shame because it doesn't have to be about God at all. But the fact remains that it *works*, and millions of people feel they owe their lives to it. Wafting around some good intentions and promises, downloading an app or three, watching motivational videos and high-fiving yourself when you go a week without getting pissed hasn't been shown to be a highly successful route to changing one's entire way of thinking. Following an actual programme yields far better long-term results for many people. Anyway, everyone has to choose the recovery path that works for them, and for Mike, it was AA.

A new, secret and mysterious world entered our lives when he joined 'The Fellowship', as it's somewhat cloakily known, filled with words and practices utterly unfamiliar to me, and I found it all quite weird and not a little intrusive, if I'm honest. There were the Twelve Steps, of course, and The Big Book, which Mike read every night now, and then there were things called 'shares' and 'chairs', there were beginners' meetings, open meetings, men's meetings and 'recovery hour meetings' (what were the rest of them, then?), there was secretive note-scribbling, one-to-one rendezvous with a sponsor, clandestine WhatsApp-tapping about God only knew what now, evening phone calls with other addicts or yet again with his sponsor, who just wanted to check in when actually we were trying to attempt some form of healthier, normal family life so could you maybe sod off for a second please, so we can do that? Everything that was shared in these so-called Rooms was kept there, and I felt no part in anything he was saying, learning or thinking. Of course, I get that only an alcoholic can help another alcoholic, because only they know what it's like, but a childish, selfish, lonely and, frankly, *worn out* side of me felt a bit put out that when I'd given everything to him for years, he was now being helped 'properly' by his new superhero alchie mates, all patting each other on the back, giving the 'real support' as only *they* could.

Having waited, begged and shouted at Mike for so long to GO TO AA, despite being very glad of the support, counsel, teaching and biscuits he was getting, many aspects of what it asked of *me* irked me to begin with.

For a start, the meetings he went to were every evening from 6 to 7 p.m. – exactly when toddlers are at their least amenable/

cooperative/delightful in any way. Having already looked after her on my own for the best part of a year, I was now required to hold the fort yet more, while he went off for an hour of mental calm, 'thinking' and healing with his fellow sobriety warriors. He'd come out from meetings in a good, calm frame of mind, having had effectively an hour of free therapy, only to be met by an exhausted mother who hadn't had five seconds of calm all day and needed to vent. If I did voice any of my own frustrations and resentments, he'd get angry because *I* had selfishly and carelessly destroyed any benefits he'd just gained from his meeting and Step Work, and an argument would ensue. I had to tiptoe round him as if he was made of glass, because we can't upset the recovering addict, can we?

I was exhausted, tired, sad and alone in a town I knew very well but in which I had no friendship network yet, I had no babysitting in the evenings or help at home for the most part, and though I needed help too, I wasn't getting any. After a few weeks of this new type of abandonment in favour of the needs of an addiction, I spent yet more evenings in tears, wondering what on earth I'd signed up to, and if I was strong enough to cope with this 'recovery' thing.

What I should have done was go to Al-Anon.

Al-Anon is a 12-Step recovery programme for anyone affected by someone else's drinking, to 'learn a better way of life, to find happiness whether the alcoholic is still drinking or not.' Al-Anon was co-founded in 1951, 16 years after Alcoholics Anonymous, by Anne B. and Lois W. – two wives of recovering alcoholics, one of those being Bill W., the founder of AA itself.

The story goes that they met while they were waiting for their alcoholic husbands to come out of yet another group meeting, and thought … hold on one second, this is a bit shit, isn't it? What about us?

Like many other 12-Step programmes, be it Narcotics Anonymous, Overeaters Anonymous, Co-dependents Anonymous and so on, Al-Anon basically took the Twelve Steps of AA almost word for word, substituting the word 'alcoholics' with 'others' where appropriate. Many of the Steps are identical, for example the famous – and, in my opinion, probably the most important – Step 1: 'We admitted we were powerless over alcohol – that our lives had become unmanageable'.

I can see why they did it this way, and these Steps have been an invaluable tool for personal and spiritual growth and a happier, healthier life for millions. I would even argue that everyone would benefit from some of its teachings, especially the bits about doing a full moral inventory of ourselves and making amends to those we have hurt.

But the carbon copy approach is where Al-Anon and I struggle to fully get along. For me, shoehorning the very specific recovery needs of those who have been affected by an alcoholic into the same mould as those required by the addicts themselves fundamentally misunderstands and almost hurtfully misrepresents both the experiences and feelings we have, which are entirely different from theirs, and what we need in order to recover from the trauma and damage. For me, this approach devalues and almost silences some of the traumas I carry, which is in direct contrast with what I need in order to recover from them – of which more later.

Some of the Steps sit comfortably with me, like those about the 'exact nature of our wrongs' and removing 'all these defects of character'. Others I'd have to ignore if I were to follow the Programme, which probably means it's not the programme for me.

The central tenet seems (to me, anyway) to be that if we could only learn to see our own faults and be more understanding of theirs, if we could only see how we make things worse by reacting the way we do to the torture they've subjected us to, we could be better people and help them more in their recovery, and ourselves in our own. Like I said, this is just the way it feels to me, but I know several other partners who feel the same way and even felt they might be failing as partners of addicts for not agreeing with the teachings or workings of Al-Anon.

While I understand the healing nature of letting go of anger, examining our own faults and not dwelling on the past, I also think there needs to be room for us to be allowed to scream, 'FUCK YOU AND FUCK EVERYTHING YOU'VE DONE TO ME, YOU LYING, ABUSIVE, SELFISH, EGOCENTRIC, MANIPULATIVE, NARCISSISTIC, PARASITIC PIECE OF SHIT. *YOU* SHOULD BE SUPPORTING *ME* AFTER EVERYTHING I'VE SUFFERED THROUGH YOUR BULLSHIT BEHAVIOUR. YOU DESTROYED MY LIFE AND YOU SHOULD GET DOWN ON YOUR FUCKING KNEES, KISS MY FEET AND BEG FOR MY FORGIVENESS EVERY FUCKING DAY.'

I might get this printed on a T-shirt and wear it round the house occasionally, just as a reminder of who gets the non-tap end of the bath, forever.

The first time I went to Al-Anon, or even heard of it, was back in the awful Summer of Madness in 2019. I was desperate for anything to hold on to that might offer me a grain of hope, support and strength in myself to survive what I was living through. But where AA is all about hope, positivity, recovery, a better future, a happier life, a determination to be stronger, healthier and ever more at one with oneself, that one hour in Al-Anon felt like a crash-course in despair. It left me so devoid of any hope of happiness I couldn't face going back for a long time.

Maybe I went to a bad one, maybe I wasn't ready (I *definitely* wasn't ready), maybe everyone that day was in a bad mood, or someone forgot the Custard Creams again or I don't know what, but it was one of the most depressing rooms I've ever been in, and the whole sad hour felt like sitting at a funeral under six feet of lead surrounded by crushed, exhausted, endlessly unhappy victims of misery who knew they were never getting out – or didn't have the energy left to try. There was no uplifting end goal, no pats on the back for another day of improvement, no marks of progress or one-week tokens to say 'well done you, you're fucking amazing', and no clear 'result', other than 'feeling less shit some of the time'. It's not much of a carrot at the end of the gnarly stick, if I'm honest, and I came out of it wanting a drink.

I did go back to Al-Anon a year into Mike's sobriety and it helped me at lot, as we'll come to later – I just think it's important to be prepared that you might not take to it immediately, it's worth trying different groups until you find one you 'click' with, and it's OK to cherry-pick the bits you find helpful and discard the rest.

In December, a month into Mike's sobriety, a new situation presented itself, which required yet another decision I didn't feel entirely qualified to make: Mike's next month of rent was due, and he couldn't pay it as whatever his source of money had been so far was now at an end. I sure as hell wasn't going to pay, and if he couldn't stay in Oxford he would have only one other option: to go back to Scotland. As his previous trips up north had gone *so* brilliantly, it was an almost dead cert that another one would set him back to square one again, or even worse.

As you already know, I am not here to tell anyone else how to live their life, what choices they should make or what's right or wrong for someone else in their own situation. This is *my* story, and only I can ever know how I felt and why I did the things I did. I weighed up and judged each hour and event as it came; I listened to the advice of others and sometimes even managed to take that advice, and I'm glad I did – but at *all* times I went with my gut and did what I felt was right for us.

There are people who will never condone, or perhaps even forgive, the fact that I let someone back into my life who had done what Mike did when he was so unwell. There are those who will always think it was reckless, selfish and unforgivable.

I respect that view, but it's not mine.

Living separately had never proved to be a positive set-up for us for longer than a week or two. Communicating by message or phone is not at all the same as face to face; it makes it easier to reflect on every word, to say things in a slightly different light to how we might if we could see the person, we can hang up and disappear and conversations are often left hanging, unresolved and festering, causing even more problems. I also found it almost impossible to relax when we were living apart, worrying as I did constantly that he might be drinking, or that sitting alone in his thoughts and anxieties might make him even more unwell. Mike didn't much like it either, frankly, being separated from his family and the life he wanted, and he always tended to regress even further into drink when on his own.

I also believe in encouragement and hope, especially when someone is making efforts to change, and Mike certainly was; he had stopped drinking, he was attending AA and his volatility had lessened considerably over the second half of this first month of his sobriety. There was no more kicking walls or throwing bikes, he was far less argumentative, he seemed more grounded in himself, much calmer and more stable, reflective and thoughtful.

There was no pressure put on me to let Mike back in, he didn't ask me to or threaten anything if I didn't. *I* made the decision to let him back into my home, because I judged that it was the right thing to do, for us all.

The house I was renting was very much *my* home, not 'ours'; there were neighbours on both sides whom I knew I could call on if ever I had to, and I knew I could, and would – and, as it transpired, *did* occasionally – tell Mike to get out quicker than he could swear at me in his most colourful Fifeisms.

And so in he came, back to sleeping in my home for the first time in over two months, since that dreadful last night in Venice. I didn't know how to *do* this 'reintegration' of someone into my life, after a period of generally enormous terribleness; should I stagger it by letting him come back for a day or two, then maybe extend to a week if nobody put their hand through a wall or left the toilet seat up? Go Full Immersion, get him a personalised mug, a star chart for good behaviour? Maybe some stickers?

I decided to take the highly scientific Gradual and Cautious approach: see how he was, stick to my boundaries as much as I could and just play each day by ear or argument.

Was I nervous? No. Was I worried something bad might happen? No, I'd never have done it if I'd worried. I was happy to feel some semblance of the life we'd always wanted to have, the house started to smell of him, have his shape and sounds in it, and it felt a little bit like a family home again – though for now one member was very much on probation and Doing Time before his monthly review.

It wasn't smooth sailing and the dry drunk was with us every day in some shape or form, there were still arguments, swearing, lies, accusations of things I hadn't said or done, twisting of reality, much storming off and nasty texts, and I had to ask him to go outside several times to cool off. I remember several abandoned trips to the local pub for pizza because he got so angry between our house and the top of the street the whole thing was called off and I ended up in tears, and we had a massive argument on New Year's Eve, which I felt was rather appropriate considering the whole of the previous year.

It was all very tiring and a huge strain on me when I needed the opposite, but the flare-ups were definitely becoming less frequent, I was getting a *little* better at handling them and so was he, and our family life, delicate though it still was, at least existed again, and that had been the focus of so much of my energy and total devotion all the way through. This *family*, these three people who were so much happier when they were all together than apart. I know it's not enough to say, 'I wanted my daughter to be with her daddy', because almost everyone wants that scenario if it's possible; but I KNEW we could do this if he could just get better, I KNEW beyond any doubt the positive effect it would have on my little girl to have a close, strong and loving relationship with her father, who adored her and was so fantastic with her when he was well, I KNEW the positive effect on him of having his daughter in his life and the devastation in him every time he had to be apart from her, and I knew that if we could make this work we could be the family we had always dreamed of. And that's what I kept on working towards.

By far my greatest fear in those early weeks and months was relapse. Any deviation from The Expected or Agreed Plan, however small, triggered a panicked flurry of where is he, why is he not answering, why is he late, was there an extra red traffic light, or is he in a pub?

None of this was helped by all the chilling relapse stories one hears of people who've been happily sober for 25 years and then walk into Tesco one Tuesday afternoon, buy a bottle of vodka and neck it before they've reached the door, with nothing whatsoever prompting it. They just *did it*.

I remember watching TV series where, in one episode, a guy who'd been sober for eight years walks into a bar and orders a double vodka, just like that, straight into relapse. I couldn't watch the rest of it, just the idea of that happening in our lives affected me so much. Oddly, at least to me, these relapse stories didn't affect *Mike* negatively at all – in fact, he sometimes said they helped him stay straight – but the awful experiences I'd just lived through were so recent and raw, my post-trauma was still coursing through my nerves like needles in my blood, I could hardly bear to hear or think about them.

I spent at least the first half a year of Mike's sobriety like a nervous child, scurrying around doing everything I could to make sure all the 'Right Things' were in place to prevent relapse. I thought that for as long as nothing rocked his boat, if I didn't let any drink into the house, didn't drink or talk about drink, didn't talk about AA, didn't nag or criticise anything he did or didn't do, basically if I became RELAPSE BALM, I could stop it from happening.

Even in sleep my mind was edgy, worrying and wondering: is today the day? It didn't matter how many 'good' months or unfucked-up events had passed, how many angst-laden work trips had gone without incident, how many AA tokens of sobriety had been added to the Hero Box: I *worried*.

I'd still look out for signs, patterns, ever-so-slightly-reddish flags, trends, slips or changes in him to suggest a relapse might be brewing: a darkness around the eyes, a jumpy leg, clenched fists, nervous fingers, sleeping badly, sleeping more, eating better, eating worse, getting fitter, not exercising, being on his phone more, being a little more snappy with me, looking distracted, listening to more music, less talk about Step Work, missing an AA meeting, then two, and saying it's 'ok, I'm fine, really', or not saying anything at all.

I knew it could happen any time, any day: on his way to work, in a lunch break, on a day off, during a quick trip to the supermarket, before a wedding, after a funeral, on the school run, on a train, in the park. It might last two hours, or forever. He might get angry, he might lose his job, fall under a bus, sleep with someone else, run up gambling debts, smash his laptop or vanish. He might die. Every day felt like rolling the Relapse Dice, and all I could do was hope it kept landing on the right number.

My worry wasn't exactly eased by Mike telling me repeatedly that if he ever *did* relapse it would be worse than the last time. Given the last time was The Worst Thing In The World Ever, as far as I was concerned, this didn't exactly put me at ease.

The first anniversary of each Bad Incident – and my God, there were a lot – was horrible; I dreaded their arrival and when each one came the memories of what had happened that day crashed me into a huge low filled with tears, flu-like symptoms, aches and pains from the PTSD, trembling and generally feeling so shit that I could barely think, eat, talk or be with Mike at all until the day had passed.

It would be so easy to say, 'Why didn't you just chill out and realise there's nothing you could do anyway, so just go with the flow?'

Well, because that's not how the mind or body work, and trauma takes years to overcome, as do deep, lifelong emotional responses to fear and detachment. I know I can't prevent relapse even if I gaffer-tape him to the sofa: if he wants to drink, he will find a way, but learning to detach from all worry and care is hard, and to be completely honest, I'm not sure I will ever stop worrying altogether, nor that I want to; the point at which I detach to the point of not caring is the point that I'm no longer in love.

By three months into his sobriety, the improvements in Mike's general well-being were already palpable and visible: he'd lost over a stone of the weight he'd gained while drinking, eating junk and lying on friends' sofas or propping up bars, he'd rediscovered some dormant abdominal muscles hiding under a pillow of beer-fat, and he'd gone back to being fully vegan again – as ever, in the way only an addict can: *obsessively*. But as obsessions go, vegetables and tofu were ones I was pretty OK with.

Around this time a piece of very good news arrived, in the form of employment; barista/photographer Mike was now Postman Mike, delivering in the local area, with working hours that fitted around our family life very well. The change this work brought to his whole outlook on life, and himself, was extraordinary: after so long in the work wilderness, he regained some routine, accountability, purpose, self-respect and responsibility, he had money coming in at last so he didn't feel like a child any more, having to ask for pocket money or crawling to friends and family for another little top-up. As a postal worker he was a valued and valuable member of the community, and he had some colleagues to chat, bitch and laugh with in the depot every morning, providing much-missed social interaction and 'banter'. It also helped *me*, because he could send me photos when he was out on his rounds and call me any time, and just knowing where he was brought me some peace of mind and calm, if my long-primed nerves got the better of me again, as they so often did – and even now, are still prone to do.

I felt very proud, watching him heading out every morning in his Post Office uniform, bag over his shoulder, off to work on his bike. *I* knew how unwell he'd been so very recently, and what a massive amount of work it had taken for him to be able to do this.

But the rollercoaster of recovery is bumpy, and one piece of good news didn't mean we were out of the choppy waters yet. There was always another shock, challenge and unexpected difficulty just around the corner, and of all of these, I think the 'sober relapses' were the hardest for me. I didn't know they could happen, I didn't even know what they *were*, and the first few times they occurred, I was completely blindsided.

The first one came just over three months into Mike's sobriety, in March 2020. Looking back, there had been a few little signs of inner unrest that I perhaps missed in all the new excitement of his job, healthier lifestyle and so on, but they *were* there: he had become a little tense and distracted again, and things he was very vigilant about started to slacken – coffee cups were left on the floor and the window ledge, his clothes, more recently hung up neatly and folded carefully as part of his recovery and self-awareness, were now piled in a dirty heap on the bed, junk food had started to creep into his diet and the daily workouts he'd started doing at home had been dropped. He mentioned that he'd started having relapse dreams for the first time, waking up in a sweat, certain he'd been shit-faced all night and had done awful things, and they were so vivid he was often withdrawn the day after, unsettled and angsty again. I suppose I thought it was all just a normal part of his transition into long-term sobriety, but he did seem to be in an uncomfortable place in himself, as if wrestling an unease, and the pressure in the home cooker had definitely risen a bit.

At this exact point in his recovery, Mike was asked to go to Edinburgh for an urgent photo shoot. I found the timing of this 'urgent' shoot somewhat coincidental, to say the least, and the location to be spectacularly unfortunate – or fortunate, perhaps, for him: being in Edinburgh was the perfect excuse for relapse because, frankly, who *wouldn't* have a pint in an old watering hole, hundreds of miles away from their partner who nagged about coffee cups and laundry? It wouldn't be his *fault*.

Edinburgh was also trigger-tastic for me, and even the thought of him going back there, so soon after the hurt of the last times, sent my anxieties and post-trauma nerves into overdrive. I mentioned my concerns, for him and for me, but he was insistent that if he didn't push himself into these uncomfortable situations, he would never get over them and move forward. Furthermore, if I didn't let him go, *I* was preventing him from making progress. Oh, *and* he promised he would give me half the money he earned.

Summary: it will be your fault if you say I can't go and my recovery then stalls, but if you let me do what I want, I'll give you some money. The manipulation, as I felt it, was phenomenal, and bar locking him in the attic, I effectively had no say in the matter at all. I remember it as being a big source of stress to me, all these triggers and painful memories, and having no power or voice to change anything.

I'll never know if something happened up there, whether Mike had a drink or not, if some memories were jogged that threw him into a bad place, but whatever it was, or wasn't, the Mike who came back was not the Mike who'd left two days before. He arrived home looking distant and stormy, and had that dreadful dead-dog look I knew so well; he was both emotionally withdrawn and more aggressive than I'd seen him for weeks, he barely talked about the trip at all and any time I asked about it he was touchy, snappy and shut the conversation down immediately with an 'It was fine, OK, and there's nothing more to say.'

He went to AA as usual that evening and seemed a little calmer afterwards, and we had dinner all together, went through the usual bath and stories routine with our daughter and settled her to sleep.

Then a row started. I don't remember what about or what prompted it, but it seemed to set fire to a touchpaper of months of pent-up resentments and stress. An explosion of emotions ensued, insults flying hard and fast, shouting, accusations, lies, old grievances and new hates, walls being hit, clothing being thrown at me, and when the old 'fuck off, you're a nutter' stuff kicked off again, I told him to leave the house immediately, because this was all completely unacceptable.

He started packing his bag, telling me what a prick I was, how I provoked him and goaded him into being like this, I was mad, I was a bitch and he'd had enough. On his way out he kicked a wooden shoe cupboard by the front door, leaving it in a heap of splinters all over the floor, said he wasn't going to work any more, and he was done with this relationship and with his life, then slammed the door behind him and went out into the dark.

Before he could have even reached the end of the road he messaged to say he was clearly not OK at all, he was still just an angry alcoholic and all the recovery stuff was bullshit:

> Everything feels so alien these days, I don't understand what I am or think or do. I hate being in my head, I hate it. I can't sit still. I'm going mad. I can't do this.

I sat at the bottom of the stairs looking at the smashed wood, the assortment of shoes spread out across the floor, my 'good vibes only' house vandalised by this ugly disease.

How could this have happened again when he'd been so well? How could this be happening, if he was *sober*?

That was the first time I understood that 'sober' doesn't mean 'cured' or 'well', it just means sober. Sober is the starting point, not the end. It's essential for recovery but in itself it is not recovery at all. That comes slowly, day by day, year by year, bump by bump, and the first whole year is so bumpy at times it's hard to stay on the road at all.

We took a few days to process what had happened, for him to talk to his sponsor and go to a few more meetings, and then to talk together. He was possibly the calmest and most apologetic I'd seen him since he sobered up, and really did seem to be shocked at what had come out of him, what was still there to be faced and mended and how angry he could be even when he wasn't drinking. It was quite sad, really, seeing the reality hit home and the enormity of recovery being recognised. It was very hard for us both, in our own ways, to have these stark reminders of what we were going through, how much we had to learn, to cope with, how much we were in our infancy in it all, and how far there was still to go. But we carried on, because every day was another day closer to the place we wanted to reach.

The word 'alcoholic' is a bit of a grenade, and sometimes the pin is pulled when you don't expect it to be – and the consequences can be pretty intense.

I've thought long and hard about whether I should include this part of our story at all, but I've always been very uncomfortable about omitting something so tied up with alcoholism and families, and which affects many people who didn't expect it either. Even in my small group of friends who live with alcoholic partners I know three other families who went through something similar, also unexpectedly and also causing much distress, and as this is a story of what happened to me and *not* something that seeks to give advice, I feel I have a duty to include it, because if I'd known what might happen and how to handle it better, it might have helped me deal with it much better.

I was feeling really quite shaken up about the stress and pressures that had bubbled up – and bubbled over – at home recently, and for the first time in a few months I started to feel emotionally in a bad place, tearful, weak, and feeling hopeless about how to deal with things. This concerned me a little, and, knowing what I do about mental health and spotting signs and asking for help, I decided it would be sensible to talk with my new doctor, just as a matter of precaution in case I should have some counselling, or some medication if I needed it to manage the emotional strains better.

During the appointment, I spoke openly about the previous few years, that my partner was an alcoholic, now in recovery and sober for four months, that I'd had an extremely difficult time of it all. When asked, I said yes, there had been arguments, some of them very unpleasant, but he was doing well at his recovery and making very good progress, and things were much better now, and progressing, albeit with bumps along the way, as is expected. I told her we were happy in Oxford, that Mike had a good, stable job, I was writing a new book, our daughter was settled and happy at nursery and at home, and life was definitely the best it had been for a long time; I just wanted to have a little talk about *my* health, to make sure I was doing all I should to manage it. All good, I thought.

Four days later, I was at home playing with my daughter in our garden when my phone rang. A woman at the other end introduced herself and began saying something about 'child safeguarding' and 'social services' and a 'referral'.

My heart rate shot up and I thought I was going to be sick. I'd had no warning about this call, I'd never heard of the agency she said she was calling from, I didn't know what they *do* or why I was even involved with them. I had no idea what was going on, I just knew that I was terrified that something was about to split this family apart, because one of us was an alcoholic and we had argued and we were deemed 'bad parents'.

This call was the start of one of the most distressing experiences of my entire 22-year parenting life at the time; out of the blue, and just when we needed a sense of security and calm, Mike and I found ourselves thrown into an agonising two months of phone interrogations, confusion and worry. Every aspect of my life was called into question and picked apart: the fact that my youngest daughter had a different father from her siblings, that I was a tenant here not a house owner, that I'd had periods of depression and anxiety, a history of an eating disorder, I'd been prescribed antidepressants in the past, I was self-employed so I didn't have an employer to give any reference as to my well-being as a human, I had been moving house a lot recently – but don't worry, they said, all of this would be discussed by 'The Team'.

If I got upset in any way, as any parent would under such unnerving circumstances, I was told I seemed 'agitated' or sounded 'upset': was I having trouble controlling my moods? Was I feeling unable to remain calm?

The calls always came without warning, and always when I was with my toddler, so a long, emotionally intense phone call was almost impossible because she'd start to get fractious and whiny that I wasn't playing with her, and *then* they'd ask why my child was upset, as if I was being neglectful. If I said it wasn't an ideal time to talk and maybe they could call back when she was asleep, it was suggested that I was trying to avoid the subject or wasn't 'able' to have a phone conversation while being with my daughter at the same time; did I find everyday life hard to handle?

I could almost hear the guillotine falling onto my family life with every word.

It's a difficult situation, because every doctor has a serious duty of care to every patient and every child of a patient, and if they have any genuine and well-founded concerns about the well-being of either, it should be looked into immediately and thoroughly. I suppose the positive message from this episode is that things *can* move very fast indeed, which is good in cases where it's necessary. But I don't believe our situation at that time should have resulted in such a referral, with no warning or even a mention of it before the call came, and it put us through months of anxiety, sleepless nights, tears, more arguments and more distress, when we needed it least.

We got the all-clear in the end and everything was pronounced absolutely fine, but I still get sick with worry sometimes about what might unexpectedly come back to bite us in the future about a time that was so difficult, but which is now well behind us.

None of this should in any way discourage someone from telling a health professional, a doctor, a counsellor, *anyone*, if they have even the slightest worry about their safety or that of their family. Everyone involved was simply doing their job – a vital job that saves many lives every year – and all I had to do was keep calm, answer their questions and it would all be fine because it *was* fine, they just needed to be sure of that. But at the time, what with everything that had been going on and the manner and tone with which it was handled, only further knocked my mental well-being at a time when I was just starting to mend it, and needed a little love and care, not more fear. It's made me cagey about the whole 'system', and that's a real shame because it's there for my protection, and the protection of all families who need it.

By four months into Mike's recovery, in March 2020, the COVID-19 pandemic was in full swing around the world and the UK went into lockdown. Overnight, we lost all the normality and routine we'd just got in place, and relied on: nursery was closed, shops, libraries and museums were closed, AA meetings couldn't take place in person any more, and we were suddenly confined to a house containing someone who needed all of the above to stay well. It was pretty much Mike's worst set-up, and I honestly didn't know how the hell we would cope.

Cue Lady Luck, fresh from her four-year sabbatical leave, stepping up in the nick of time to transform what could have been another disaster into a blessing. For a start, as a postman Mike was classed as a 'key worker' so he carried on working throughout the whole of lockdown, allowing him to maintain some daily routine and purpose. Secondly, all AA meetings were now online, which turned out to be a huge bonus for *me*: all he had to do was pop upstairs and log in, leaving me holding the fort on my own for less time, and also safely in the knowledge that he was actually *there*.

Lastly, and maybe most unexpectedly, with no ability for either of us to go anywhere, go missing anywhere, be unaccountable or out of reach, we found ourselves in a strange little lockdown cocoon of time together. A lot of time.

We started talking about everything that had happened in the last two or three years, and for the first time ever he was able to shove his addict's ego into the corner for a minute, and listen to how it had been for *me*.

It was very hard for him to hear, I'm sure, and not everyone can do it – at least not so early into recovery. But he *did* listen, and for the first time since it had all kicked off, way back before I'd even got pregnant with our now two-year-old, he was able to self-analyse and criticise, be accountable for his own actions and their consequences to me, take blame where it was due, say sorry and *mean* it (quite the revelation), see when he wasn't being honest with himself and silence his own guilt enough to let my side of things have their moment to be heard.

Of course he could still get angry when he felt frustrated or his own recovery progress was harder or slower than he wanted, but the difference was that he could say sorry afterwards and mean it, and the little flurries of harsh words and sighs were now short-lived and calmly resolved.

PART NINE

Lockdown and Breakdown

Leonard Cohen said there's a crack in everything, and that's where the light gets in. Unfortunately, for me, that little crack is also where my darkness sneaks out, and, somewhat annoyingly, this often happens when there's a pause in all the stress and struggle, and I find a moment to rest, and STOP.

For all its inconveniences and restrictions, lockdown brought the first period of rest from all the incessant stress and *doing* that I'd had for several years: the book I'd been writing in Venice had now been published, I'd recently pitched a new book idea to my agent – you've nearly finished reading it, by the way – and while we were waiting to hear back from the publishers she'd sent it to, there was nothing much I could do. I suddenly found myself with no deadlines, no work pressures, and lots of *time* … to *be*. The weather was glorious, a proper hot English May, my daughter's nursery was closed for lockdown, and we went for long walks in the park and along the river every day, she'd skip through the buttercups and delight in ripping catkins off the willows before stuffing them into her pockets, as toddlers do; we watched dragonflies carpet-bombing the lily pads and dipped our feet in the river, ate ice cream and lay on the trampoline watching white clouds against blue sky. I started keeping a daily diary of things I was grateful for, challenges I had coped with well that day, and things I intended to do better.

As the pace of my life slowed down and all my self-protective, truth-filtering blinkers were dropped, I began an unexpected sort of 'unpicking' of the whole story of me and Mike, looking back over everything that had happened between us through a new, revealing filter: every event, conversation, decision and argument, his ever-changing work schedule back in Cambridge, the frequent and sudden trips to the shop, all those delays on his way home, unaccountable hours and vanishing money.

I felt stupid and cheated, for all the things I'd believed, or not known about: the bottles and cans hidden above my head or behind the sofa in Venice; the litres of wine downed while I read stories to our baby, the thousands I'd given him that turned out to be gambling debts; the hours I spent alone while pregnant or with a newborn so he could work more, when all that money was going elsewhere; the stag do, the gig in London, the work leaving drinks, that awful day I went to IKEA and he got so hammered, throwing him out of the bar in Via Garibaldi, the rugby event he'd insisted on going to, passing out on his birthday, running away to Barcelona and Scotland to 'clear his head', the efforts made to help him and let him have what he said he needed, and all the time it was lies, excuses, and deceptions everywhere.

Had he said *anything* true to me since we met? Had he even *wanted* a baby or was that yet another fantasy to try and create a family life he thought he should want? Did he even mean to get engaged, or was that yet another method of trying to construct a Mike he wanted to be, but wasn't?

Was he too drunk to have been present at most of the key moments in our lives together? *Did 'we' ever actually exist at all??*

All of this unpicking and re-writing in my mind was made all the worse when I started writing this book, and I had to go back over all of our messages, the hundreds of photographs I'd taken through every day of this car crash, videos of Mike falling about the streets of Venice, heart-breaking voice messages of love, despair and rage. I had to piece it all together, relive it all, word by word, event by event, trauma by trauma.

The hundreds of questions this raised in me tormented me for months as the jigsaw we'd made together started coming apart and rearranging itself, pieces I'd loved being thrown out and replaced with new, hideous ones. I wanted to know what our *true* picture looked like, what colours and shape it had, what it was even a picture *of*; I wanted to see it for what it was, get to know it and love it again – but I couldn't tell what was truth and what was lies any more, what was real and what I'd imagined. So I couldn't finish it and get any sense of closure or peace, and the whole process knocked me to the floor.

As Mike was going through his spiritual metamorphosis from fucked-up caterpillar to reasonably functioning butterfly, as the year wore on, the summer of lockdown dragged strangely through its timeless weeks and months and I re-lived so many painful feelings and memories in the writing of this book, I sort of ... fell apart.

It was as if someone had told me I could let go now, so I did. Completely. Having shouldered, carried and coped for so long, I felt too tired, too weak, too broken to be able to hold up a life in which I could never properly rest, never know when the next relapse would come, where I'd be constantly aware that the ground could be kicked from under my feet at any second without warning. I think I was even *jealous* of him for looking so well, clear-skinned and bright-eyed, with a good job and a support network while here *I* was, washed-up, skinny, ragged and aged, and even if I did find the energy to meet up with anyone I had far too little confidence and too much social anxiety now to see it through.

I shrank further into myself, stripped of all confidence about any part of myself from my work to my appearance, my relationship with Mike, friendships and even myself as a mother, and as I withered emotionally, so my old, self-destructive control mechanisms saw their chance to come back, just as all his were going away.

I was already thin but I got thinner. Dangerously thinner. I wanted to shrink away and become invisible – but maybe more than that, I think I wanted my suffering to become unmissably visible to *him*; I wanted him to notice *me* for once, to step up, come to me, take the reins, be my bloody 'rock' or whatever they call it. I wanted him to *help* me and give me love as I'd given it to him.

But it didn't work. Of course it didn't: you can't help someone else if every grain of your energy is needed to help yourself, and an addict in early recovery still has no space for anything but their own needs for a long time. Far from coming closer and being any form of rock for me to lean on, Mike was more like quicksand for me to drown in; he retracted from me as I became more unwell, as if it was too much for him to have someone else's problem to deal with, while having to focus all his energies on his own.

He *was* concerned for me, and said as much, but he had no idea what to do, and was finding it hard to deal with. I'll never know if it was because I'd stopped holding everything together or if it was going to happen anyway, but almost exactly one year into Mike's sobriety he had a major relapse in his mood and behaviour.

Things had got a little strained in the week or so leading up to it, I'm not entirely sure why, but there were work worries and deadlines to think about. By now it was November so it was dark and cold, we were still in semi-lockdown in the UK so there wasn't anything to *do* – all the shops and cinemas, swimming pools and restaurants had now been closed for months – and I guess both of us were getting frustrated and bored with life. I was working hard on this book to get it finished on time, Mike was still doing his postal job but there was a strong atmosphere of frustration in him, as if his lack of creative fulfilment, topped with my work pressures, and lockdown and the weather and having a toddler who was also quite fed up with lockdown, was all just too much.

He'd become a bit snappy again of late, but he didn't appear to be down on himself as he'd often been before, rather there was a sense that life was holding him back, and he was ready to break free and achieve great things. He started making grand plans to chuck in his job and set up a shop in town to sell T-shirts and hoodies he'd been designing and was going to open a coffee bar in it too, and run the place himself. He'd even contacted some commercial real estate agents about prime properties in the centre of Oxford, and when I asked about the *cost of all this* given I was still covering by far the majority of the household bills, rent and childcare, he said he'd be making a profit almost immediately because 'I know all about these things, OK?' These bizarre, new delusions of grandeur, an urgent need to *do it now* and a palpable frustration at being held back from global domination by everything and anything were all horribly similar to his past addictive traits of lack of proper planning or any hook on reality, abandoning projects, quitting jobs or buying things he had to have but never used.

One mid-November morning, while our daughter was at nursery, we had our first major argument for months. Mike announced that our relationship was over and he was leaving, again, and started *listing* reasons why.

He said now he was sober he could see everything clearly for the first time and he didn't think he was the kind of person who should be in a relationship with anyone. He said the recent downturn in my well-being had made me withdrawn and difficult, he couldn't connect to me any more, my PTSD made things too hard for us to mend, all the damage he had caused was irreparable and we would never be free of it or happy together. He said we had nothing in common, didn't like the same music or even like the same parts of town – all very rational reasons for two parents to split up – but, worst by far, he said he felt no empathy for me and didn't even care that I was so unwell – in fact if anything, it annoyed him.

Oh, and he wasn't done yet; he said he'd already found a room to rent for a few days so he could get his head straight and work out his future, and he had an appointment to view a house in a town nearby that he might want to rent longer term. He wanted fifty-fifty shared custody of our daughter because he was just as responsible as me now, in fact maybe *more* so because I wasn't very well, so arguably she should live with him, really, and he could afford the childcare now because she was nearly three years old so she'd qualify for 30 hours a week free at nursery.

I stood in our living room shaking, taking blow after blow of shock after shock, delivered calmly and coldly. I didn't understand. Who *was* this person, destroying me again, now seemingly in such control, while I was crumbling?

How could he do this when he was *sober*? How could he say these things, *sober*??

He could say them, because he wasn't saying anything he meant: it was just a massive emotional relapse, a panic about everything he had to keep together now, everything he had to do, everything he was, and feared and couldn't handle. It's happened a few times since, and NOW I know what it is. But I didn't then, and in my weakened state it was all too much. I couldn't take another split, another round of pain, and my mind cracked.

I started screaming. Like *really* screaming, soul-emptying, air-smashing screaming, scratching my arm and hitting my head with my hands to smash away everything I could feel. I'm embarrassed and ashamed that a grown woman, a *mother*, could behave like that, but it's what long-term trauma can do, especially when re-ignited.

Mike didn't come to console or calm me. He put on his coat, told me I was a nutter and left.

He stayed in a bed and breakfast in town for two weeks after that, and I found it very hard to cope with, to be honest. While he had all the time in the world – again – to sit on his bed and think, attend his AA meetings, call his sponsor and be entirely self-absorbed, I was back where I'd been so many times, left to cope on my own with my work and a child, and a shocked heart and nerves. Almost a year to the week since I'd packed up our whole Venice life and driven to Oxford in that van, here I was, on my own, again, in tears. I remember going to the market in town one morning to buy some flowers to cheer myself up, and I looked so bloody awful and was crying so much they gave them to me free of charge. I went and sat on the steps by the Bodleian Library, exactly where I'd been a little over a year before when Mike had left for Scotland again, calling me a dick as a parting gift, and I'd heroically decided to start my life over, like the superwoman I was. And here I was now, in tears yet again. Well done me.

That final, temporary break-up in November reminded me of the words of the French lady at Stansted airport: 'The only person in the world you can rely on is yourself.'

But *could* I? I didn't seem able to rely on myself at all, except to fall apart.

I sat and thought about who – and *how* – I was, not only as a result of the last few years, but before that even: my eating problems as a teenager; the episodes of depression and panic I'd had in my thirties; the self-harm I inflicted upon myself by starvation, bulimia or, more recently, cutting myself; the increase in my drinking in the last year or so, when I was stressed or depressed; my attachment and detachment issues, nervous disposition and increasingly volatile, uncontrollable moods.

A student walked past, carrying books and a takeaway coffee. He had a confidence about him that said he knew he could have a good life ahead and was striding forward to make it happen. I thought about what kind of a future *I* wanted, if I wanted one at all, and something about that student and his air of limitless possibility really hit home. I *did* want a future, but it didn't look like this, and if I wanted it to look better I'd have to do some major self-examination, ask myself some difficult questions about my thought patterns, mental health, addictive tendencies, unhealthy coping mechanisms and general well-being – or unwell being.

In a way, I had to do exactly what Mike was doing. And if he could do it, then so could I.

While he checked into his bed and breakfast, I checked into a new place too: myself. My own truths and problems, my own recovery and my own coming clean.

There are as many ways to go into recovery as there are ways to fall over in the first place, but I think the key to long-term success is to find what works for YOU. If you need a programme, follow a programme; if you need to be told what to do, do that; if you prefer a more flexible, self-motivated approach, then do that. As long as it *works for you.*

Whether it's independent-minded or downright stubborn I'm not sure, but I'm not a great follower of doctrine and I don't tend to respond well to imposed Rules and Systems. For better or worse, I like to follow my own instinct – as you might have noticed – and retain the freedom to do what feels organic and right for *me*. If I could just work out what that was.

Personal Revolutions don't happen overnight and it's hard to start an epic *Grand Designs*-style renovation of your entire being, if 'you' don't exist. How can you identify with yourself if your whole self has become wrapped up in someone else? What and who exactly are you trying to change, what are you trying to create and how the hell do you find the right Allen keys?

I wasn't even aware of the extent of my 'Self Houdini Act' until I took step one of this self-created Plan Me and got myself a psychotherapist. I hadn't spoken with a therapist since those crazy days in Venice, but it really felt to me that this was the right time to do it again.

After four sessions she asked me if I was aware that I hadn't mentioned myself once outside of the context of Mike: Mike's drinking, Mike's behaviour towards me, my life with Mike, my traumas with Mike, my love for Mike, my *everything* connected to Mike.

I hadn't noticed this, no, but now she'd mentioned it … maybe she had a point? (She did. That's her job.)

My entire identity, self-worth and confidence had been so reduced to rubble by gaslighting, lies and fear, I didn't know who I *was* any more. Even when pressed, I found it impossible to say what I thought, wanted or even *felt*, separate to other people, notably Mike. Compassion is a desire to reduce someone's suffering, and empathic people make excellent compassion-givers to others. In doing everything to reduce Mike's suffering, I'd done nothing at all to lessen my own. I had given *my* needs almost zero value and let his dominate everything, and the weaker I'd got the less I'd fought back, and the more I'd tried to silence my sadness through destructive distractions because I hadn't learned – or hadn't put the work in to learn – any other ways of coping with stress or distress.

Even when I'd *tried* to focus on myself – going to Scandinavia, telling him to get out of my flat, 'starting over' in my new place in Oxford, buying bath bombs and candles – it was always a new start or a break *away from him*, which is not at all the same as a new start *towards myself*.

I was a mess – a high-functioning mess, certainly, but a mess all the same – and the task for me now was to find ways of valuing myself, giving myself some love, care and compassion, and focusing on my needs, not always his. This is much easier said than done, but as the weeks went by and I talked, listened and learned from my therapist, I slowly began to uncover and re-connect with a 'me' who had disappeared and lost her voice a long time ago. She's a long way from being fully back yet, but I know she's in there, and bit by bit, I'm finding her again, and giving her some new wings.

One of the most useful things I did to help my own recovery and understand Mike's better was speaking not only to other partners of alcoholics, but to other alcoholics in recovery. This happened initially through social media, as I started to follow the recovery journeys of people on Twitter or Instagram, tentatively liking a post or asking a question, and eventually engaging in

conversation. The honesty I found there was amazing: strangers
opened up to me about the thinking patterns of alcoholics, the
lies they tell themselves and how these spill into lies to others,
how many of them had said or done similar things to Mike, had
also had horrible dry-drunk episodes and behaved abominably
to their partners or families, then regretted it. I learned why
it can happen, where it can stem from and how recovery is so
much about self-'unpacking', honesty, awareness, accountability
and learning new ways to think and react. Hearing all of this
from people to whom I wasn't emotionally connected and
by whom I hadn't been hurt, from voices on the outside who
had been in Alcoholics Anonymous or Narcotics Anonymous
long enough to become less prickly or defensive than many
newcomers can be – and Mike was too, until some way into his
second year of recovery – was hugely helpful to me, and I think it
made a very significant difference to my recovery, and to the way
I supported Mike in his.

It was a window into the workings of the whole illness, not
just one person's expression of it, and I think it was key to our
eventual recovery *together* rather than apart, as it so easily could
have ended up.

I also went to a few AA meetings in person, not when Mike
was there, of course, to see how it works and try to understand
it better – and, in truth, to see if I might need something like this
when my own destructive, addictive behaviours come back, and I
don't feel I can manage them on my own. I sat quietly at the back
and listened to the stories, saw how it worked and what Mike did
in there week after week, how much work it took for everyone
there to stay clean every day, how humble and respectful they
were of their addiction and how much they were there to support
each other as much as themselves. It humbled me too, and I
understand far better why he goes, why he *has* to go, and just
how precarious the line of recovery really is.

Some people regularly go to meetings with their recovering
partners, some alcoholics go to Al-Anon meetings, and

there are recovery programmes specifically for couples, and I think all of this mutual support and sharing of experiences is to be encouraged, where it can happen: the more we can understand what we *each* go through, the greater our chance of recovery all round.

PART TEN

Recovery

And so here we are. The end of all that, and the start of whatever comes next.

I'd love to say I've reached a state of honey-coated Zen, that I'm stronger than I've ever been, I'm invincible now, my resilience is like steel, I've forgiven and forgotten it all and I'm sitting here now basking in gratitude with glowing skin, bouncy hair and a broad smile.

I'd love to say all that, but that's not how real life and recovery work – at least, not in one year. I naively thought that by this time I might have risen phoenix-like from the wreckage, strong and well, reborn and reconstructed, and I *have* had some good periods of feeling much better. But breakdown lasts, and it's turning out that recovery from the effects of someone else's alcoholism is as long as recovery from the addiction itself, and there's still almost no part of my life that isn't affected by what happened.

Physically, I'm slowly mending: the scars on my arms are fading, though the bigger ones still show clearly if I'm tanned, and the exhaustion-wrinkles on my face are softening. My teeth suffered a lot from all the grinding at night caused by anxiety (I had three extractions and numerous root-canal treatments in the two years of Mike's worst drinking – go figure) but there's been no more damage since then and they just are what they are now. I'm still a little underweight and my heart still has palpitations and arrhythmia, which they think was caused by chronic stress and anxiety, plus the weight loss, but my body really *is* getting healthier as time passes and a bit of recovery is taking place.

The psychological damage is still major, and not getting a whole lot better yet, to be honest, and I think my PTSD and heightened anxiety are probably the most prominent and regularly debilitating after-effects for me.

Not a day goes by when there isn't some trigger or reminder of a trauma or fear, a pang of sadness or anxiety. Sometimes I can pause, and then carry on; other days my nerves are more sensitive and my mind goes into a spin again, I call him just to be sure he's at work and not on a plane to Edinburgh – or Barcelona, or I have a little cry.

This isn't helped by the fact that Mike is so early in his recovery he still exhibits a lot of behaviour traits that send warning signals to my brain: buying things he doesn't need when he'd just said five times he won't do that any more; suddenly going to an extra AA meeting 'just because I feel I should', saying things that don't quite match up to what he said the day before, and so on.

My therapy has helped me deal with this a little better, and as I get more practised at not spiralling into negative thinking I'm finding that my calmer, more controlled responses are slowly becoming the norm.

The loss of my trust, not just in Mike but in almost everything, really, is a huge hurdle for me to overcome. When everything you believe to be true is broken, it's hard to fully put one's faith in anything or anyone again.

Trust is a fundamental part of being free, and I used to think about my mistrust and fear a lot; I wondered if it was fair on either of us to be in a partnership where old uncertainties can muddy a perfectly clear day, spoil a nice event or restrict freedoms, and I used to be frustrated with myself for still worrying and being suspicious of bad things going on: why couldn't I just let go of the past and enjoy the good things we had now? Why did I have to dredge it all up at every opportunity, panic when nothing bad had happened and suspect the worst? How was this *helping* us?

It wasn't, and it doesn't; but it's just the profound effect of repeatedly broken trust, of being let down by people you love, by the medical system and by everything you thought would be there to catch you, and unless you're entirely emotionally disconnected from any sense of self-preservation, it's probably sensible not to trust after all that.

The only *truth* I know is that I will never know the truth of much of what happened, and the only person who can decide how to live at peace with that is me.

My trauma will take many, many years to heal, but I know it can if I put the work in, do the therapy, read the books, practise my self-care, be kind to myself, give it time, and keep working to get better.

So easily written, *so* hard to do. But all I can do is want to try, and keep trying.

The whole subject of alcohol is now pretty much wrecked for me, which I find very sad. I used to enjoy a drink with friends or at home, and it was never a big issue, a source of guilt or concern. Now it's a constant, background fridge-hum of problems, almost as jarring when it falls silent as while it's chugging away.

I haven't had a drink at home for at least two years. I used to without any problems at all, but now I would feel very uncomfortable drinking in front of Mike. *He* says he doesn't mind at all and I believe him, but to me it's all a bit like waving the bomb that nearly killed him right in his face.

Socialising is also a minefield of anxieties now. We went to a barbeque with friends when Mike was nine months sober and I spent the whole evening worrying that this kind of laid-back 'summer chill-out with mates' vibe was exactly the kind of thing that would make him yearn to crack open a beer and he might decide to just give it a go, now he was 'better'. We are yet to tackle a wedding or Christmas party, and if any of his friends have a stag do, I'll be downing Valium for the duration.

Mike always says he's fine being around drink and it doesn't bother him one bit to see others drinking. That's great and everything, but it bothers *me* because I'm not in his head, I'm not in control of his thinking, cravings and wobbles, and I worry he might suddenly decide to have that 'one safe beer' when he's out with his mates or on a photo shoot and the after-work pints are being handed round, and the devastating consequences of that to our lives.

Conversely, I also dread *not* going out and having so little fun that one of us will combust if we don't GO THE HELL OUT AND HAVE SOME FUN – after all, we might find someone else to do it with. So I feel a bit doomed if we do and doomed if we don't, but all I can do is see how it all goes over time.

In recovery, people talk about finding the similarities not the differences between each person's experiences with addiction and recovery, in a bid to avoid the old, 'yeah, but I'm not like *that* person' excuse for carrying on with bad habits. The old 'yet' game, again. But as the partners of addicts, our recovery, and what it needs, is very different to an addict's.

Firstly, we are recovering from the effects of someone *else's* actions, not our own, and that requires a lot of forgiveness, detachment and letting go of resentments.

Secondly, we don't really have a *target,* as such, except 'getting by a bit better than we did before', and that's very different to the motivation and sense of achievement of counting the successful sober days or going to meetings where people are celebrating theirs.

Lastly, and this is a very big, significant difference, most of us can't share what we are going through openly, without implicating or exposing someone else. There are quite a few support networks out there, notably those on social media, that some partners and family members of alcoholics I know don't feel they are able to use or interact with because it would mean 'outing' their partner or friend or family member. I am lucky, in that Mike actively encourages and supports me to talk about his alcoholism in public, to try and highlight what partners go through, and give some hope and support to others. I receive many private messages from people who want to say thank you for what I share about our journey, but they can't reply on a public platform or even become part of a community online that might give them real support and advice, because they can't talk about it openly.

Protecting someone else's anonymity is essential, and that's one of the reasons why Al-Anon exists. But it does mean that our side of the story is often kept quiet and secret, and some partners don't feel able to tap into a rich source of support from which they might really benefit. The resources out there in the addiction recovery community are immense, and people's sobriety journeys are immensely supported by sharing their number of days sober, their feelings and worries, the things that help them stay dry and so on. But those on the other side can't slap a post on Twitter saying, '175 days since my partner last swore at me before passing out on the stairs, pissed – #recoveryfromthem' and get 400 people saying 'go you, you got this, you're doing so well.'

It is how it is, but I do feel sad for those who could be getting much more support if their partners felt able to let them share it, as I have.

One thing I know for certain is that the more we talk to each other about what we feel, our pains and grievances, our worries and fears, the better the chances for our recovery.

The couples I know who mutually support each other without fear of reprimand, and with total honesty, have, for the most part, gone on to have a strong, happy relationship; those who felt they couldn't, or weren't 'allowed' to speak openly either with their partner or with others, eventually went their separate ways.

Aside from our own recovery, remaining in a relationship with a recovering addict means also supporting theirs, not only practically but also in the way they choose to go about it – assuming it's working, obviously.

It took me a while, but I've learned not to criticise or question anything about the path and programme Mike has chosen for his own recovery. Whatever hesitations, irritations, criticisms or general what-the-fuckisms I might have about AA don't matter: it keeps him alive, it keeps many people alive and that's all that matters. It's a *lifeline* and it's not for anyone else to turn someone's off, and for every day Mike is still sober and well, I'm right here beside him, feeling damned grateful.

As he put it to me one day:

Liz, I can't go into meetings questioning it – I can't *ever* question it. I have been given this curse, I don't choose it, and AA is what has to be done for me to stay sober and alive. I will do it and accept every part of it for the rest of my life.

So I now do that as well, and that's much better all round.

When you've lived with an active alcoholic and your alcoholism radar is set to Extremely Bloody Sensitive, it's easy to fall into the trap of *defining* someone by their alcoholism and assigning every imperfection, bad mood, questionable decision or inconvenient action to it.

I did this for quite a while: every time Mike had even the slightest rise in temper or drop in mood, slipped a little on the health front or forgot to replace the toilet roll, I put it squarely down to the fact that Mike is an alcoholic, and obviously he *only* did this because he's an alcoholic and oh God, what if everything is about to go wrong again?

But the bottom line is that addicts are also *people* and they are *allowed* to be angry or frustrated, to make mistakes or forget things, be moody or changeable, just as we all are, and it doesn't mean it's a sign of a Problem or because they're an alcoholic. It might just mean they're in a bad mood or they forgot the toilet roll thing. Again.

THE QUESTIONS

I still live daily with questions I'd never had to ask myself before:

Should we stay together or not? That one is ongoing, and always will (and should) be. For now, yes.

Do I hate him for what he did to me? Sometimes, of course I do. The memories and scars are there for me to see every day, but it's getting much less so with time.

Can I forgive him? I haven't managed to forgive it all yet, because a lot of it could have been dealt with far better and more kindly to me, but time is healing a lot and I'm much better at letting go and moving on.

Do I think he will relapse? I'd be very naive not to think he might relapse at some point. That's no criticism of him or his willpower, but I've heard enough stories from other addicts now, and also from Mike and the things he watches, reads and hears, to know how common it is even in people who were sober for a long time and had no apparent 'reason' to relapse. So I find it hard now to imagine that in his *whole* life ahead, with all the unforeseen work problems, injury, illness, deaths, arguments or one personal stress or another, he will never turn back to drink, even for a short period of time. If he does, he does: I can't control it.

Do I worry about my child inheriting alcoholism? Yes, of course I do. But I also think she's lucky to have parents who can educate her about mental health issues of all kinds, addiction, compassion, resilience and recovery, and who will be there for her in all the ways she might ever need us to be.

Will I ever forget Drinking Mike? When you've looked into the eyes of someone who says they want to stab you, it's hard to un-see it. I can still look at him sometimes when we're sitting together on the sofa or he's chopping vegetables in the kitchen, and if a dark cloud passes behind his eyes, if he seems jumpy or irritable or we have a little spat and I hear that angry voice again, I can sometimes have a little flash moment of wondering if he is really better now, or if his demons lie so close to the surface still, they could come back out. So no, I won't 'forget', but I only remember when I'm reminded, and then I remind *myself* that those days are over.

Did I do the right thing by sticking by him through it all, even to my own detriment? Yes, I believe I did.

Are we all susceptible to addiction? I think so, yes, and certainly the more we understand about it and talk about both sides of it, the more people we can help through it.

There is no healing without forgiveness – not just of others, but of ourselves. It's easy to torture ourselves over whether we should or could have prevented our loved one from substance abuse, stopped it, dealt with it better, been better able to cope with it, shielded our children from it and never allowed it to come into all our lives in the first place, and blame ourselves for much of what happened.

I've often asked myself how much *I* might have been if not exactly 'to blame', then certainly a contributing factor in Mike's ultimate descent: if I hadn't been as calm, helpful or supportive as I might have. If I hadn't listened carefully enough to what he was trying to say through his drinking, spotted his depressions soon enough and tried to help more with the causes instead of trying to fix the symptoms. If having a baby had been a bad idea because he wasn't ready to look after himself yet, let alone a child.

I've wondered if my own insecurities, my postnatal exhaustion, periods of depression or disordered eating had made me so difficult to live with that he'd drunk more than he might otherwise have, and whether my own breakdown had fuelled his. I've even wondered if the person *I am* was bad for him.

A year or so into his recovery, I talked with Mike about this and he said this: 'Liz, I was a piece of shit. Whether I was ill or not, I was a piece of shit, and it caused some abhorrent behaviour in me, which resulted in your being incredibly damaged. That's just a fact. You didn't cause any of this, my disease did, and all I can do is spend my life trying to make up for the damage, and being better.'

Alcoholism makes monsters of us all, and the fact is that neither of us was our best self for a long time. It doesn't *excuse* any of it but it also doesn't mean that we are bad people, or we 'caused' any of it. It's what can happen, I forgive him and I forgive myself, and that's the only way I can find peace with it.

In the end, we have a choice: we can stay with our alcoholic partner, or leave. If we choose to stay, we sign up for a life that is, shall we say, a little less simple and easy than it might otherwise be. But if it's a life we would rather have, warts, bumps, possible relapses and all, then it's up to us to live it.

Despite all the damage, many good things came out of this story that I take forward with me every day into all aspects of my life, and I think I *have* come out of it a little stronger in some ways, and also, perhaps, a better person than I was before.

I've learned things about human fallibility and strength; I'm far more informed about and understanding of alcoholism, its causes and what strength goes into recovery every day; I'm more patient, honest with myself about what I'm thinking and feeling and the causes of my resentments and responses; I'm far more aware of the positive things in my life – and I feel grateful, not resentful, and that's a massive step.

I cope with anxiety and fear a little better now and I've learned things I can share with others to help them too.

Of course, I still carry anger and resentments, because I'm a human being and a lot of really awful shit has happened to me, which still causes problems. The financial fallout is staggering – I did eventually add up everything I gave directly to Mike in the form of money (which he drank), plus all associated costs of the effects on my life of his alcoholism, and it's somewhere close to £25,000 – I know I will never get any of it back – and every time I look in the mirror I'm reminded of how tired I am, how much weight I lost in the last two years and how much thinner my hair is. But these are just little things, in the grander scheme of life, and I try not to dwell. It's hard sometimes, but I'm getting there.

There are moments every day where I'm almost brought to tears by how lucky the three of us are to be in our lives, when we so nearly lost it all. It's all the schmaltzy, peachy stuff: watching Mike teach our daughter to ride a skateboard, hearing her say 'I love you, Daddy', listening to him read her stories, seeing his smile, hearing him sing in the shower, feeling his kiss on the back of my neck as he walks past me in the kitchen, smelling his skin when we're on the sofa, sharing a laugh, asking each other for advice and giving support or a cuddle when we need it. These are the things I fought so hard for, and always believed we could have back, if he could just get better.

And what gets me through each day? Well, I'm definitely a work in progress and there's a long way to go, but I try my own little version of the Twelve Steps – though it's more 'Twelve Things That Help Me Cope A Bit Better':

1. I remind myself that there's nothing I can do to stop Mike drinking. If he wants to drink, he can. That's on him.
2. I remember that I exist both as a part of us and also separately to him. I might still feel it sometimes, but I know I'm not dependent on him, and I can survive on my own if I have to.
3. I try to 'stay in my lane' and not let *his* moods and behaviours dictate my day or my well-being.
4. I try to stick to my personal boundaries, albeit with varied degrees of success. It's something I still find very difficult, but I'm getting much better at it now, in all walks of my life.
5. I talk to people. Friends, strangers, therapists, dental nurses, people on Twitter, cashiers, scaffolders, bank clerks, anyone. Vocalising a fear, sadness or anxiety reduces that feeling immediately, and often the person I'm talking with knows exactly what it's like too, and is glad to have someone to share it with.
6. I say my daily gratitudes every evening, out loud. It feels a bit 'woo-woo', but it really does have a positive effect on my mental state. It can be anything from

getting the last seat on the train, being thankful that
the rain stopped and the sun came out just in time for
the nursery run, finding some leftover curry in the
fridge when I had a major curry craving, and so on. It's
amazing how many good moments there are in every
day, and focusing on them makes the difficult stuff
seem far more manageable.

7. I try to be honest with myself about why I say and do what
   I do, where my emotions and reactions stem from and
   how to react better and be kinder – both to myself
   and others.

8. If I feel angry or hurt about something, I write it down,
   go outside and shout it to the sky, go for a run or just
   take five to breathe. Speaking in anger has never brought
   anything good to this family, and I'm very mindful of
   keeping the 'good vibes only' as much as I can.

9. I try to respect both my own need for mental space and
   calm, and Mike's. If he seems stressed out or irritable,
   I'll take some of the pressure off and make sure he finds
   some inner calm again. No resentment, no jealousy, just
   an understanding of what a person in recovery needs.
   Likewise, if things are getting a bit too much for me, I'll
   say so calmly, and take five instead of soldiering on until
   I crack.

10. I try to let go of the negative feelings still in me. There
    are many, and I'm happy to admit that, but there's
    no point harbouring grudges or living in regret or
    mourning for what's been lost. It's gone and there is only
    going forward. That's hard to do sometimes, but just
    remembering it can help.

11. I try to find five minutes every day to stop thinking, stop
    worrying about the future, stop being anywhere but *in
    the moment* and to breathe slowly. It calms my mind,
    grounds me and makes me feel more able to deal with
    whatever comes next.

12. I remind myself every day that I am in recovery too. It's a very long, slow journey, and I have to be patient. I will have better days and worse days, but they are all a part of it, and I don't beat myself up when I'm not functioning as well as I'd like to. Every day is a little further away from the bad times, and a little closer to better ones we are creating.

Epilogue

I wrote the whole of this book in COVID lockdown, and during Mike's first year of recovery – and mine – and as I write these words, he is a year and a half sober.

In a box in my bedroom I still have Mike's 'Be Better' Post-it note, my bent engagement ring, the first postcards and letters we ever wrote to each other, and a bottle top I found in one of his coat pockets in Venice. I also have his One Year Sober token, which he threw across the room and said he didn't want any more, that day he left for the bed and breakfast in November.

My apartment in Venice is being sold, and that chapter is closed forever. In a way, *our* chapter has only just started.

This book has an end, but our story doesn't. Mike and I are still living it and it's evolving every day. The ups and downs come unexpectedly, some are harder than others, but we ride them better now than ever, and we do it together.

Come back to me in a year, even a month, and Mike might be drinking again, I might be in the throes of depression, we might not even be together any more. Or, we might be very happy, and planning our wedding.

Nobody knows what their life will look like in an hour, let alone the next 20 years, but this is where we are now, and this is where I stop this story.

I haven't really had a proper chance yet to take time to heal, or 'recover' properly; writing this book was a huge emotional strain as I went over every pain and trauma again and again, and it really did make me unwell at times. But it's done now, it's going out into the world and it's for others to take from it what they will. I hope it will do some good and help others who live through anything like we did, whichever side of addiction they are on.

Now it's *my* time to start my own recovery. One day at a time, and all that.

THE END

Resources

ORGANISATIONS

AA – self-help organisation for people fighting alcoholism, with branches worldwide. alcoholics-anonymous.org.uk; www.aa.org (US)

AL-Anon – a mutual support organisation for the families and friends of alcoholics, especially those of members of Alcoholics Anonymous. al-anon.org

Club Soda – global mindful drinking community underpinned by behaviour-change science. Joinclubsoda.com

Nacoa – National charity providing information, advice and support for everyone affected by a parent's drinking. Helpline: 0800 3583456. nacoa.org.uk

National Domestic Violence Hotline – US organisation offering free, confidential advice: 1-800-799-SAFE. thehotline.org

Refuge – provides specialist services to survivors of domestic abuse in the UK. 0808 2000 247. refuge.org.uk

Samaritans – organisation providing emotional support. Helpline: 116123. samaritans.org

Shelter – national organisation offering resources and support for people facing homelessness. shelter.org.uk

Women's Aid – UK national charity working to end domestic abuse against women and children. Womensaid.org.uk

BOOKS

Al-Anon (2014) *How Al-Anon Works for Families and Friends of Alcoholics* (Center City, MN: Hazleden Publishing)

Alcoholics Anonymous World Services (2013) *The Twelve Steps and Traditions* (New York: Alcoholics Anonymous World Services)

Hardin, Rosemary (ed.) (2014) *SMART Recovery Handbook*, 3rd edition (OH: Alcohol & Drug Abuse Self-Help Network)

Tolle, Eckhart (1997) *The Power of Now: A Guide to Spiritual Enlightenment* (San Francisco, CA: New World Library)

van der Kolk, Bessel (2015) *The Body Keeps The Score : Mind, Brain and Body in the Transformation of Trauma* (London: Penguin)

APPS

I Am Sober – sobriety counter app. Along with tracking your sober days, it helps you build new habits and provides ongoing motivation.

Pink Cloud – sobriety companion, connecting you to 181,000+ Alcoholics Anonymous, 46,000+ Narcotics Anonymous, 600+ Crystal Meth Anonymous and 13,000+ Al-Anon meetings worldwide.

Sober Time– sober day counter with a built-in community.

HASHTAGS

Recovery
Recoveryposse
Mindfuldrinking
Sober
Soberlife